THE SUN KING

LOUIS XIV AT VERSAILLES

DEDICATED TO
RAYMOND MORTIMER

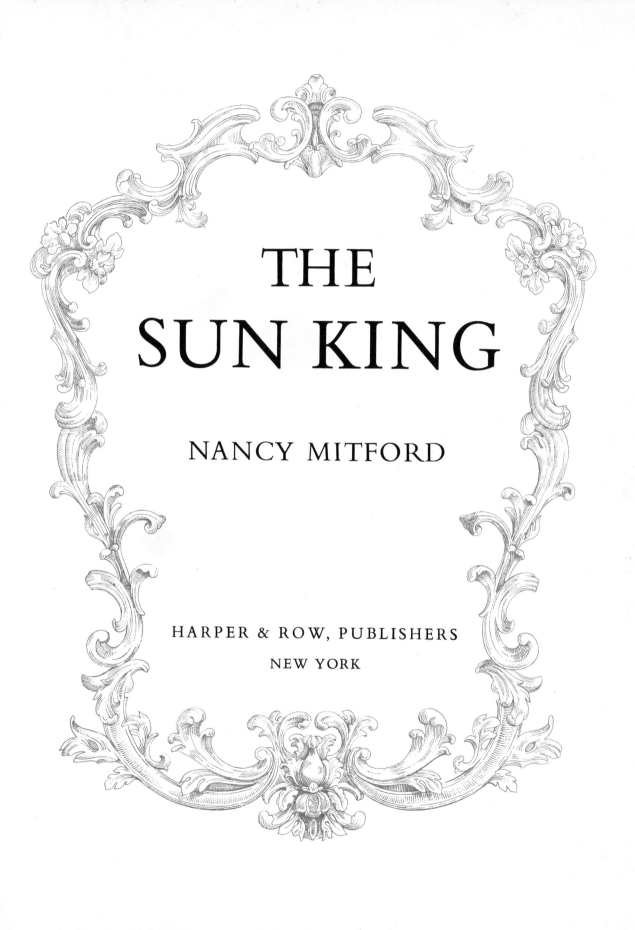

THE
SUN KING

NANCY MITFORD

HARPER & ROW, PUBLISHERS

NEW YORK

This book was devised and produced by
George Rainbird Limited,
2 Hyde Park Place, London W.2, England

Designed by Ronald Clark

Composition by Filmset Ltd, Crawley;
printing and color reproduction
by Amilcare Pizzi S.p.A., Milan,
and binding by
Legatoria Editoriale Giovanni Olivotto S.p.A.
Vicenza

Library of Congress Catalog Card Number
66-18954

CONTENTS

ACKNOWLEDGMENTS

The author's grateful thanks are due to Mr Raymond Mortimer, Comte Jean de Baglion, Mr Ian Dunlop and Professor John Lough for kindly reading and advising upon the text. M. Gerard van der Kemp, Conservateur en Chef at Versailles; M. Jean Féray, Inspecteur Général des Beaux Arts; Mme Chantal Coural of the Conservation at Versailles; Prince Clary; Mr Francis Watson, Director of the Wallace Collection, London; Mr Tom Wragg, Librarian of Chatsworth; Mr John Hadfield; Mme Gaudin; Miss Irene Clephane; Mrs St John Saunders and the Librarian and staff of the London Library have all given valuable assistance. Comtesse Carl Costa de Beauregard harboured the author for months while the work was in progress. Finally Mrs Joy Law has been indispensable; the book in its present form would never have seen the light of day but for her.

LIST OF ILLUSTRATIONS

COLOR

7

MONOCHROME

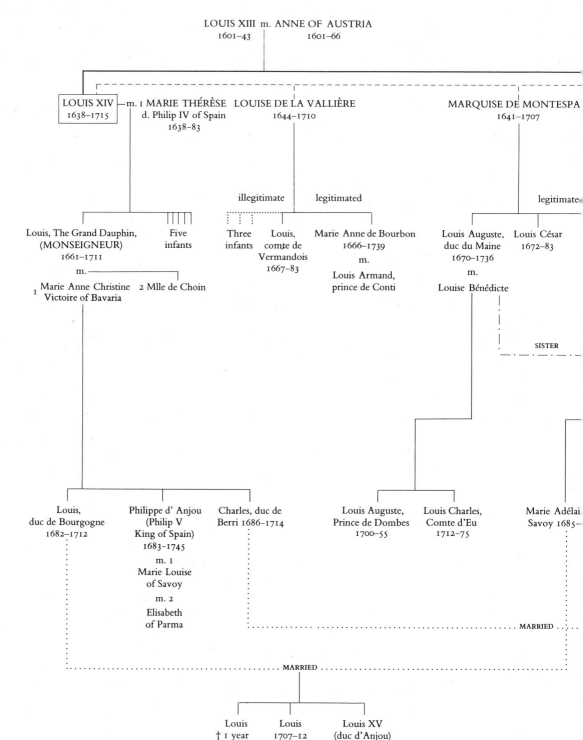

LOUIS XIII m. ANNE OF AUSTRIA
1601–43   1601–66

LOUIS XIV —m. 1 MARIE THÉRÈSE   LOUISE DE LA VALLIÈRE   MARQUISE DE MONTESPA
1638–1715   d. Philip IV of Spain   1644–1710
                    1638–83

illegitimate   legitimated   legitimate

Louis, The Grand Dauphin,   Five   Three   Louis,   Marie Anne de Bourbon   Louis Auguste,   Louis César
(MONSEIGNEUR)   infants   infants   comte de   1666–1739   duc du Maine   1672–83
1661–1711   Vermandois   m.   1670–1736
m. ————————————————   1667–83   Louis Armand,   m.
1 Marie Anne Christine   2 Mlle de Choin   prince de Conti   Louise Bénédicte
Victoire of Bavaria

SISTER

Louis,   Philippe d' Anjou   Charles, duc de   Louis Auguste,   Louis Charles,   Marie Adélai
duc de Bourgogne   (Philip V   Berri 1686–1714   Prince de Dombes   Comte d'Eu   Savoy 1685–
1682–1712   King of Spain)   1700–55   1712–75
            1683–1745
            m. 1
            Marie Louise
            of Savoy
            m. 2
            Elisabeth
            of Parma

.... MARRIED ..

.... MARRIED

Louis   Louis   Louis XV
† 1 year   1707–12   (duc d'Anjou)
                  1710–74

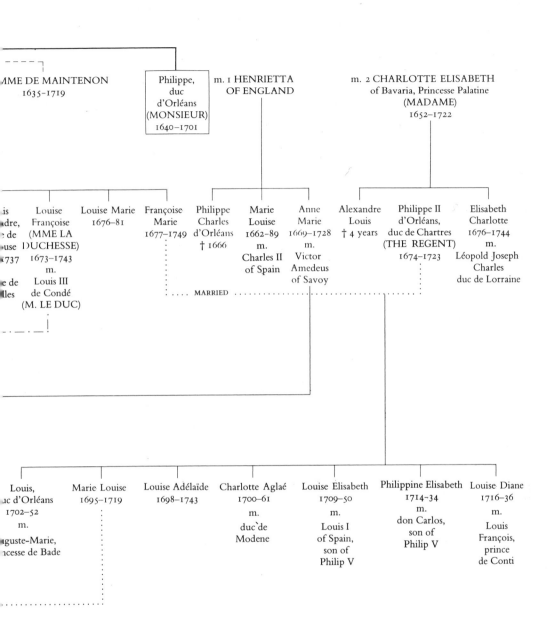

Philippe,
duc
d'Orléans
(MONSIEUR)
1640–1701

m. 1 HENRIETTA
OF ENGLAND

m. 2 CHARLOTTE ELISABETH
of Bavaria, Princesse Palatine
(MADAME)
1652–1722

Lis
dre,
e de
use
737

Louise
Françoise
(MME LA
DUCHESSE)
1673–1743
m.
Louis III
de Condé
(M. LE DUC)

Louise Marie
1676–81

Françoise
Marie
1677–1749

Philippe
Charles
d'Orléans
† 1666

Marie
Louise
1662–89
m.
Charles II
of Spain

Anne
Marie
1669–1728
m.
Victor
Amedeus
of Savoy

Alexandre
Louis
† 4 years

Philippe II
d'Orléans,
duc de Chartres
(THE REGENT)
1674–1723

Elisabeth
Charlotte
1676–1744
m.
Léopold Joseph
Charles
duc de Lorraine

. . . . MARRIED . . . .

Louis,
uc d'Orléans
1702–52
m.
uguste-Marie,
ncesse de Bade

Marie Louise
1695–1719

Louise Adélaïde
1698–1743

Charlotte Aglaé
1700–61
m.
duc de
Modene

Louise Elisabeth
1709–50
m.
Louis I
of Spain,
son of
Philip V

Philippine Elisabeth
1714–34
m.
don Carlos,
son of
Philip V

Louise Diane
1716–36
m.
Louis
François,
prince
de Conti

The family tree of Louis XIV

I

THE HOUSE

Et l'on peut comparer sans crainte d'être injuste
Le siècle de Louis au beau siècle d'Auguste

CHARLES PERRAULT

Louis XIV fell in love with Versailles and Louise de La Vallière at the same time; Versailles was the love of his life. For years before he lived there it was never out of his mind. When he was at the seat of government or away on hunting visits or with his army at the front he had to be sent a daily report on the work in hand on his house down to the tiniest details; and he never stopped adding to and improving the place while there was breath in his body. This 'undeserving favourite' as the courtiers called it is part of his legend but in fact the Sun King only lived there during the meridian and the sunset years: in his great morning he held his court, consisting of a few dozen officials, at the Louvre and Saint-Germain-en-Laye, where he was born, with visits to Chambord, Fontainebleau and Vincennes. Like a feudal king, he was always on the move, generally at war, and his court was a bivouac between two campaigns.

Nobody ever knew when this secret man first conceived the design by which his father's little hunting lodge was to become the hub of the universe, perhaps as early as 1661 when he began to give parties in the gardens there for his young mistress and a band of friends, whose average age at that time was nineteen. He was twenty-three, had been married for a year and already had a son, but his kingdom had hitherto been governed by Cardinal Mazarin his godfather; and his behaviour was still regulated by his mother, Queen Anne of Austria. He liked to disport himself away from the eye of the older generation and Versailles was a perfect place in which to do so, though the parties there had to take place in the garden; the house was much too small. The weather was always fine in those happy young days, the freshness of evening a welcome change from the heat of noon.

Louis XIII's house at Versailles had some twenty rooms and one big dormitory for men. It was perched over a village which clustered round a twelfth-century church, (where the Orangery is today; the Pièce d'Eau des Suisses was the village

Louise de La Baume Le Blanc, Duchesse de La Vallière by Jean Nocret, about 1663.

pond). Some poor little hamlets in the neighbourhood were called Trianon, Saint-Cyr, Clagny. Versailles, on the main road from Normandy to Paris, was more prosperous than they were; farmers and their cattle passed through it and it possessed three inns. The surrounding country was full of game, and Louis XIII who, like most Bourbons, practically lived on horseback, so often found himself at Versailles after a day's hunting that he built the house to save himself the choice between staying at an inn or riding home to Saint-Germain after dark.

No doubt Louis XIV's famous visit to Vaux-le-Vicomte gave him his first idea of what Versailles might become. Like many people of mixed blood he was a strong nationalist; at the newly built Vaux he first saw the perfection of contemporary French taste, free from that Italian influence which had hitherto been fashionable. Its master, Nicolas Fouquet, gave a house-warming there, 17 August 1661, and invited six thousand people to meet the King. It proved to be his own farewell party; the King, with mingled admiration and fury, examined the establishment in all its sumptuous detail and decided that Fouquet's ostentation (*luxe insolent et audacieux*) was unsuitable for a subject and intolerable for a minister of finance. He did not modify this view as the evening wore on and such gifts as diamond tiaras and saddle-horses were distributed to the guests. Louis returned Fouquet's hospitality by clapping him in gaol and we seldom hear of other people giving parties for the King. Mazarin had just died and Fouquet's real crime was ambition: he was intriguing to make himself head of the government. Had Louis XIV been the man everybody supposed him to be, Fouquet would have ruled both King and country; Louis however had other ideas and to put them into practice he was obliged to get rid of this clever, unscrupulous statesman. He thus gave a second indication of his own implacable ambition, the first having been his marriage with Marie-Thérèse of Spain when the wife he wanted was Mazarin's niece, Marie Mancini. She said to him as they parted 'You are the King; you love me and yet you send me away'. He was always to be the master of his mistresses and of himself, as well as of France. Marie-Thérèse eventually brought the crown of Spain to the Bourbons – who shall say that Mazarin's brains would not have been a greater prize? They were to prove a precious legacy to many another family.

So Fouquet went to his long martyrdom in the fortress of Pignerol. His sins were not visited on his children. His daughter, the Duchesse de Béthune, was always kindly received at Court; under Louis XV, his grandson the Maréchal de Belle-Isle became a rich and respected soldier while his, Belle-Isle's son, Gisors, was a French Sir Philip Sidney. But the King took a certain amount of loot from Vaux-le-Vicomte and thought himself justified by the fact that its contents had been paid for out of public money, in other words his own. Archives, tapestry, brocade hangings, silver and silver gilt ornaments, statues and over a thousand orange trees found their way to the royal palaces. The orange trees alone represented a considerable sum; a

Vaux-le-Vicomte. An engraving by Adam Perelle.

The title-page from the engravings of the *Plaisirs de l'Ile Enchantée*, 1664, showing Versailles from the south.

VEUE DU CHASTEAU DE VERSAILLY

Les plaisirs de l'Isle enchantée, ou les festes, et divertissements du Roy, à Versailles,
Divisez en trois journées, et commencéz le 7.me Jour de May, de L'année 1664.

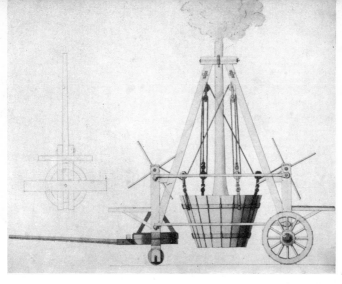

Drawing of a machine for transporting the orange trees in their tubs by Nicodemus Tessin.

sizeable one even nowadays costs a hundred pounds. The King was passionately fond of them and had them in all his rooms, in silver tubs. (Perhaps if one were exiled from France the single object most reminiscent of that celestial land would be an orange tree in a tub.) Eight of Louis XIV's own trees still exist in the Orangery at Versailles to this day. He also appropriated the three remarkable men who had created Vaux: Le Nôtre the gardener, Le Vau the architect and Le Brun, the artist of all work. He needed them to help him in the realization of a project which was now beginning to occupy his thoughts.

Louis XIV seems to have known that he would live to be old. His plans, both artistic and political, were for a long term; they ripened slowly and were confided to nobody. Why, having decided to build himself a house, he chose Versailles as a situation remains mysterious. The material difficulties of building on a large scale there were considerable. He insisted on keeping his father's little lodge, poised on a sandy knoll whose surface was forever shifting, and building his own mansion round it. As the house became more and more vast the hill itself had to be enlarged. The water supply, too, was always a problem. Then why, as he wanted a house of his very own, to be a monument to his reign, did he build on to an existing one, whose style had become unfashionable? His architects all begged him to pull down the old house because it made their work so difficult. His answer was that if the old house disappeared for any reason he would immediately build it up again brick by brick. No doubt Versailles had some special charm for him; his courtiers never could imagine what it was; their complaints and criticism grew more and more vociferous as his purpose, which was to make them all live there with him, became evident. As much as they dared they even protested to his face. 'There is no view.' But he loved the view, so typical of the Ile de France: a great cutting through woodlands quietly rolling away to the western horizon and ending in two poplar trees. It had always

Vaux-le-Vicomte.

Overleaf: Bird's eye view of Versailles from the east in 1668 by Pierre Patel showing the château before its transformation by Le Vau and Mansart. The King is shown arriving in a carriage drawn by six horses, and the Queen in the following carriage.

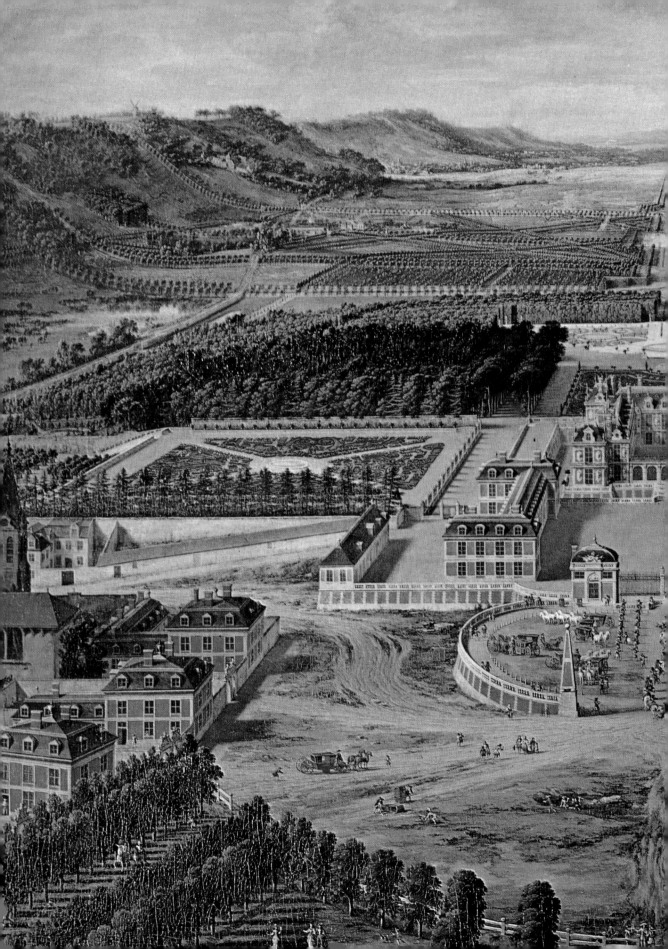

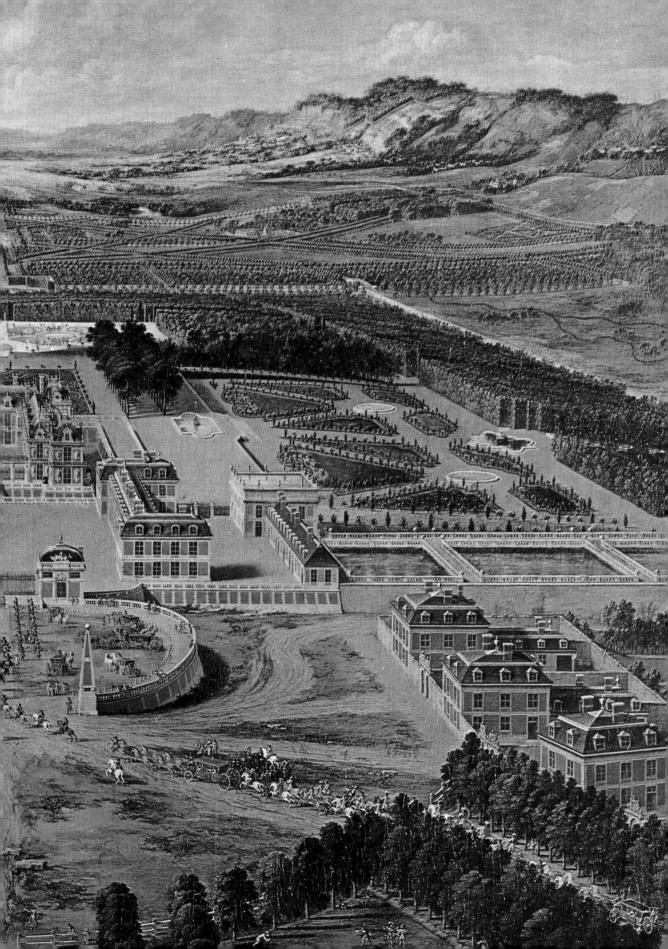

Bonne, Ponne and Nonne: the King's shooting dogs by François Desportes for the antechamber at Marly.

been the same, and though he was to lighten it with the canal he never would put statuary to replace the poplars. 'There is no town' was another complaint. So much the better – wherever the King lives a town will spring up; this one can be properly planned and laid out. 'It is unhealthy.' The King feels perfectly well there.

More serious objections were put forward by Colbert, the King's chief political adviser. Backed up by Chancelier Séguier, a grand old man for whom Louis had considerable respect, Colbert wanted to see the King of France living in his capital. Quite naturally, in that age of building, Louis XIV would want a modern country residence, but why choose Versailles? In the early days Colbert had no notion of what the house would become; even so he grudged the money and the manpower which in his view, ought to have been used to make the Louvre a fitting residence for a great King. But Louis had no intention of living in Paris. He was not afraid of the Parisians as has sometimes been said – fear was left out of his nature. Nor did he neglect Paris; on the contrary he lavished care and attention on all aspects of its development, turning it from a medieval slum into a beautiful and supremely habitable city. True he had no intention of allowing another Fronde, the civil war between the great nobles which had raged during his childhood putting him, his mother and his brother in awkward, if not dangerous, situations. Too much stress may have been laid on the traumatic effect the Fronde had on the King's young psychology; no doubt it was his policy to keep power out of the hands of the aristocrats, and he liked to have them under his eye, but with his dominating personality he could have done so wherever he chose to hold his court; that was not a question of geography.

Louis XIV was a country person. He excelled at all sport and could hardly bear to be indoors; he spent hours every day hunting or shooting. The year before his death he brought down thirty-two pheasants with thirty-four shots, a considerable

Chancelier Séguier by Charles Le Brun.   21

An engraving showing construction work at the Louvre.

Detail of the marble bust of Louis XIV by Lorenzo Bernini, 1665.

A performance of Molière's *Le Malade Imaginaire*, at Versailles, 1674. Engraving by Le Pautre.

feat with the primitive gun of those days. He thought nothing of riding from Fontainebleau to Paris, going to see the building in progress at the Louvre and Vincennes, dining with his brother at Saint-Cloud, inspecting the improvements there and riding back to Fontainebleau. In old age he became more and more interested in gardens. Such a man would have been miserable, cooped up in a town.

Having fallen in love with Versailles the King never made the mistake of improving away the very atmosphere which had attracted him in the first place. He built the greatest palace on earth but it always remained the home of a young man, grand without being pompous, full of light and air and cheerfulness – a country house. Indeed it is called *le Château*, never *le Palais*. (*Château* in French means gentleman's seat, a castle is *château-fort*.) To begin with he did more work in the gardens than in the house, following the lines already laid out by Louis XIII, greatly enlarged and elaborated and with the addition of much water; he added more and more green rooms which led off the central alley or *tapis vert* and which he used for ever larger, more elaborate parties. These had nothing in common with the *fêtes champêtres* of the next century; there was no whiff of hay, the farmyard played no part in them; nature was kept in her place and the trellised drawing-rooms were decorated and furnished with oriental luxury. It may be imagined how passionately invitations to these parties were desired; the King had already begun to enslave his nobility by playing on the French love of fashion. In 1664 he gave a fête called *Les Plaisirs de l'Ile Enchantée* which lasted from 7–13 May. This really caused more pain than pleasure, for the guests had nowhere to sleep and were obliged to doss down as best they could in local cottages and stables. In 1665 he was spending one day a week at Versailles, generally coming over from Saint-Germain to see how the work was getting on, to hang a few pictures in the house, run round the gardens and then divert himself with his friends.

This was the time of Bernini's visit. He was invited to France to make plans for finishing the Louvre which was then an amorphous cluster of buildings, of many different dates, more like a village than a palace. The King was bent on tidying up Paris and he succeeded with the town but there has always been something unsatisfactory about the Louvre, beautiful as are many of its component parts. Bernini's plans were not liked; the King thought them too baroque, unsuitable for the sober skies of northern France, while Colbert raised practical difficulties such as where would the servants sleep? How was the food to be brought from the kitchens? The King got on well with Bernini, cleverly allowing him to think that his failure was all Colbert's doing; but Bernini was rude and arrogant with the French artists, architects and civil servants, whom he thoroughly disliked and who loathed him – the old story of Frenchmen and Italians unable to appreciate each other's merits. After some months he went home, loaded with money and thanks; his voyage would have been waste of time had he not made a bust of Louis XIV which is one of the greatest treasures of Versailles and the only effigy to illustrate contemporary descriptions of the King's appearance.

Unfortunately the pictures of Louis XIV are not attractive, possibly because of the perriwig which always seems frowsty, very different from the flowing curls of the bust. If one looks carefully at the face it often has a humorous and kindly aspect, (for instance in the Mignard of the Louvre) but is never handsome – in some portraits it is decidedly oriental (Louis XIV most probably had both Jewish and Moorish blood through the Aragons). But the many people who wrote about him at first hand, either, like the Venetian ambassadors, to describe him to their governments (a physical description of those in power was considered important) or in diaries or memoirs intended to be published after his death, if at all, or in letters, do not seem to have noticed an alien or exotic look. They agree that he was tall and dark, with an excellent figure, perfect legs, feet and hands, small but brilliant eyes which he hardly ever opened wide but which gave the impression, truly, of seeing everything. The salient feature was his nose; it was a good shape, though rather pinched above the nostrils; it only became Jewish when he was old. All speak of his noble look and extraordinary grace; he never made an ill-considered or meaningless gesture so that he seemed like a deity (or, according to some, an actor of genius ever on the stage). These characteristics are evident in Bernini's bust and such was the appearance of Louis XIV. It is to be hoped that his strange character will emerge during the course of this book.

Genealogical tree showing Louis XIV's Aragon ancestors.
Charles V was his great-great-grandfather.

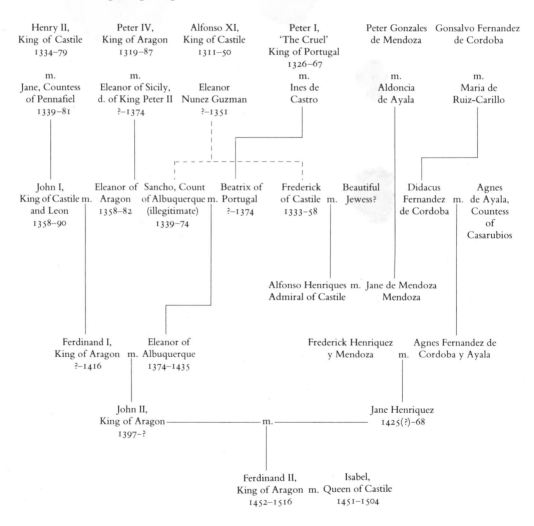

Marble bust of Louis XIV by Lorenzo Bernini.

He was delighted with the bust and commissioned an equestrian statue of himself which Bernini was to create at his leisure when he got back to Rome. It arrived at Versailles some nineteen years later and was unpacked in the Orangery. The King hated it. He prided himself on his excellent horsemanship and thought that he was portrayed as sitting all wrong in the saddle. He wanted to break up the statue. In the end he got Coysevox to make a few alterations so that it appeared to represent, not the Sun King but a Roman emperor and banished it to the end of the Pièce d'Eau des Suisses where it still is, gloriously beautiful in spite of a nearby railway line, much litter and the scribblings of Versailles plebeians. It is too seldom visited.

The King's existence as a grown-up, independent man only began in 1666 after the death of Anne of Austria. She was old enough to have been his grandmother, having been married for twenty-three years when he was born, and was a highly civilized, polite person whom he greatly admired. She held a court better than any queen in Europe and had always been too lazy, or too clever, to have anything to do with politics. During the long minority of Louis XIV, who came to the throne when he was five, she had left the conduct of affairs entirely in the hands of Cardinal Mazarin who was perhaps her lover, possibly her husband. It was a measure of Louis XIV's own exquisite politeness that he waited to become the ruler of France until the Cardinal had died in 1661 – unlike his ancestor, the Emperor Charles V, in similar circumstances. He was careful, too, never to shock his mother or hurt her feelings – his mistress and bastards were carefully kept out of her way. He knew that she feared petticoat influence for him.

Anne of Austria's death was distressing; she was eaten with cancer. At the end, when the King and Queen knelt, weeping, by her bed she murmured: 'Such children——.' But really they were both twenty-eight, not children at all. Queen Marie-Thérèse had good reason to cry, her best friend was leaving her. She was Anne's brother's daughter and the King's first cousin twice over since her mother was the sister of Louis XIII; Anne was fond of her, perhaps the only person in France who was, and always took her part. The King, with whom, unfortunately for her, she was in love all her life, was not bred to be a faithful husband, either on the Spanish or on the French side. The family tree of the Aragons is an amazing succession of illegitimacies while in France it had long been the custom for the King to have a wife and a declared mistress who was almost a second queen. Henri IV's bastards, powerful dukes, were a living proof of this as they swaggered about the Court; the last of his sons only died in 1682.

As soon as his mother's sufferings were over, the King stopped crying. (In the whole of his long life he was only to be affected by one death, that of the Duchesse de Bourgogne.) He immediately recognized Mlle de La Vallière as his titular mistress, made her a duchess and legitimized their baby daughter, Marie-Anne. Their first child had just died at the age of three; he had been called Louis de Bourbon,

with no title. Modest Louise, who blushed to be a mistress, a mother, a duchess, was now brought into the glare of public life; it did not suit her. She was a woman to be kept hidden away, visited by moonlight at her house in the rue de la Pompe at Versailles or encountered as by chance in some forest glade while the hunt went crashing by – a simple country girl, an excellent rider, puzzled and perplexed in the Byzantine atmosphere of the Court, though by no means averse from the financial benefits to be picked up there. She is supposed to have been responsible for more *placets*, (petitions to the King usually concerned with obtaining some lucrative sinecure, which were a feature of Court life) on all of which she took a comfortable percentage, than any of the other mistresses. In the early days of love, when she ought to have been happy, since the King, whom she worshipped, was at her feet, her large blue eyes used to fill with tears for no particular reason. Then her tears had melted his heart; now they bored him. Inadequate in the rôle of declared mistress, she was not the mate for a Sun King.

The King seems to have put off his major schemes for Versailles until after his mother's death. This occurred during the Guerre de Dévolution with which he sought to implement his wife's claim to the succession of the Spanish Netherlands. Having conquered Flanders and signed the Peace of Aix-la-Chapelle (1668) he set to work in earnest on his house. He gave a *Divertissement* to say good-bye to the old establishment, during which Molière produced his *George Dandin* for the first time. Three hundred of the women present were invited to a sit-down supper. Louise de La Vallière, pregnant, melancholy and dull, was next the King; his look was not upon her but on another table which the Marquise de Montespan and Mme Scarron, her great friend, were keeping in a buzz of laughter. They were the two liveliest women in society at that time. Years later, people remembering the *Divertissement* said it had contained the past, the present and the future.

Marie-Thérèse and Anne of Austria, Queens of France, by Simon de Saint André, 1664.

Cardinal Mazarin by Philippe de Champaigne.

Louis amongst the ladies at Court. An engraving from the Almanack of 1667.

The pattern of the King's three principal love affairs was the same, the new mistress was provided unwittingly by the existing one. When his flirtation with his sister-in-law Madame (Henrietta of England) began to cause gossip she told him to pretend that he was courting one of her ladies, Louise de La Vallière for instance. The pretence became reality. He had not cared for Mme de Montespan at first but Louise could not be without her. He saw her every day and she was determined to conquer him; she stirred up Satan himself and triumphed. As she was the most beautiful and most brilliant woman at the Court she ought to have been able to succeed without the help of such a compromising ally, but it is a curious fact that she was making no headway until she brought him into the affair. Then Mme Scarron, the future Mme de Maintenon, was thrust upon the King by Mme de Montespan. He could not endure her but she stirred up God and triumphed in her turn, though she took longer. Louise de La Vallière was the youngest of the three, three years younger than Mme de Montespan who was six years younger than Mme Scarron. None of these women really shared the King's aesthetic tastes. Mme de Montespan patronized artists in a desultory way; the others took no interest in the arts – indeed Mme de Maintenon grudged the money which was spent on beautifying the King's houses; Louis XIV never had a Mme de Pompadour.

A few days after the *Divertissement* Versailles was given over to workmen and what was called the *enveloppe* put in hand. The King had decided, with the collaboration of Le Vau, to envelop his father's house, like a precious jewel, in his own. Le Vau left the east front of brick and stone as it was, flanking it with wings and leading up to it with pavilions which were to house the ministers. For the west, or garden, side he designed a new stone front in a more majestic manner to consist of two wings joined by a terrace on the first floor. The King also turned his attention to the town. It was laid out by Le Nôtre and land was given to people who under-

27

took to build houses to an approved specification. Three wide avenues starring out from the Place d'Armes were planted.

During the years which followed the *Divertissement* of 1668 the King gave himself over to his favourite occupations, war and building. Having bought the alliance of his English cousin Charles II he set about conquering Holland. In those days it was hardly realized that if two rich countries lived side by side in peace, greater prosperity for both could result. A state of war was the natural condition of nations; during the whole of the seventeenth century there were only seven years of peace in Europe. As soon as trade began to expand, it was choked off by cut-throat quarrels.

Co-operation with the Dutch did occur to Louis. He offered his baby daughter Marie-Anne to be the wife of William of Orange and received a humiliating rebuff. William said that in his family one married the legitimate daughters of kings, not their bastards. (He was the son of one Mary Stuart and about to be the husband of another.) So Marie-Anne stayed at home, married the Prince de Conti and became an ornament of her father's court. Louis XIV, always touchy on the subject of his illegitimate family, never forgave William the insult. He had three further reasons for disliking the Dutch: the republicanism which seemed ingrained in their character, their Protestantism and their pamphlets. His own press was strictly censored, but disagreeable observations on himself, his policy and his family never stopped coming off the printing presses of The Hague and Amsterdam. Furthermore he was always obsessed by the Rhine. His foreign policy never altered in its main objective which was to secure, as France's frontiers, the Rhine, the Mountains and the Sea. Leibniz was forever saying that Louis XIV had no need to fight for France to become mistress of the world and rich beyond dreams, he only had to stay quietly within his existing frontiers; but that if he must go to war, to occupy the young men, why not do so in other parts of the globe? Egypt, Asia and America were all waiting to be conquered, far more interesting prizes than a few German villages. But Louis cared not a fig for these exotic places and who, nowadays, can blame him for that? It was the frontiers that interested him, the mountains and above all the Rhine. Each time his eye slid down this river on the map he was annoyed to be reminded of little Holland. He put on his feathered hat and went off with his great generals Condé and Turenne to bring her down. When he thought he had succeeded and was within sight of Amsterdam, the brave Dutch opened the dykes and the King found himself at the edge of an inland sea. Holland was saved, though at a dreadful cost. Various countries now came to her assistance and the tide turned very slightly against the French. Under the leadership of William of Orange the Dutch were never conquered, though there were at least two occasions on which Louis seemed to have them in his power. Each time he turned away at the crucial moment: as usual with him there was no explanation. The year 1675 saw

Building in progress at Versailles, with Colbert in the foreground, by Antoine van der Meulen.

A map showing the French frontiers in 1648.

Henri de la Tour d'Auvergne, Vicomte de Turenne by Charles Le Brun.

the death of Turenne, killed in battle to the despair of his soldiers who loved him so much that the whole French army was sobbing and crying that night. This loss was followed by the retirement of Condé. The Peace of Nimeguen, 1679, gave Louis XIV Franche-Comté and most of the Spanish Netherlands; it marked the apogee of his military glory.

Meanwhile Versailles had become an enormous workshop. The house was covered with scaffolding and buried in dust; the gardens were like a quarry, full of mud, stones, drain pipes, men and horses. Thousands of good-sized forest trees were being planted; those which died, about half, were immediately replaced. Marble and bronze statues lay about waiting for the King to say where he wanted them. He was in such a hurry to see the results that the building still suffers from hasty, ill-completed work. He dragged the Court there from time to time; the courtiers slept where they could and he himself was not comfortable. By the grandeur of the new schemes it was beginning to be clear that Versailles was intended to be one of the main royal residences.

At this time France, in the words of Lord Macaulay, had 'over the surrounding countries at once the ascendancy which Rome had over Greece and the ascendancy which Greece had over Rome'. Louis XIV's great house was to be the outward and visible sign of that ascendancy.

Louis, wearing his feathered hat, at the wars, 1662.
Detail from the Gobelins tapestry; after Charles Le Brun and Antoine van der Meulen.

II

THE BUILDERS

C'est la voix de génie de toutes les sortes qui parle au tombeau de Louis;
on n'entend, au tombeau de Napoléon, que la voix de Napoléon.

CHATEAUBRIAND

There were four men without whose collaboration the King could never have built Versailles: Colbert, Le Vau, Le Nôtre and Le Brun. They were all much older than he, must indeed have seemed to him like old men; remarkable as they were he dominated them and was the spirit of the whole tremendous enterprise. He knew exactly what he wanted; his eye had been trained by Mazarin who had surrounded him in childhood with beautiful objects, and he had a personal taste which developed and improved year by year, stamping itself on everything he undertook.

When Mazarin died he left his fortune to the King, saying that the pictures, the books, the houses, the eighteen enormous diamonds known as *les Mazarins* and the money (even, he might have added, the nieces) were nothing – the precious legacy was Colbert; and so it proved. He was the most remarkable minister in the history of France. If the French are divided into Franks and Gauls, Franks, serious and rather cold, the builders and Gauls, adorably frivolous, the destroyers of this nation, Colbert was the very type of the Frank. He was born in 1619, the son of a wool merchant of Rheims. His emblem was the humble grass snake – the antithesis of Fouquet's squirrel which can be seen climbing higher and higher, all over Vaux-le-Vicomte. Unlike Fouquet who was a jolly man of the world and a great lover of women, Colbert concealed his brilliance beneath a dour reserved manner – he frowned more often than he smiled, and never tried to charm. But people knew where they were with him; and those who, hoping to get off paying some tax, went behind his back to the King, to be received with infinite grace and told, with a delightful laugh 'Sir, you will have to pay!' would say they rather preferred Colbert's frown. Early in life he saw that economics are a sure if unspectacular road to power; he began his career by putting order into the private affairs of Mazarin which he found in an incredible muddle; then, still under the Cardinal, he turned

Jean-Baptiste Colbert by Claude Lefèbvre.

33

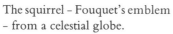
The squirrel – Fouquet's emblem
– from a celestial globe.

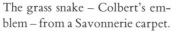
The grass snake – Colbert's emblem – from a Savonnerie carpet.

his attention to the national finances and established them on a solid foundation. When the King was a boy he taught him to keep accounts; he was the first King of France who had ever done such a thing. Colbert made him write down how much money he had got at the beginning of each year and then subtract expenses from it. When it ran out too soon, as it always did, he would borrow for him, from Mazarin! He realized that a new world was dawning in which a country must export or die; and he instituted a Council of Commerce, presided over by the King, which met every fortnight. He hated Versailles, but he alone was capable of producing the enormous sums of money which it swallowed and as soon as he saw that the King was determined to live there he bowed to the inevitable and began to think of ways in which the house could be made to further French commerce.

The prestige of Louis XIV and the fame of Versailles mounted year by year; other European princes and magnates wanted a Versailles of their own, down to the smallest details of its furnishings; Colbert exploited this fashion to help his exports. He erected a rigid customs barrier, nothing was allowed to be imported that could be made in France. Factories were set up to supply the linen, lace, silk, glass, carpets, jewellery, inlaid furniture and other articles of luxury that used to come from foreign lands, mostly from Italy; all these were soon of a superior quality to any that had been seen, since French craftsmen, then as now, were the best in the world. The finest examples of their work went to Versailles and were shown to the foreign visitors who flocked there; the château became a shop window, a permanent exhibition of French goods. It made an enormous contribution to French supremacy in the arts, as nowadays some great aeroplane, not in itself a paying proposition, can advance the technical progress of aeronautics. But soon there were not enough workmen so Colbert took measures to increase the working population. Families of over ten children were exempt from tax. He thought too many young people were taking religious vows and raised the age at which they might do so. Workmen were forbidden to emigrate and foreigners, especially Protestants who were persecuted in their own countries, were encouraged to come to France. He always said that the men should not be too strictly directed but allowed to do what they thought best. He had difficulties with the Gauls however. The great nobles refused to invest in his companies for trading overseas; the workmen were not easy, they refused to give up their sixty public holidays a year, (apart from Sundays) and there were strikes. He himself worked fifteen hours a day seven days a week and his holographs would fill a hundred volumes. Though his only real interest was commerce, he ran every government department except that of war. His work bore fruit; in the ten years between 1661 and 1671 the national revenue was doubled. In 1683 it was four times that of England and nearly ten times that of the Venetian republic. But the richest of all European countries was Holland. The prosperity of this tiny state, troubled by England beyond the sea, by the sea itself and by its European neighbours (the Spanish menace hardly over when the French menace began) was a perpetual source of wonder. Colbert, like his master, but for different reasons, was obsessed by Holland. The Dutch had two citizens to one peasant, and that one produced heavier crops to the acre, fatter pigs and higher yielding cows than were to be found anywhere else. Like bees, the Dutch seemed to gather honey from all around them: Norway was their forest, the banks of the Rhine and the Dordogne their vineyard; Spain and Ireland grazed their sheep; India and Arabia were their gardens and the sea their highway. Their enormous riches and enviable way of life were achieved by commerce, banking (the Bank of Amsterdam dates from 1609), insurance, printing and the fact that they were a seafaring nation situated between the new world and the old. Also there were no Gauls in Holland. Colbert would have loved to rule such a land! His greatest handicap was the war that raged on the frontiers during almost the whole of Louis XIV's reign. A hundred and fifty thousand men were kept under arms even in peace time – men whom Colbert could have employed over and over again on different schemes for enriching the country. He hated war, and not out of humanity, for he had none in his make-up. He did little or nothing to help the French peasants through a period of agricultural depression; indeed low farm prices suited his policy of cheap exports. The gap between the peasantry and the rest of the population first became serious under Colbert; it was not bridged, as in England, by country gentlemen. He encouraged the slave trade and though he did insist on certain humanitarian measures, this was only to keep down the death rate of such valuable cattle. Worst of all perhaps he increased the number of galleys in the French navy from six to forty, each containing two hundred unhappy souls. Since black people were useless for manning them (they had no stamina and died at once) he employed French criminals and Turks caught in the Barbary wars. When the Turks were worn out they were sold in America for what they would fetch. Young, solid Frenchmen accused of capital offences were often sent to the galleys for life instead of being executed. Minor criminals, if they were able-bodied, were never released at the end of their sentences – they could only be freed if their relations could afford to buy a Turk to replace them. Colbert thought that too many of his galley slaves died – the Intendant of the Galleys swore that they were well fed but said they died of grief and boredom. We can imagine these two rich, comfortable courtiers conversing together on the subject in some golden drawing-room.

A profound knowledge of literature, science and the arts was part of this extraordinary man's make-up, though possibly he regarded them as an adjunct to trade, part of the French prestige which was to attract the world markets. He was a member of the Académie Française and the famous *fauteuils* there were due to him. (The *fauteuil* had an almost mystical significance in seventeenth-century France. The only people ever allowed to sit in one when the King was present were his wives, King James II of England and the King's grandson, Anjou, when he became King of Spain.) Some noble Academician brought one for himself to the Académie when it was in session; next time he came he found that Colbert had provided *fauteuils* for all forty Academicians. Colbert created the French school of painting and sculpture in Rome; the Observatory in Paris, bringing the astronomer Cassini to work there; he founded the Académie des Sciences; he bought quantities of books to add to the royal library. Finally, as Surintendant des Bâtiments, he directed the works at Versailles.

Colbert had one unexpectedly romantic side to his nature: he was a snob. His ancestors the wool merchants bored him and he began to look for something better. To the general merriment the Northumbrian St Cuthbert was brought into play and Colbert deposited various old deeds with d'Hozier, the King's genealogist, which were supposed to prove that he descended from the saint and his 'Scotch wife Marie de Lindsay of Castlehill, Inverness.' Unkind people said that these deeds looked as if they had been at the bottom of the sea for years, they were mildewed and illegible; however they served their purpose and the genealogy was duly registered. (It only took him back to the wool trade after all – one wonders if Colbert knew that St Cuthbert was the son of a shepherd.) Then he removed his grandfather's tomb at Rheims, on which the word 'wool' figured, and replaced it with an old stone inscribed, in the language of a former age, with the virtues of one Colbert, of Scotch descent: 'Cy gist ly preux chevalier Richard Colbert dit l'y Ecossois. Priez pour l'âme de ly. 1300'. Some time later the great man and his three sons-in-law, all dukes, were seen kneeling by it in fervent prayer. Nevertheless, Mlle d'Aligre whom the King forced to marry Colbert's eldest son, the Marquis de Seignelay, died of a broken heart at having made such a *mésalliance*. Colbert had six sons; they were a worry to him in youth but after their father's death turned

The siege of Tournai, 21 June 1667, by Robert Bonnard. Sketch for a Gobelins tapestry.

out well: Seignelay was Ministre de la Marine, the Marquis de Blainville, Surintendant des Bâtiments; there were three soldiers, all killed in battle, and the Archbishop of Rouen. They were all rather lazy. Of his brothers, one was a bishop, one a general and the third, Colbert de Croissy, an able diplomatist.

Though Colbert was twenty years older than the King he was deeply in awe of him. When he left his country house, Sceaux, to go to Versailles, this powerful, authoritarian personage before whom all France trembled, would take a piece of bread down to his park and throw it at the canal. If it got to the other side it meant that Louis XIV would be in a good temper; if it fell in the water Colbert knew that the day would be stormy.

Colbert's hatred of war was only equalled by his hatred of Louvois, the war minister. This horrible man was the King's evil genius. He and Colbert were obliged to meet and collaborate every day under the eye of Louis XIV, who used their rivalry for his own ends and was not above teasing them. On one occasion Louvois, who wanted the Foreign Ministry for himself, ruined the existing minister, Pomponne, by stealing letters he had written to the King, and then pretending that the King had purposely been kept in the dark as to their contents. Louis knew quite well what had happened; but he used the affair to get rid of Pomponne who was not very brilliant. Then, to the fury of Louvois, he gave the ministry to Colbert's brother, Colbert de Croissy.

At the beginning of Louis XIV's reign the French army was a disorganized mob which had never been taken in hand since feudal times. It was turned into the first-class fighting machine with which the King implemented his foreign policy, by two men, Le Tellier and his son Louvois, who became his father's chief assistant, at a very early age in 1654. Able as he was, Louvois was not a genius. If he had been, he would have reformed the army from top to toe; but he winked at many abuses

37

which grew worse and not better and which finally became a stone round the neck of Louis XV. For years the King, who thoroughly understood the art of war, kept him well under control; unfortunately as they both grew older Louvois began to conceal things from Louis who, perfectly truthful himself, was always too much inclined to believe what he was told. The two greatest scandals of the reign, the atrocities in the Palatinate and those committed against the Protestants in the south-west of France, were the responsibility of Louvois. When Louis XIV found out the horrors which were going on in the Palatinate he went for Louvois with the fire irons of his room. Probably he never really knew the full extent of the Protestant persecutions. Louvois had a part in the building of Versailles since, at the death of Colbert in 1683, he took over as Surintendant des Bâtiments.

Le Brun was born the same year as Colbert, and worked with him most of his life. The two men shared the capacity for turning their hand to any job. Le Brun was found at the age of ten by the Chancelier Séguier, painting scenes from the apocalypse, on vellum. The Chancellor put him into Vouet's studio. At fifteen he was already painting for Cardinal Richelieu and at twenty-three he and Poussin went to Rome together; Poussin stayed there for most of his working life but Le Brun returned to France after four years, having been profoundly influenced by the Carracci gallery in the Palazzo Farnese. His first important commission, in 1649, was the decoration of the Hôtel Lambert, the Paris house of a rich magistrate. Then he worked for Fouquet at Vaux-le-Vicomte; in 1662 he was appointed the King's painter-in-chief and put in charge of the decorative art at Versailles. He was director of the Gobelins, the great factory which made not only the tapestry but nearly all the furnishings for Versailles. Le Brun was never more than a second class painter but he was a decorator of genius. He himself designed everything for the château, chairs, tables, carpets, panelling, silver and tapestries, even keyholes; he painted

Charles Le Brun by Nicolas de Largillière.

the ceiling of the Galerie des Glaces and those of the Salons de la Guerre et de la Paix, and the façade of the King's little house at Marly; he decorated the prows of galleys and the settings for fêtes. He also found time to paint immense pictures with religious and mythological subjects. He loved allegories and battle scenes and was rather indifferent to nature.

Le Brun and Le Vau worked in perfect harmony. Le Vau's best known buildings are Vaux-le-Vicomte, the Hôtel Lambert and the Collège des Quatre Nations which was built to his design after his death by Darbay. Most of his work at Versailles has been covered up by that of Mansart but the inspiration is his, greatly enlarged and one must say not improved. His château, when the *enveloppe* was finished, was a gem.

Of these men, the greatest charmer was Le Nôtre. He was born and bred to be a royal gardener; his grandfather spread manure in the parks of Marie de Médicis; his father was head gardener at the Tuileries and his sisters were married, one to Anne of Austria's nursery gardener and the other to the man who tended her orange trees. Le Nôtre thought he would like to be a painter and started life in Vouet's studio but he soon went back to gardening. He succeeded his father at the Tuileries and gave a new aspect to the gardens there. Fouquet then took him off to Vaux where Louis XIV saw the quality of his work and immediately made him director of all the royal gardens. We owe him not only the park of Versailles but also those of Chantilly, Saint-Cloud, Marly, Sceaux, the celebrated terrace at Saint-Germain-en-Laye, many private parks and gardens, Bossuet's garden at Meaux, in the shape of a mitre, and the great sweep up the Champs Elysées from the Louvre. He also laid out the town of Versailles.

Le Nôtre was one of the people Louis XIV liked best in the world. He felt more at ease with his servants than with the sophisticated aristocrats and pompous bourgeois by whom he was surrounded – in a way Le Nôtre was to him what John

The *Trianon de Porcelaine*, a reconstruction by
Ian Dunlop from contemporary drawings

André Le Nôtre by Carlo Maratta. He is wearing
the Order of St Michel.

Brown was to Queen Victoria. He had a perfectly direct natural manner and never
minded disagreeing with his master. In 1678 he went to Italy to study the gardens
there and obtained an audience with the Pope. Somebody told the King that Le
Nôtre had given the Holy Father a good hug; the King said he was not at all surprised;
'he always hugs me when I come back from a journey'. He offered Le Nôtre a coat
of arms but the idea was treated with derision: 'I've got one already, three slugs
crowned with cabbage leaves'.

Le Nôtre hated flowers as much as the King loved them. He greatly objected to
the parterres which he was obliged to plant in front of the royal palaces, saying they
were fit for nursery maids to look at, out of upper windows. Neither nursery maids
nor their charges ever got so much as a whiff of fresh air in those days, and Le Nôtre
had no doubt seen white faces behind glass looking wistfully down at his bedding-
out. The King's passion for flowers led to the building of the first Trianon, a pavilion
in blue and white porcelain, which was embowered in blossom. His favourites were
tulips – when he was not at war with Holland he used to import four million bulbs
a year from the Dutch nurseries – then came orange blossom, tuberoses, stocks and
wallflowers (both of which are called *giroflées* in French), daffodils and jasmin.

Le Nôtre never lost his interest in painting and the arts, and his lodging at the
Tuileries was full of beautiful things, including much Chinese porcelain. When he
was out, this delightful man would leave the key of his house on a nail so as not to
disappoint any amateurs who might call to see his collection.

A minor figure at Versailles was M. de La Quintinie who made the King's
kitchen garden there. He began life as a lawyer at Poitiers but his only interest was
fruit trees and vegetables. His book, *Instruction pour les Jardins Fruitiers et Potagers*
must be one of the best gardening books ever written; it makes the reader long for a
kitchen garden; the instructions are so precise that a child could follow them;

The King's gardener, Jean de La Quintinie, from the frontispiece to his book.

the work for every month is clearly set out. La Quintinie is interested in soil – he notices that when you transplant a tree it is no longer nourished by its old roots but by small new ones which it puts out. His greatest love is for pears. He lists every one of the five hundred best pear trees in the King's garden; his favourite is *Bon Chrétien d'Hiver* on which he writes a poetic eulogy. For one thing there is its ancient lineage – it was already known to the Romans who called it *Crustumeria*; and it always figured at their banquets – then its illustrious name, given in the early days of Christianity. Thirdly, nature has bestowed on us no more beautiful fruit than this pear, so surprisingly large and symmetrical, often weighing more than a pound, and of a lovely yellow colour, with a pink blush on the side which gets the sun. It can easily be kept four or five months in a greenhouse, rejoicing the eyes of those who come to look at it, as they might visit a jewel or a treasure. As for taste, it is incomparable, with brittle, slightly scented flesh and sugary juice. It is not true to say that this pear can only succeed against a wall; M. de La Quintinie gives many reasons and much data disproving this universal belief – but he does think that if it is kept in the eternal calm of the greenhouse it will bear a great abundance of fruit. As for other sorts of pears, there are good, less good and mediocre but he does not know of any bad tempered (*méchant*) pear. He goes on to say that a true gardener will spend the public holidays walking round the beds with his assistants, pointing out their failures and noticing their successes.

The King was very fond of M. de La Quintinie, ennobled him, gave him a house in the kitchen garden and often went there for his daily walk. It is still quite unchanged today, including the door labelled 'Public' where the burghers of Versailles came to take away, free of charge, those vegetables not wanted at the château. Until 1963 when they had to be dug up, two of M. de La Quintinie's pear trees still existed at Versailles. In the nineteenth century many of them flourished

An illustration from *Instructions pour les Jardins Fruitiers et Potagers*.

there, surviving winters which killed other fruit trees. When La Quintinie died he was succeeded by his son.

The hereditary system was the foundation of the Versailles social structure from the highest to the humblest. The great appointments of the Court went from father to son, as well as the ministries, if the son was considered adequate – if he did not take on his father's charge, he sold it. Public offices, including the military ones, were inherited or bought, with the King's consent. The same applied to menial jobs. The mole-catchers were always of the Liard family. The engineers who built fountains were called Francine, pronounced Franchine; they descended from an Italian Francini brought to France by Henri IV as an expert on waterworks. His grandson, François Francine, designed the fountains at Versailles as well as the aqueduct of Arcueil which brought water to Paris (a good deal less of it than was used in the King's gardens). The last of the Francines was guillotined during the Terror. Jean-Baptiste Bontemps was *valet de chambre* to Louis XIII, his son Alexandre to Louis XIV; his grandson Louis-Alexandre, his great-grandson Louis and great-great-grandson Louis-Dominique were all *valets de chambre* to Louis XV. The Bontemps came to an end in 1766 with the death of Louis-Dominique after more than a hundred years in their powerful position. They were known as *Les Bontemps de Tout Temps*. Mouthier *le jeune* was Mme de Pompadour's cook; he was the son of Mme de Montespan's Mouthier *l'aîné* whose father, Mouthier *l'ancien*, was one of the Grand Condé's cooks. Such examples could be given indefinitely.

III

THE MORTEMARTS

Et vous, conspirez à la joie
Amours, jeux, ris, grâces, plaisirs
Et que chacun de vous s'emploie
A satisfaire ses désirs

RACINE

'You know,' the King once said to his sister-in-law 'I like clever, amusing people' (*les gens d'esprit*). This was true of him all his life. Nobody could have been cleverer and more amusing than Athénaïs de Montespan and the other members of the Mortemart family. She, her two sisters and their brother were always together; they were extremely brilliant. They had a way of talking which has unfortunately never been precisely described but which people found irresistible. Their lazy, languishing, wailing voices would build up an episode, piling unexpected exaggerations upon comic images until the listeners were helpless with laughter. Among themselves they used a private language. They were malicious, but good natured; they never really harmed anybody; they liked laughing and had the precious gift of making other people sparkle.

Mme de Montespan was christened Françoise but, rightly, considered that the name did not suit her and changed it to Athénaïs. She first came to the Court in 1660, the year of the King's marriage, and was maid of honour to his sister-in-law, the first Madame. Nearly all his women originated in the household of his brother's wives, so that this came to be known as 'the nursery garden of the mistresses'. Three years later she married Montespan but she always had her eye on the King and must have found it hard to bear that he should have picked another flower, Mlle de La Vallière, out of the same garden. Athénaïs cleverly courted Louise and became her greatest friend so that she saw the King every day. But years went by and she got no further with him. At last she felt the need of a little supernatural assistance. She firmly believed in God, was in fact very devout, but unfortunately it is against the rules to ask Him to give one the chance of committing double adultery. So she went to consult the fashionable fortune-teller, Mme Voisin; what happened between the two women is not known for certain but the present writer believes it to have been more or less as described in the following pages.

Athénaïs de Mortemart, Marquise de Montespan,
in front of her gallery at Clagny, artist unknown.

Mme Voisin, whose kind, motherly face in her portrait by Le Brun shakes one's faith in the art of physiognomy, did not live in some sordid back alley. She was a comfortable bourgeoise and had a villa in its own grounds near Saint-Denis, where she gave elegant parties, to the music of resident violinists. She had friends in many walks of life; minor noblemen and the public executioner were among her lovers; her daughter's godmother was the respectable Mme de La Roche Guyon. She gave excellent advice to her clients and did what she could to help them, catering for little feminine desires such as larger breasts and smaller mouths, white hands and luck at cards. When unwanted babies were on the way she was very understanding. If wishes concerned an inheritance there were certain powders; for unrequited love various forms of magic. No doubt she began by advising Mme de Montespan, by talking over the situation – and who, longing to be loved, can have enough of such talks and such advice? But nothing happened; the King remained indifferent. At last Mme Voisin said they had better try spells. Unfortunately any really efficaceous spells entailed calling in Satan, with the attendant risk of hell fire. In those days faith, which was general, included belief in the Devil. There he was, just round the corner, with his horns and his tail and his dreadful fascination, waiting to pounce. If God refused a prayer, Satan might well grant it, though at the price of eternal flames. Athénaïs, young and healthy and with all her life before her was not, yet, unduly preoccupied by the next world; her thoughts were centred on this one. In 1667 she had been married for four years and had two children; the time had come to realize her ambitions.

Mme Voisin knew a priest who was willing to help. He read the Gospel over Mme de Montespan's head; there was some nonsense with pigeons' hearts under a consecrated chalice; and she prayed: 'Please let the King love me. Let Monseigneur le Dauphin be my friend and may this love and this friendship last. Please make the

Engraving of Mme Voisin.

The siege of Lille, 1667 by Antoine van der Meulen. Painted for Marly.

The Marquis de Montespan by Nicolas de Largillière.

Queen sterile; let the King leave La Vallière and never look at her again; let the Queen be repudiated and the King marry me'. It was all rather harmless and undeniably successful. The King seemed to become aware of Athénaïs for the first time. He went off to besiege Lille (June 1667), taking her in the capacity of lady-in-waiting to the Queen. Louise de La Vallière was not invited. In despair she followed the royal party and caught up with it as the camp was being pitched. When she came face to face with the King he put on a terrifying manner and said 'Madame, I don't like having my hand forced.' She had to go away again, deeply humiliated. During this campaign Mme de Montespan became his mistress. Her sacrilegious prayer seemed well on the way to being answered. The King loved her now; so did the Dauphin aged eight (and his affection never changed). The King's looks in the direction of La Vallière were getting fewer and colder, though this did not prevent him from giving her another baby as a parting present. The Queen was far from sterile; she had six children, but all except the Dauphin were dead by 1672, two as infants and the other three at a few years old. They were murdered, not by Mme de Montespan's spells but by the Court doctors. As for the King's remarriage the time for that was not yet.

So the *Divertissement* of 1668 to usher out the old Versailles ushered in a new mistress but the King had to be careful that this should not be too apparent. In the eyes of the Church and of his subjects, double adultery was a far greater sin than a love affair with an unmarried woman. Athénaïs, Marquise de Montespan, was not only a wife but a mother; furthermore M. de Montespan, unlike the usual run of men whose wives were honoured by the King and who built up enormous fortunes on this favour, minded. He made a song and dance. He boxed his wife's ears; when he was with the King he talked loudly about David and Bathsheba; he drove to Saint-Germain-en-Laye with a pair of horns wobbling about on the roof of his coach and there took leave of his friends and relations. Then he went into mourning and referred to the Marquise as his late wife. The King, who very much disliked being embarrassed, was furious; but Mme de Montespan only laughed and said scornfully that her husband and her parrot seemed to amuse *la canaille* about equally.

Montespan's uncle was the Archbishop of Sens; he took his nephew's side. He found a married woman, in his bishopric, who was living in open sin with another woman's husband and made her do public penitence. He put up notices in all his parishes drawing attention to the laws on adultery. The French bourgeoisie was made aware, by these and other means, of what was happening; it was shocked. However the King had his own way. He forced the Parlement of Paris to sanction a deed of separation solicited by Mme de Montespan; finally, as scandals do, the scandal lost its interest and everybody got used to the situation. But at first there were some nervous moments. The lovers were driven to pretending that the King was still attached to Louise de La Vallière while Mme de Montespan was in full fling with the Comte de Lauzun. Lauzun was the great amuser of the King's little set; he and the Marquise played their parts with enthusiasm; but Louise suffered. The others really could not see why; she was a rich duchess; Mme de Montespan was adorable to her, walked arm-in-arm with her and turned on full charm. For some reason none of this made up to Louise for the King passing through her room to find his new love and throwing her his little dog as he went. In 1671 she could bear it no more; she fled to Chaillot, the famous convent where the Palais de Chaillot now stands, and wrote to the King to say that, having given him her youth she wished to sacrifice the rest of her life to God. The King cried. He sent Colbert, bearing vague threats to the Mother Superior of what might happen to Chaillot if the nuns kept Mlle de La Vallière there. She was returned to Saint-Germain. Louis was alone with her for an hour and then, both crying, they went to see Mme de Montespan who was in floods of tears; she held out her arms, Louise fell into them and there was a total reconciliation all round. After this she stayed on, in good odour with the King and seeming much happier. Mme de Sévigné describes her at a Court ball with her beautiful little girl Marie-Anne, aged six, dressed in black velvet. Mme de Sévigné noticed that they called each other Mademoiselle and Belle Madame.

Mme de Montespan, who was a prolific woman, was soon expecting a baby. (She had, in all, nine.) The King, by now very much in love, looked forward to having a child of hers but feared that Montespan, the legal father, might claim it as his own. That would have been a pretty revenge exactly in the style of the Marquis. So Mme de Montespan concealed her condition as best she could and the lovers decided that some safe, reliable woman must be found who would take the infant at birth and look after it secretly. Mme de Montespan knew the very person, her own greatest friend, a poor, pretty, well born widow of thirty-four, noted for her piety, who was in difficult circumstances and lodging in a Paris convent – that same Mme Scarron

Louis XIV at the Establishment of the Academy of Science and the Foundation of the Observatory, 1667. Detail from a painting by Henri Testelin.

who had been with Athénaïs at the *Divertissement*. The King was not in favour of the idea. He did not like Mme Scarron; he thought she was a blue-stocking and he always sensed disapproval when she was there. Also he hated her friends. Nor did she show much enthusiasm for the job. She was proud, concerned with her own reputation and though by no means averse from a foothold at Court she only wanted it on regular terms. Underhand transactions involving new-born bastards did not appeal to her at all. At the same time she desperately needed both the money and the security which were offered to her. Mme de Montespan in such a dilemma might have gone to a fortune teller; Mme Scarron went to her confessor. He said that if the King himself asked her to take the child she could not very well refuse. And so it was. The King pocketed his prejudice and she her pride.

A house was bought in what was then a remote suburb between Paris and Vaugirard, (it still exists, No. 25 Boulevard du Montparnasse, buried in other houses and shops but of recognizably beautiful architecture). It was furnished; servants were engaged and Mme Scarron moved there from her convent. When the child, a girl, was born, Lauzun, in a cloak-and-dagger scene which he and Mme de Montespan must greatly have enjoyed, smuggled it out of Saint-Germain and handed it to Mme Scarron who sat waiting in a hackney cab. The baby was then settled into its secret nursery. In a very short time a little brother appeared, the future Duc du Maine. Mme Scarron loved children; they brought out the best in her curious nature; and she was an ideal governess. To her despair, the girl soon died. In those days most people took the death of an infant very lightly, especially if it was a female – not so Mme Scarron. The King was more moved by her grief than by his own loss and thereafter he liked her better.

While looking after the children Mme Scarron was able to go out in Paris society, as she had always done from her convent. She was a brilliant member of the brilliant circle presided over by the Comtesse de Lafayette and the Marquise de Sévigné. These famous writers were rather cut off from Court life; they were real Parisians, many of their friends had been compromised in the Fronde; and both of them had been intimate with Fouquet. The King looked upon the whole set with no good eye, though he thought them more tiresome than dangerous. It would not be true to say that they were satisfied with this state of affairs; they might have congratulated themselves on having escaped from the Court and its futilities but in fact they hankered after it.

Mme Scarron often dined with these friends and sometimes they would take her home as far as the park gate of the mysterious house where she was now living. No doubt they knew perfectly well why all of a sudden the poor widow had a house, a coach and servants of her own; why her plain, almost nun-like, though elegant gowns in the dark colours she always affected, were now of the finest cloth and embroidered with real gold thread. Mme de Sévigné tells all this in her letters but

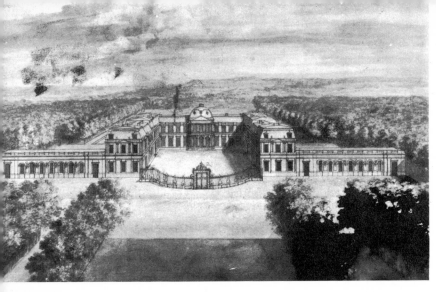

Drawing of the château of Clagny.

without any explanation. Better not to write such things since the mail was apt to be read by the police. Presently Mme Scarron began to amuse her friends with tales of that 'village she knows so well' (the Court); the tempers of Lauzun; the grief and woe and appalling boredom that often assailed the women there, 'from which she who is most to be envied is by no means immune'.

In 1673 the King went to the front with Mme de Montespan, heavily pregnant, Louise de La Vallière and the Queen, all lumbering after the army in the same coach, so that the peasants, amazed, used to tell how they had seen three Queens of France. It cannot have been a very cheerful trio; Marie-Thérèse, mad with jealousy, had vapours most of the time. Mme Scarron and the little boy were also of the party. Athénaïs had her new baby at Tournai and was obliged to be up and about two days later.

When the campaign was over the King thought it would be safe to recognize his two children. He gave them the titles of Duc du Maine and Comte de Vexin and took them to live with him. Mme Scarron came too.

Mme de Montespan was establishing her empire. At Clagny, a stone's throw from Versailles, the King built a house for his love. Unfortunately it was not large or grand enough to please her, she said scornfully that it was the sort of thing one gave to opera singers, so it was pulled down and a new young architect called Mansart, a protégé of Colbert's, designed a château on a more suitable scale. 'Armide's palace,' says Mme de Sévigné, after having visited it, 'the house is getting on fast, the garden is ready. You know Le Nôtre – he has left a little, dark wood which makes a perfect effect; there's a forest of orange trees in large tubs – then, to hide the tubs, on both sides of them there are palissades covered with tuberoses, roses, jasmin and carnations; a beautiful, surprising, enchanting idea – everybody loves this spot.'

Athénaïs's family shared in her glory. Her brother, the Duc de Vivonne, was

50

made Captain-General of the Galleys and Governor of Champagne and the Duc de Mortemart, her father, Governor of Paris.

Her sisters were the Marquise de Thianges, the eldest, and Mme de Fontevrault the youngest of the family; there was a fourth, a nun at Chaillot, but she had a true vocation and never appeared at Court. Mme de Thianges regarded herself as nature's masterpiece. Her husband bored her and she left him in order to join forces with Mme de Montespan, falling into bed with the King from time to time. She was a tremendous snob; two French families alone counted in her eyes, the Mortemarts and the Rochechouarts – the latter only because of their many marriages with Mortemarts. She used to make the King laugh by telling him that the Bourbons were decidedly *parvenus*. At parties Mme de Thianges would group all her relations together to show how wonderful they were and how superior to everybody else.

Mme de Fontevrault was the most beautiful and cleverest of the sisters. She was a nun without a vocation; the King made her abbess of the important convent of Fontevrault, where she ruled over both nuns and monks. He loved her company but she would never go to his parties, although she always saw him when she visited Athénaïs. She was a good nun, an excellent abbess and a learned woman; in her spare time she translated Plato. Like the rest of the family she loved a joke. When she was in Paris she used to take Mme de Montespan to hear the sermons of a certain Jesuit who was the double of the Duc de Vivonne. It made them shriek with laughter to see what seemed to be their naughty brother, dressed in a soutane, delivering himself of holy thoughts and priestly gestures.

Abbé Testu used to say of these sisters, 'Mme de Thianges talks like a woman who reads, Mme de Montespan like a woman who dreams and Mme de Fontevrault like a woman who talks'.

Mme de Montespan arranged for her penniless pious young niece, Mlle de Thianges, to marry one of Mazarin's nephews, the Duc de Nevers, who, according to Mme de Sévigné, always had his hands in unexpected places. He practised the 'Italian vice' (sodomy) and is said to have corrupted Monsieur, the King's brother. When he was young he was put into prison for baptizing a pig. Now the King gave him so many lucrative jobs that it was as though he had married a huge heiress. This marriage most unexpectedly turned out to be a happy one.

Mme de Montespan and Mme de Thianges obtained a percentage on the meat and tobacco sold in Paris, and numerous other benefits with which they were to make their fortunes. All the same, Mme de Montespan had some pride – she never would take jewels from the King. May this have been because the ones he lent her were even larger and finer than any he would have given away?

IV

THE ENVELOPE

Le luxe est la discipline de la prospérité

ANDRÉ GIDE

In 1674 the King began going to Versailles for prolonged visits; the enlarged house was more or less habitable and he was able to take his family, some of the courtiers and the government officials. The ministers now had lodgings of their own so that they could bring the archives, as they always had to do when the Court went for the annual visit to Fontainebleau, many waggon-loads of them, and work there properly. Louis XIV, his wife and his mistress were comfortably lodged at last. He lived on the first floor of the old château, behind the windows of his father's rooms which faced both east and west, since the Galerie des Glaces had not yet shut up the western wall. His private sitting-rooms were at a right angle to his bedroom, facing south over the Cour de Marbre. This courtyard was the business side of the château, the scene of comings and goings; all the Kings who lived at Versailles liked to keep an eye on it; Louis XV had a secret window through which he could see and not be seen; Louis XVI went so far as to set up a telescope. The Cour de Marbre was sometimes called the Cour du Louvre because it was only available to those who had the privilege of bringing their coaches into the great square courtyard of the Louvre – princes, dukes, marshals of France and ambassadors.

The Queen's rooms, also on the first floor, were in the southern part of the 'envelope' or new building and the beautiful 'Queen's staircase' led to them, through guard-rooms and antechambers which are now one big picture gallery. Her bedroom and drawing-rooms looked across the Orangery and Pièce d'Eau des Suisses up to the wooded heights of Satory. Here she herself died and so did one other Queen, Marie Leczinska, and two Dauphines, and here nineteen royal children were born. Versailles was fated never to have a Queen who could sustain the rôle as envisaged by Louis XIV, there was never to be another Anne of Austria. He wanted somebody who would not only shine in society, with infinite politeness, and ornament the royal pageant, but also rule over the courtiers and take an interest

Detail from a door in the Salon d'Apollon in the Grand Appartement.

Meeting between Louis XIV and Philip IV of Spain at the Ile des Faisans, 7 June 1660, to ratify the peace treaty between them following Louis' marriage to the Infanta Marie-Thérèse on 3 June at Fontarbie. With Louis are the queen-mother Anne of Austria, his brother Philippe Duc d'Orléans, Cardinal Mazarin, and the Prince de Conti. Behind is Marie-Thérèse wearing an embroidered white satin dress and holding a bouquet of emeralds with diamonds, a present from the king.

in their human problems. Marie-Thérèse knew very well how to behave at ceremonies and if her husband had no reason to be proud of her he had no reason to be ashamed either. But she had the mentality of a child, liked to play with little dogs and half-mad dwarfs and never learnt to speak French properly; she made no impact on her subjects. In spite of a pretty face she was not attractive; she had short legs and black teeth from eating too much chocolate and garlic. The King was fond of her and treated her in a fatherly way; and she worshipped him, though she avoided being left alone with him, it embarrassed her. One kind look from him made her happy all day. She believed everything he told her and the courtiers knew that she always repeated things to him. She suffered agonies of jealousy. At the beginning of the King's affair with Louise de La Vallière she had tried to assert herself by refusing to sleep with him. This was a very bad idea; it alienated him completely – months, and the intervention of the Queen Mother, were needed before their relationship became normal once more. 'The Lady of the Manor' as Mme de Sévigné called her, never tried that again. According to various contemporaries, the King and Queen had a black daughter who was kept in a convent near Melun. Certainly a little 'Moor' existed there and was regularly visited by the Queen and women of the royal family when the Court was at Fontainebleau. Whether she was really the daughter of Marie-Thérèse and Louis XIV will probably never be known.

The King's brother, the Duc d'Orléans, always known as Monsieur, had temporary rooms in the château of 1674 and a much grander suite when Versailles became even bigger. Until the Dauphin grew up Monsieur was the most important person at the Court. Louis was devoted to him though he regarded him as a joke and sometimes as a bad joke at that. Physically he was a caricature of his brother, three-quarters his height and more oriental-looking, swarthy, with eyes like black

Marie-Thérèse as Infanta by Velasquez.

Monsieur, Philippe, Duc d'Orléans by Jean Nocret.

currants. In spite of being one of history's most famous sodomites, Monsieur had two wives, a mistress and eleven legitimate children of whom seven died in infancy or were born dead; and he is the 'grandfather of Europe'. Every Roman Catholic royal family has him among its ancestors; all the Kings of France after Louis XIV, as well as Marie-Antoinette and the son of Napoleon descend from him. He modelled himself on the exquisite Henri III, even to the point of being devout, though this also came from his love of ceremony. Carefully brought up by Mazarin and Anne of Austria in total ignorance of public affairs, so that he should not embarrass his brother with political ambitions, his interests in life were clothes and jewels, parties, etiquette (on which he was sound), objects of art and boys. He loved his château at Saint-Cloud, which was perhaps the most attractive of all the royal country residences; the King also gave him Richelieu's town house, the Palais Royal.

In his youth Monsieur was partial to battles. He would arrive rather late on the field, having got himself up to kill; painted, powdered, all his eyelashes stuck together; covered with ribbons and diamonds – hatless. He never would wear a hat for fear of flattening his wig. Once in action he was as brave as a lion, only afraid of what the sun and dust might do to his complexion; and he proved an excellent strategist. But he soon found warfare too fatiguing; he was the only member of his family not to require violent exercise; he never went out hunting and seldom put his nose out of doors if he could help it.

Monsieur could be amusing – he was a chatterbox and at family gatherings his was the voice mostly heard. Louis, who had no small talk, said he was glad of it when he thought of the rivers of nonsense spouted by his brother. He treated the King with an infinitely respectful familiarity; he knew his place and stayed in it; the King responded affectionately but with more than a hint of condescension. 'Now we are going to work; go and amuse yourself, Brother.' He always called him Mon Frère – Monsieur called the King Monsieur. Sometimes the two of them would quarrel, that is to say Monsieur, who was extremely touchy, would behave rather like a Pomeranian yapping at a lion, for their set-tos were always of his making. This sort of thing was typical: a gentleman of his household, M. de Flamarens, offended Monsieur in some way and he dismissed him on a slender pretext. (The little court at Saint-Cloud is described by contemporaries as 'stormy'.) Soon afterwards Flamarens appeared at one of the King's evening parties. Monsieur, shaking with anger, went to the King and said 'Monsieur, Flamarens is being disrespectful to me. I did not forbid him your house as I know it would not be in order for me to do so, but I forbade him to appear before me and I find it very strange and insolent that he should be here.' 'But, Brother' said the King 'it's not my fault!' Monsieur then became so furious that the King said they had better talk about it when he was calmer; but the subject was never raised again and Flamarens continued to appear at Court.

Monsieur's first wife was his cousin Henrietta of England, much loved by all except him. She was the subject of Bossuet's sermon, delivered to a loudly sobbing Court: 'Madame se meurt; Madame est morte——' (1670). It was freely said in England that Madame was dead because she was poisoned by Monsieur's two minions, the Chevalier de Lorraine and the Marquis d'Effiat and that her husband was an accessory before the fact; but nobody who knew the little man believed this. Very probably she was not murdered at all. Her health had always been bad; all her eight children but two were still-born, one of them quite rotten, or died immediately; she was opened after her death and found to have an abcess on her liver. Be it as it may, Monsieur was ruled by Lorraine and d'Effiat to the end of his life. The King himself, who hated sodomites as a rule, was partial to the Chevalier de Lorraine, beautiful to look at and an amusing scoundrel.

After a year of freedom, Monsieur married again, another close relation of the English royal family, Princess Elizabeth-Charlotte (Liselotte) of the Palatinate. She was a Protestant and had to be converted to Roman Catholicism in order to marry a French prince; as a result she lost her claim, which was better than that of George I, to the throne of England. She did not mind at all – she disliked the English if possible even more than she did the French and became a good Catholic, although retaining a certain Protestant manner during her devotions. She found the French Catholics less bigoted than the Germans. 'Whoever wishes may read the Holy Scriptures and one is not obliged to believe in nonsense and stupid miracles. The Pope is not adored here and no value is set on pilgrimages and such things.'

Madame the second was a great blonde Teutonic tomboy; delicate little Monsieur seemed to be his wife's wife. When he first saw her he told his friends, despairingly, that he would never be able to manage. However, by dint of hanging holy medals

The *tapis vert* at Versailles.

Overleaf: Louis XIV visiting the Gobelins Manufactory, 15 October 1667;
tapestry after Charles Le Brun. Le Brun is presenting the craftsmen to the King.

in a certain place, rather impeding any pleasure Madame might have felt, he did manage and they had three children. After that, by mutual consent, they slept in different beds. He liked Liselotte better than Henrietta who was an intriguer and, he thought, might have had lovers. The courtiers noticed that the King too seemed fonder of her. Their short flirtation over he had never paid much attention to Henrietta. Liselotte had one great advantage in her husband's eyes; she did not care for diamonds, so that he was able to plaster his own clothes with all he had. Somebody asked their little boy, the Duc de Chartres, if he was fond of dressing up. 'I like it better than Madame does, but not as much as Monsieur.' She never bothered about clothes; she only had full dress gowns and riding habits.

Madame adored hunting; she rode hard, eight hours on end, looking like an enormous policeman, until well over sixty. She was fond of animals and had many pets; little dogs and a tame duck; she hoped they had immortal souls, while doubting whether anybody had. She also collected medals and geological specimens. The rest of her time was spent in a small room lined with portraits of German princes, writing letters – at least thirty pages every day to various royal relations all over Europe, including Henrietta's two daughters, the Duchess of Savoy and the Queen of Spain, whom she loved like younger sisters. She is one of the best sources of information about Versailles, but her letters, entertaining as they are, are not quite reliable. Like Saint-Simon, who arrived at the Court twenty-three years later than she did, she was full of prejudices and was inclined to invent all sorts of lies with which to justify them. She complained bitterly about the French. 'People only have to marry in France and the desire to laugh will leave them.' But she liked Versailles; she said it was so comfortable having everything under the same roof and the hunting at one's door. She hated Paris.

Madame knew quite well that her letters were opened by the King's police and often read by him – she used them in the rashest way, to let off steam or tell home truths as she never would have dared, to his face. She was obsessed by him; probably in love with him. Monsieur and Madame were both very fond of Mme de Montespan. Madame does not seem to have been jealous of her, as she was of the King's later attachment. She was already established as mistress before Madame arrived in France, besides which Athénaïs got on with everybody.

Madame described her day as follows: she gets up at nine and goes where you can guess; then says her prayers, reads three chapters of the Bible, dresses and receives visits. At eleven, she reads and writes for an hour. After chapel comes dinner, over at about two. Then, on days when there is no hunting, she reads and writes until the King's supper at a quarter to eleven. He often doesn't appear until half past. At twelve-thirty he says goodnight. When there is a play it is given at about seven (the King grew to like the theatre less and less but Monsieur and Madame greatly enjoyed it and in the end he only had plays at Versailles when they

Queen Marie-Thérèse and the Dauphin by Pierre Mignard.

were there). On hunting days Madame gets up at eight and goes to church at eleven.

At the beginning of Mme de Montespan's reign she and the King received their friends at Versailles in a large and beautiful flat on the ground floor called the Appartement des Bains. It contained a sort of Turkish, or Roman bath, with rooms for washing and for resting and one with a large marble basin, filled with warm water, where people, having already washed, could disport themselves. The inhabitants of Versailles were by no means as dirty as has sometimes been said, although then, as now, some people were cleaner than others. The King and his brother were almost fanatically clean in their persons; they were rubbed down with spirits every morning, before the ceremonial *levée*; and they changed their linen three times a day. Mlle de La Vallière and her daughter, too, were clean to the point of fussiness; Mme de Montespan was a grubby woman. The Queen's chief pleasure in life was long, hot baths. (The soap which they used was made at Marseilles from olive oil.) As for the château, Madame thought it rather dirty, and with such crowds milling to and fro it could hardly have been polished and shiny like some small German palace. But it is certainly not true to say that people relieved themselves on the staircase; there were privies in the courtyard where the W.Cs are now. When crowds came down from Paris for balls or fêtes there was sometimes a queue for the public conveniences and then a rich bourgeois in a hurry would pay a nobleman's servant as much as four *louis* to be conducted to his master's privy. Versailles was not unique in depending upon the chamber-pot and the *chaise percée* for all sanitation; most houses and palaces did so until the twentieth century. The present writer well remembers arriving at Buckingham Palace to be presented, in 1923, after a long, chilly wait in the Mall; and finding that the only possibility offered was a chamber-pot behind a screen in the ladies' cloakroom.

Mme de Montespan was lodged next door to the King's own flat, in rooms looking south onto the courtyard. They have been completely refashioned by subsequent occupants in the eighteenth century and are now shown as the Cabinet Doré of Mme Adélaïde and the library of Louis XVI. But the windows are the same. When Mme de Montespan and Louis XIV were known to be together behind these windows, the courtiers would do anything sooner than pass underneath them – they called it going before the firing squad. Both she and the King frightened people; she was a tease, a mocking-bird, noted for her wonderful imitations and said to be hard hearted. This meant that she regarded serious events with a cheerful realism; she was not sentimental. When her coach ran over a man and killed him the other women present all cried – they reproached Athénaïs for seeming unmoved. But she pointed out that they only cried because they had seen the thing happening; they never gave a thought to the men who were run over every day. She received a message from Mme de Maintenon to say that her children's house was on fire.

Louis XIV. Detail from the *Resurrection of Christ* by Charles Le Brun, 1674. A painting commissioned by the Merciers of Paris when he returned 50,000 livres they had loaned him for the war in French-Comté.

Overleaf: allegory of the royal family by Jean Nocret.

As she was at Saint-Germain-en-Laye and the house was in Paris there was nothing she could do about it – she remarked that no doubt it would bring the children good luck and went on playing cards.

As for Louis XIV, it would be impossible to exaggerate the terror which he inspired, and with good reason. He had a ruthless side to his nature, especially when he was young. This came partly from lack of imagination and partly because he thought it was his duty to uphold the dignity of God's representative on earth. A poor woman once shouted crazy insults at him. Her son had been killed in an accident during the building of Versailles and people thought that when the King heard the whole story he would surely forgive her. But he had her whipped. People talked under their breath of the Man in the Iron Mask, that prisoner of quality kept in solitary confinement, of whom nobody knew either the identity or the crime. Some courtiers lost out hunting were welcomed, warmed and fed by a mysterious gentleman whose house they came upon in the forest not twenty miles from Versailles. He turned out to be an old Frondeur who had lived there peacefully ever since the rebellion, an event so remote that it seemed like history to the new generation. The King's friends thought to amuse him with this adventure; to their horror, and in spite of all their protests, the man was arrested and executed. One of Louis' small, intimate set, Lauzun spent ten years in a fortress either for wanting to marry the Grande Mademoiselle, the King's cousin, or for going too far with his jokes – in short, for being altogether above himself.

Louis XIV took no account of feminine weaknesses. If one of his mistresses was pregnant she was told to conceal the fact; when her time came she had better have the baby quickly and silently and join the other courtiers as soon as the child had been smuggled out of sight. 'Why so pale, Mademoiselle?' the Queen unkindly asked Louise de La Vallière, knowing quite well why. 'Too many tuberoses and lilies in my room, Your Majesty.'

When he travelled from one of his houses to another he only took women with him in his coach – his mistresses, later on his daughters or great friends. He thought if he spent several hours alone with a man he would be sure to ask some boon and embarrass the King. These journeys, except for the prestige they gave, were a real torment to his companions. In the coldest weather all the windows had to be kept open as he could not bear stuffiness. The ladies were expected to be merry, to eat a great deal (he hated people to refuse food) and to have no physical needs which would force them to leave the coach. If by any chance they were taken ill, fainted, or felt sick, they could expect no sympathy; on the contrary, disfavour set in. One of his closest friends, the Duchesse de Chevreuse, Colbert's daughter, went alone with him from Versailles to Fontainebleau, a journey which took about six hours. Hardly had they left Versailles when she was seized with a pressing and seemingly irresistible need to retire. She knew that there was nothing to be done, though every mile that went by increased her misery. About half way there the King stopped the coach and a meal was served; she ate and drank as little as she possibly could but even that little made her condition worse. She cast longing glances at a peasant's house nearby but dared not go to it. They started off again. Several times she nearly fainted, but she hung on and at last they arrived. Her brother-in-law, the Duc de Beauvilliers, was waiting in the courtyard to meet them and she hissed in his ear the state she was in, saying she would never be able to get as far as her own room. He hurried her to the chapel and mounted guard while she relieved herself there.

There were few who did not tremble before Louis XIV; his sister-in-law and cousin, the first Madame, had trembled when they were boy and girl together – even the great Condé did. People who went to Court for the first time were told that it was better to get used to seeing the King before daring to address him, since the first contact with his personality often struck dumb. This terrifying side was the reverse

62

Henrietta of England, Duchesse d'Orléans, the first Madame, holding a portrait of her husband in her hand by Antoine Matthieu, 1664.

Elizabeth Charlotte, Princess Palatine, Duchesse d'Orléans, the second Madame, by Nicolas de Largillière.

Antonin de Caumont, Duc de Lauzun wearing the Order of the Garter, by Peter Lely.

Michel Le Tellier, Marquis de Louvois, by Sebastien Bourdon.

of the medal. The King could be most human. When he gave an audience, even if it was to somebody who had displeased him, he would listen attentively and with goodness, only interrupting in order to understand the point which his interlocutor was trying to make. He was polite – perhaps the most truly polite king who ever lived. He always took off his hat to women, even to some small little housemaid, though raising it higher according to their rank. With men, the hat was brought to a fine art; for the dukes it came off though only a little, for others it was tilted, or rested a moment on his ear. If he was in his carriage and saw a priest with the viaticum he would get out, whatever the weather, and kneel on the ground. He was only seen to lose his temper to the point of physical violence three times in his long life, with Louvois, with Lauzun, when he broke his stick and threw it out of the window so as not to be tempted to strike a gentleman and, when, deeply upset at hearing of the cowardice of his son du Maine, he struck a footman for stealing a biscuit at his table. 'This prince', says Saint-Simon, 'so even-tempered and so perfectly controlled, gave way on this unique occasion.' The astonishment of the bystanders spoke for itself.

Louis XIV loved a joke and in his dry fashion could be very witty. The best way of getting out of a difficult situation was to make him laugh; Mme de Montespan's hold over him was partly due to her funniness. She was never frightened of him, only of losing him.

This year, 1674, Mlle de La Vallière accepted the fact that she had lost him; asked and received permission to leave the Court for good. She threw herself at the Queen's feet in public and begged forgiveness; then she entered Orders as a Carmelite. All her friends at the Court went to see her take the veil; the spectacle was touching. She said that she left the world without regret though not without pain, 'I believe, I hope and I love'. She was only thirty; and she expiated her sin with much mortification of the flesh for another thirty-six years. So it was that she who had once been the very soul of Versailles never had a suite of rooms in the château and never saw it completed.

There was still not enough room at Versailles for all the people by whom the King would have liked to be surrounded but at least he could now hold his Court there; the splendid suite of seven reception rooms known as the Grand Appartement was ready. The walls and ceilings, decorated by Le Brun and his pupils, are exactly as they were then, but the furniture, the hangings and curtains, of embroidered velvet in winter and flowered silk in summer, the silver candelabra and chandeliers from which flickered a hundred thousand candles, so that the whole place appeared to be on fire, have vanished; and the pictures are in the Louvre. They were: Giorgione's *Musicians*, Antonio Moro's *Portrait of a Man*, all the Leonardos of the Louvre including '*la femme d'un Florentin nommée Gioconde*', Andrea del Sarto's *Tobias*, Mantegna's *Virgin*, Titian's *Entombment, Last Supper, Christ and the Pilgrims at Emmaus, The Virgin and St Agnes, Portrait of a Man, Andromeda*, Veronese's *The Pilgrims at Emmaus, The Virgin, St John and St Catherine, Judith and the head of Holofernes, Flight into Egypt, Woman presenting her son to Christ, David and Bathsheba*, Guido Reni's *Labours of Hercules, Flight into Egypt, The Good Samaritan*, Guercino's *Virgin and St Peter*, Raphaël's *St John, La Belle Jardinière*, Carracci's *St Sebastian, Aeneas carrying his father*, Poussin's *Our Lady of the Columns, Rebecca at the Well* and seven others, Rubens's *La Tomirice, Labour of Hercules, Marie de Médicis*, Domenichino's *The Musicians*, Bassano's *Noah's Ark*.

Many of these pictures came from the collection of François I, but Louis XIV also collected. When he came to the throne he owned about two hundred – when he died over two thousand. He liked the Venetian and Bolognese schools – in his bedroom he had Caravaggio's *St John the Baptist*, Guido Reni's *Mary Magdalene*, a self-portrait by Van Dyck (it is still there), Domenichino's *St Cecilia* and Veronese's *St Catherine*.

The Grand Appartement was essential to the routine of Court life as planned by the King, since the whole establishment could foregather here, and did so every morning for the procession to Mass and three times a week for an evening entertainment which was called *Appartement*. The gambling without which it would have been impossible to keep the courtiers amused and happy took place in the Grand Appartement. Versailles was often known as '*ce tripot*' (gambling den) and indeed resembled a casino. The nobles played high and, unless the King happened to be in the room, when they more or less controlled themselves, those who were losing fell into audible despair; they howled, blasphemed, made dreadful faces, pulled out their hair and wept. They cheated shamelessly and were not specially blamed for doing so. Those who could remember St François de Sales said that he cheated worse than anybody in his worldly days, though in all other respects the best of fellows. The few who never lost their self control at the tables were remarkable, they

64   The entry of Louis XIV and Marie-Thérèse into Arras, 30 July 1667.
Detail from a painting by Antoine van der Meulen for Marly.
The King, with his brother, follows the coach with the Queen and ladies of the court.

A promenade in the gardens at Versailles; detail from a painting by Jean-Baptiste Martin.

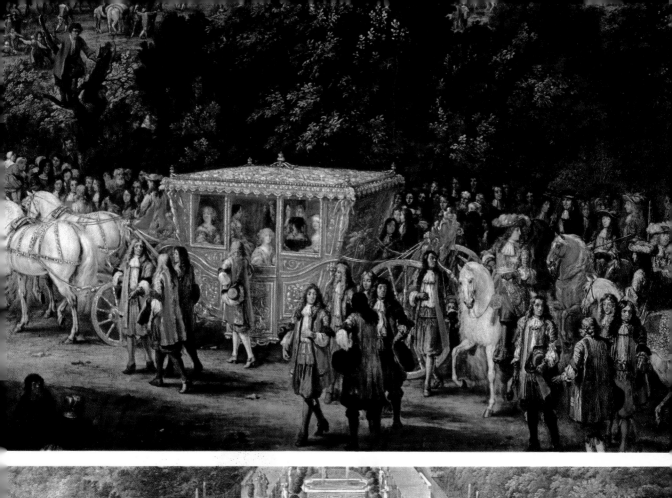

The ladies gaming; with Monseigneur, the Princesse of Conti Douairière, the Duc and Duchesse de Bourbon and M. de Vendôme. Engraving by A. Trouvain.

Louis XIV playing billiards; with the Ducs de Chartres, Toulouse, Vendôme, and MM. d'Armagnac and Chamillart. Engraving by A. Trouvain.

included Mazarin's niece the Comtesse de Soissons, the Venetian Ambassador Giustiniani, the Marquis de Beaumont who gambled away everything he possessed at a single sitting without making any observation, and the Marquis de Dangeau, for years the best card player in France, who generally won and was never suspected of cheating. Dangeau was the author of the dullest but most reliable diary of the period; it was annotated after his death by Saint-Simon, who freely used it in the composition of his memoirs. Voltaire said it was written by Dangeau's servants, and indeed the entries are in different handwritings.

Whist had not yet been invented; ten or eleven different games were played, of a simple variety, rather like *vingt-et-un*. It paid, however, to have card sense, even if but little skill was required. The Queen, who loved gambling and was as stupid at cards as she was at everything else, invariably lost. As well as cards they played Hocca, a sort of roulette at which people lost such enormous sums, and which was generally so crooked, that two Popes forbade it in the Papal States and so did La Reynie, head of the police, in Paris. To his annoyance, the King not only allowed it at the Court but even played it himself. His favourite card game was Reversi, which Napoleon also liked, but Louis preferred billiards to playing cards as it made him fidgety to sit still for any length of time. A billiard table was set up in one of the rooms (Salle de Diane) of the Grand Appartement.

As well as the gambling there were plays, concerts and dances. The King was devoted to music and seldom without any – a band or orchestra was generally playing within his earshot; he woke up to the sound of a band in the courtyard. On summer nights he and his friends would go on the canal in gondolas, followed by Lully and his fiddlers on a sort of floating platform. These gondolas, complete with gondoliers, were sent to the King as a present from the Venetian Republic. He built a village for them called Little Venice, on the water.

The Baptism of the Dauphin; detail from a Gobelins tapestry after Charles le Brun.

Marly, the east or entrance front; a reconstruction by Ian Dunlop from contemporary drawings.

In 1679 Louis XIV with his architect Jules Mansart, began to build Marly, a small house near Versailles where he could go in order to be quiet and peaceful, taking a few friends. The château itself was large enough for him and his family and there were twelve pavilions, eleven which housed two married couples in each and one which was kept for bathrooms. These pavilions were connected with each other and the main building by arbours of sweet-scented shrubs. The etiquette at Marly was quite different from that at Versailles and much easier. Whereas at Versailles no man but Monsieur ever sat down to dine with the King, at Marly the Dauphin and, later on, his three sons, Monsieur and his son Chartres could do so, though generally the Dauphin presided at a second table and the King had the women at his own. The men all ate together at a third. The day at Marly was spent looking at improvements in the gardens, where the King amused himself for the rest of his life turning lakes into forests and forests into lakes; the whole place was a bower of blossom. In the evening there were balls, parties, concerts, plays and, of course, gambling.

Invitations to Marly, where one lived so intimately with the King, were much sought after; he liked people to ask for one, so that when it became known that a visit there was in prospect, he would go down the Galerie des Glaces on his way to church to the sound of 'Sire, Marly?' from many throats. In fact the same people were asked over and over again, those with whom he felt easy. As at Versailles he gave parties in the garden before the house was ready – he slept there for the first time in 1686.

All the buildings at Marly, except one or two lodges and gardeners' houses were destroyed after the French Revolution, but the site is still one of the most beautiful parks in the Ile de France.

Jules Hardouin Mansart by François De Troy.

V

THE GOVERNESS

Sa compagnie est délicieuse

MME DE SÉVIGNÉ,
OF MME SCARRON

In 1674 Mme Scarron began what in later life she used to call her 'long struggle for the King's soul'. In this struggle her chief adversary was Mme de Montespan and her most powerful weapon the little Duc du Maine. He was a particularly fascinating baby who had inherited all his mother's looks and charm. Mme Scarron brought him on, taught him to read at a very early age and never punished or frightened him, so that he was confident with grown-up people. The King loved him much more than his other children and he responded naturally. It was the greatest pity that Louis never took such a fancy to the Dauphin, who was much better human material but was being ruined by a different sort of upbringing. His father, whose own schooling in practical government, with Mazarin's brilliant manoeuvres as an example, had been unique, but whose book-learning left much to be desired, was particularly anxious for the Dauphin to have a good general education. He appointed Bishop Bossuet, the greatest living manipulator of French prose, as his tutor. His governor was the Duc de Montausier. No doubt from excellent motives these two men beat the Dauphin cruelly, every day at his lessons. On one occasion it was even thought that they had broken his arm. Montausier was a brute but Bossuet ought to have known better. Presumably he had no understanding whatever of children. The Dauphin was far from stupid – some of his contemporaries go as far as to say that he was a brilliant little boy – but all this punishment put him off books for ever; he became timid in society and terrified of his father; and of course this reacted on the King. As a result his natural fondness for children was concentrated on his bastards, especially on du Maine.

Mme de Montespan, for all her brilliance, was a bad psychologist. She thought that when golden curls, blue eyes and high spirits are not enough to hold a lover he must be brought back by spells; she never saw an alternative close at hand in the form of a little boy. But Mme Scarron knew that nothing links two people as much

Françoise d'Aubigné, Marquise de Maintenon by Pierre Mignard.

as a child – the dullest woman can hold a man, particularly if he is not very young, by talking to him about that extension of himself, his son; she saw the King every day in order to do so. He had got over the aversion he used to have for her and she was quite at her ease with him. Presently their conversation began to include such subjects as the state of his soul. 'Sire, you love your musketeers. Now what would you say if one of them left his wife and lived with a married woman?' The King laughed. 'I spoke to him as a Christian and as a real friend of Mme de Montespan.'

Years later she defended her behaviour in these terms: 'Mme de Montespan and I were the greatest friends in the world; she loved my company and I, in the simplicity of my nature, gave myself up to this friendship. She was attractive and brilliant, I was in her confidence and she told me everything. Then, there we were, on bad terms, without however wanting to break off relations. It was certainly not my fault and yet if anybody had a grievance she had; she could say, with perfect truth, "I put her where she is, I made the King like her; then she becomes the favourite and I am sent away." On the other hand was I wrong to accept the King's friendship? Was I wrong to give him good advice and to use my influence to make him lead a virtuous life? If, loving Mme de Montespan as I loved her, I had launched an intrigue for wicked reasons, if I had given bad advice as regards either God or the world; if, instead of urging her to break with the King I had shown her the best way of keeping him, then indeed I would have given her ammunition with which to destroy me. Am I not right in saying that there is nothing so clever as not only not being in the wrong but having always and with everybody an irreproachable conduct?'

The King's thoughts were turning towards reconciliation with the Church. Bossuet and the other great preachers of the day had been admonishing him from the pulpit for years. He put up with their criticism but he could not be said to like it. He had a great respect for God, whom he regarded as his feudal overlord, and was grateful to Him for the military successes and civilian splendours of his reign; he wanted to show his gratitude. Besides, if God became really angry He might take away what He had given. Long, interesting conversations with Mme Scarron were the order of the day.

Mme de Montespan began to be uneasy. She wanted now to get rid of her friend, not that she regarded her as a rival, but the King was spending hours with Mme Scarron when he might have been with her; the thought of their deep talks together bored her, besides, she was not at all anxious for him to become godly. However, Mme Scarron was not a nursery maid who could be given notice; she would clearly have to have an enormous reward for her services. Athénaïs thought she might like a husband. She cast about and presently found an old Duc de Villars-Brancas who, for the kind of dowry recently bestowed on Nevers, was ready to marry. Mme Scarron refused. Mme de Montespan then suggested a nunnery; the King could make her the abbess of some rich foundation. She energetically refused and the King was displeased – he told Mme de Montespan that he had no wish for Mme Scarron to leave the Court. He had a better idea: he would give her an estate and a title. A large and beautiful château near Chartres was purchased, Mme Scarron took its name and was henceforth known as the Marquise de Maintenon.

Mme de Maintenon kept Bossuet informed of the King's new frame of mind and he now brought up all his ammunition. The year 1675 was a jubilee of the Church and the priests were anxious that Louis should go to his Easter duties for once. Bourdaloue came to Court to preach the Lenten sermons; of all the divines he had the most influence over a congregation. His sermons were noted for their length (women who were not certain of being able to hold out for the necessary hours used to arrive at the chapel with a small china receptacle which they concealed under their skirts and which was called a Bourdalou) but this did not put people off them; they were profound, solidly composed and delivered at enormous speed; intensely stirring. Maréchal de Gramont was so much affected during one of them that he burst out with: '*Mordieu*, he is quite right' upon which Madame gave a huge guffaw, Bourdaloue lost his place and all was confusion. He did not mince his words during this Lent; he said right out that the King must give an example; he even spoke of debauchery. The courtiers trembled; Louis appeared to be unmoved.

But when Easter came he sent Mme de Montespan to her house at Clagny. Both he and she confessed and communicated. When he went off to join the army without saying good-bye to Athénaïs, everybody thought the love affair was over.

Mme de Montespan took the whole thing very calmly. She was no longer irked by the presence of Mme de Maintenon, who was at a watering place in the south with du Maine. The little boy had a half paralysed leg, shorter than the other, which seemed to be getting worse. The doctors tortured him for years during his childhood, pulling the short leg with a sort of rack until it was longer than the good one and very weak; he bore everything with courage and patience. Mme de Maintenon devoted herself to him, she was determined that he should be cured and in the end he was, more or less, though he always limped. During their tour he was received by the provincial notables and common people exactly as if he had been a legitimate prince of France, with wild enthusiasm.

Meanwhile his mother was enjoying herself at Clagny, where there were still twelve hundred workmen, inside and out, who greatly diverted her; she spent a good deal of time at Saint-Cloud, playing cards with Monsieur, and went for a while to take the waters at Bourbon. The Queen paid her a visit at Clagny: she went all over the house and gardens, inspected the nursery, where Vexin lay ill (he was delicate and died at the age of twelve), expressed the greatest interest in everything she saw and spent an hour alone with Athénaïs in her room. She was not the

only visitor; Bossuet often called on Mme de Montespan. She treated this awe-inspiring man in a most lively way; carrying the war into the enemy's camp and accusing him of wanting to reform the King out of spiritual pride. When he did not bother to defend himself she made violent scenes; then she put on charm and finally tried bribery, holding out hopes of great ecclesiastical honours. Of course none of this had the slightest effect; she cannot really have expected to get round Bossuet. She had to find some other way of winning her cause.

Mme Voisin also went to Clagny, with some constructive suggestions. She sent to Normandy for the receipts of a certain Galet, who trafficked in all sorts of interesting drugs such as love philtres and *poudres à héritage*, a kind of medicine for disposing of old, rich unwanted relations. Rivals in love were also dealt with by M. Galet. Mme de Montespan's case was rather special since there seemed to be no rival; the issue was between God and Satan. If she really had Black Masses celebrated on her account it was now that she began; she certainly tried more spells. Several different love philtres, in the form of powder, a black, a white and a grey, were delivered to her at Clagny.

At last the King returned from the front. Bossuet, who had heard certain disturbing rumours, went, religious grief written all over his face, to meet him on the road, only to hear from his own lips that Mme de Montespan's rooms at Versailles were indeed being prepared for her. The Bishop was not much reassured when Louis added something about living together in Christian chastity. In fact, the desires of a returning warrior, excited by Galet's splendid powders, soon undid the work of Mme de Maintenon and the divines. The King arranged to meet Athénaïs in the presence of respectable, elderly women of the Court, who were to witness the transformation of love into friendship. The two former lovers began by exchanging a few platitudes for all to hear, but then they went over to a window embrasure, away from the crowd. They were both seen to be crying. Suddenly he led her to the door of her bedroom; they bowed to the company and disappeared. After that, everything was perfect, though the King, for some unaccountable reason, began to have appalling headaches.

On 29 July 1676, Mme de Sévigné spent a day at Versailles and wrote an account of it to her daughter, Mme de Grignan. She went down with the Villars: first they assisted at the Queen's toilette; went to Mass and then watched the royal dinner. At three o'clock everybody assembled in the Grand Appartement. The King, the Queen, Monsieur and Madame with Monsieur's eldest daughter, Mme de Montespan and her people, all the courtiers, all the ladies – in other words, the Court of France – were in these beautiful rooms. It was not the least bit too hot; you wandered about as you liked, no feeling of being crowded. The King was with Mme de Montespan who was taking cards; the Queen, at her own table, had Monsieur, Mme de Soubise, Dangeau and Co., Langlée and Co., all playing with gold *louis* and no counters – a thousand *louis* were on the table. Dangeau let Mme de Sévigné sit by him so that she was very comfortable and she watched him and saw how badly everybody else played compared to him. He never looked up from the game – was completely concentrated – never missed a trick or let the smallest opportunity escape him, so that luck or no luck he couldn't help winning – the proof was that he had been credited in the book with ten thousand *louis* in ten days.

Mme de Sévigné curtseyed to the King in the way Mme de Grignan had shown her – had she been young and pretty he could not have responded more kindly. The Queen asked how she was after her illness and talked about it at length with as much interest as if it had been childbirth. In fact everybody had a kind word for her.

Mme de Nevers is very pretty and modest – M. de Nevers has not changed a bit but his wife is madly in love with him. Her sister, Mlle de Thianges, is more beautiful but not so nice. M. du Maine is incomparable, so funny and clever and says such unexpected things. Mme de Maintenon and Mme de Thianges together are like the Guelphs and the Ghibellines. Madame most friendly. Mme de Montespan talked of the cure she was doing at Bourbon and asked about Vichy. She said she took one bad knee to Bourbon and came away with two. Her back is perfectly straight and her looks are amazing. She is half the size she was but neither her skin, her eyes nor her mouth are any the worse for that. Her dress was of French needlepoint lace, her hair, in a thousand curls done up with black ribbons; she wore huge diamonds and enormous pearls – in short a triumphant beauty to dazzle the ambassadors. She knows that people have felt she prevented them from seeing the King, so here he is, she has given him back to them – Mme de Grignan can't imagine how gay and beautiful it all was. So all this charming, easy-going yet orderly confusion of the cream of society lasted from three till six. The post arrived in the middle of it and the King went off to read his letters but he soon reappeared. There was music all the time. At six o'clock the gambling stopped – no need to bother with accounts as they were playing with gold. Then everybody got into carriages – the King, Mme de Montespan, Mme de Thianges and Monsieur in one, the Queen and the Princesses in another followed by all the rest. From six to ten the whole company floated on the canal in gondolas to the music of a band. At ten o'clock the play began and at midnight there was supper. So passes a Saturday at Versailles.

Mme de Maintenon had returned to the Court, leading du Maine by the hand. He was better, could walk alone and much bigger. The King was delighted to see them both and gratified by the reception his little boy had had in the provinces, but Athénaïs was not so pleased to find Mme de Maintenon at her elbow again. Mme de Maintenon herself complained to her confessor, the Abbé Gobelin, 'I can't believe that it is really God's will that I should have to put up with Mme de Montespan – she is incapable of friendship'. She said that whatever rules she made for the children were immediately reversed by their mother. Mme de Maintenon also complained to the King, who took her part – Athénaïs naturally found this unendurable and furiously reproached them both. Then she knew that they went away and talked about her behind her back, so she made more scenes. She was no Louise de La Vallière to bear everything, a slow trickling tear her only form of protest.

Very soon the whole world was talking about the two women, their quarrels and their reconciliations. These were astonishingly frequent because in fact the Marquises were fascinated by each other. When it seemed as if they had broken for ever, Mme de Maintenon would go and stay at Clagny or Athénaïs at Maintenon. This old *château-fort* was being modernized; and the King sent Le Nôtre to see what he could do with the garden. Having inspected the improvements in each other's houses, apparently on the best of terms, the two women would come back to the Court and refuse to speak to each other. On one occasion, after many scenes and sulks, they were obliged to travel from Versailles to Fontainebleau together alone in a coach. Athénaïs, settling herself comfortably for the long drive, said 'Do let's forget everything and chat as we used to – might as well enjoy ourselves while we can'. They laughed the whole way, but after their arrival were on the same bad terms as before – worse, indeed, because the King made Mme de Maintenon tell Athénaïs that she had better begin thinking about her salvation. Nothing loath, she did tell her, to be rewarded by a storm of insults. She said this was most unfair; Athénaïs ought to be grateful for being rescued from the results of her irregular life – she seemed not to like her old friend any more. To say that she did not like her was putting it mildly; the mere sight of Mme de Maintenon now made Athénaïs choke and secrete black bile.

At the end of 1676 they were both worried about the King, who seemed to have lost interest in them and had become startlingly promiscuous. He had always been inclined to go to bed with any woman who was handy, had done so in Athénaïs's own antechamber, if she kept him waiting, with her maid Mlle des Oeillets or with Mme de Thianges, but such passing fancies, all in the family so to speak, had never bothered anybody and the public knew nothing of them. Now he threw caution to the winds and had a series of violent, unexpected and costly love affairs in the full light of day: a pretty face seemed able to do anything with him. Mme de Sévigné said one smelt fresh meat at Mme de Montespan's – her star was setting – there were tears and grief mingled with affected gaiety. Princesse de Soubise, beautiful and dull, was in love with her husband the head of the great Armorican Rohan family. He was poor; she longed to be of some practical use to him. So she encouraged him to go and look after his estates and as soon as his back was turned she put on her emerald earrings, a prearranged signal which showed the King that the coast was clear. The result was that the Soubises became enormously rich and built the lovely house which is one of the glories of Paris to this day. The King's affair with Mme de Soubise lasted off and on, always rather tepid because she bored him, for several years. She lost a front tooth; she seemed not to mind but the effect was odd and after that there was less talk about her and Louis. Then she got King's Evil, not, it was said, for want of having been touched by the King. They always remained on friendly terms; her son, Cardinal de Rohan, was most probably the fruit of this attachment.

Meanwhile various other women had turns and the next major upset was caused by Mme de Ludres, a maid of honour from Madame's nursery garden who, having taken religious vows, was called Madame, not Mademoiselle. She was quite lovely and had been the mistress of Vivonne. The Queen noticed that when Mme de Ludres came into a room the Duchesses present rose to their feet, although she was an unmarried nobody, while Mme de Thianges was extremely rude to her. All this could only mean one thing.

Mme de Maintenon sulked but Mme de Montespan acted – she sent for Mme Voisin. She may have resorted to Black Mass – in any case Mme Voisin was keenly working on her problem. The two Marquises retired to Maintenon together. Athénaïs, in the family way as usual, was out of spirits and Mme de Maintenon not at all kind to her; a certain coldness which was part of her character was in evidence during the whole visit. She and her guest went to church a great deal, and Mme de Maintenon told a correspondent that people thought she was trying to bring Athénaïs to God. 'I would like to, but am not hopeful. There is another heart, of better quality, of which I have greater expectations.' This was not the view at Court; the King seemed well on the way to becoming a dirty old man.

Athénaïs was brought to bed, at Maintenon, of the future Duchesse d'Orléans, the 'Jubilee Baby'. Meanwhile the King had gone to join the army and nobody doubted that this time her sun had set for good and all. She thought so herself and awaited his return in a mood of unusual pessimism. She was anxious to get Mme de Maintenon and the little boy out of the way – they were going to the Pyrenees again for du Maine to do another cure – so as to have the King to herself without the eye of the governess ever upon them. Her holy influence seemed to be directed, most unfairly, against Athénaïs more than against the temporary mistresses. However, Mme de Maintenon elected to stay; she said du Maine must embrace his father before such a long journey. So she was obliged to witness the displeasing spectacle of Athénaïs victorious, happy and glorious, for, to the general amazement, the King suddenly seemed more in love with her than he had ever been before. Mme Voisin had worked very successfully indeed.

'What a triumph at Versailles!' Mme de Sévigné wrote to her daughter. 'What redoubled pride! What a solid establishment! What a Duchesse de Valentinois [Diane de Poitiers] . . . I was an hour in her room; she was on her bed, dressed and her hair done up, resting before supper. I gave her your messages, she was all sweetness and praise; her sister was happily teasing poor Mme de Ludres and laughing at her for daring to complain. Just imagine how pride without generosity can act

Anne de Rohan-Chabot, Princesse de Soubise, French school, seventeenth century.

Marie de Rabutin Chantal, Marquise de Sévigné by Robert Nanteuil.

in a moment of exultation and you will be in the picture.' During the next weeks she said that Athénaïs and the King were behaving as they used to at the beginning. 'Mme de Montespan was covered with diamonds the other day, such a brilliant divinity that one's eyes dazzled. The attachment seems stronger than it has ever been; they're at the stage when people can't stop looking at each other. There can never have been another example on this earth of love starting again like theirs.'

Athénaïs was in luck. She gambled for huge stakes every evening and she always won. In Paris as at Versailles nobody could talk of anything but this amazing turn of affairs.

The governess and her charge went to Barèges. Everybody loved this little boy for his jokes and high spirits and his sayings were much repeated by the courtiers. He had been forbidden to call Louis XIV Papa. One evening when the royal family were all supping in gondolas he drank a lot of red wine and then, making his gondolier row him over to the King, he called out at the top of his voice: 'Long live the King my father!' Screaming with guilty laughter he then flung himself into the arms of Mme de Maintenon. While they were at Barèges she collected some essays and letters he had written and had them printed, an edition of seven copies, in a little volume called *Works of a Seven Year Old Author*. The title page bears no date; the book is dedicated to Mme de Montespan and the letters are to her and the King.

Barèges 1677. I was so happy, Belle Madame, when I saw that you hadn't forgotten your Mignon. You know how much I love getting letters and I'm enchanted to have one in your beautiful writing, full of kisses for me. I'm going to write to little de Rochefort but I've begun by you because my heart tells me many things for you. Pray, Madame, don't let the King forget the Mignon.

Barèges 1677. I was jealous, Sire, of the letter you did Mme de Maintenon the honour of writing to her; I so long for signs of your friendship that I can't bear you to give them

Marie-Adélaide de Scorailles de Roussilhe, Duchesse de Fontanges, by François De Troy.

to other people. Belle Madame's letter makes me anxious to keep up the reputation I flatter myself I have got, since there is nothing in the world I want so much as to please Your Majesty.

Barèges 1677. I have received a letter from the King which fills me with transports of joy; nothing could be more obliging. I shall not do as you did when at Maintenon [at the time of Mme de Ludres] you burnt one from him . . . Adieu, Madame, I love you passionately.

Barèges 1677. Thank you humbly, Belle Madame, for the goodness you have shown my wet-nurse, please continue it, she is a woman I love very much. Mme de Maintenon says you have taken her to Fontainebleau and I am very happy that you have . . . I want to ask you another favour, may they stop dressing me in skirts? I should walk much better so I beg you to allow this, Belle Madame.

Barèges 1677. Mme de Maintenon spends all day netting and if one allowed her to she would spend the whole night at it, or else writing. She works every day to make me clever, she hopes to succeed and so does the Mignon who studies as hard as he can, since he dies to please you and the King. I read the Life of Caesar on the way here, also Alexander's and yesterday I began Pompey. Mme de Maintenon had migraine and only got up for Mass. M. Fagon [the King's doctor] scalded me yesterday in the little bath; I do hope he will be more moderate another time and not make me scream so loudly. The *tartufferie* of our chaplain continues and will divert you when he gets back. I am the man who loves you most in all the world.

Indeed he seems to have worshipped his mother at this time: 'my dearest heart, my dear child, you were as beautiful as an angel' and so on. But it was Mme de Maintenon who did everything for him. When he was taken away from her, at the late age of ten, and handed over to a male governor, she advised about his health which she understood so well. Don't make him eat when he is not hungry; try and stop him from over-eating at night. He should have several different kinds of soup; not too much meat; plenty of raw fruit and no sweets between meals. His teeth are

The Hôtel Carnavalet; town house of the Marquise de Sévigné.

so bad that he is not very fond of dry bread. Plenty of fresh air is necessary for him and at least nine hours' sleep.

In 1678 du Maine wrote to the King from Saint-Germain:

> I was sad, Sire, to see you go so soon and I shall never forget the honour of the look Your Majesty gave me on leaving. The courtyard is melancholy and our lodgings even more so since you are here no more; I ardently desire the return of Your Majesty. The Mignon.

The King, the Queen and Mme de Montespan and no other women at all had gone to the siege of Ghent. Athénaïs left the party after a few weeks and retired to Clagny to bring the Comte de Toulouse into the world. Mme de Maintenon was so disapproving about the appearance of the two last babies, Toulouse and his sister, that the King did not dare ask her to look after them and they were handed over to Mme de Louvois.

Sad to relate, after this birth Athénaïs definitely lost her power over the King. She grew enormously fat and, in spite of two or three hours of massage every day, it was seen, when she got out of her coach, that each of her legs was the size of a thin man. She was always inclined to be blowsy, now she used too much scent, which the King hated. He was so used to her, so proud of her and so much amused by her; she was such a help to him in holding his Court and such an integral part of Court life, that none of this, probably, would have mattered had she been amiable. Her tempers had become truly appalling. She still had her flat next to the King's and he still spent a good deal of time there with her, but the courtiers could walk with impunity under the windows now. The two of them never sat any more looking to see who went by and with whom, laughing, probably mocking, happy and in love. Inside the gilded rooms there were tears and angry reproaches. He hated scenes, which embarrassed and upset him – he went to Mme de Maintenon more and more for a little peace. The relations of the two women again became as bad as they could be, Athénaïs attributing her troubles to this viper she had nourished in her bosom.

People were now talking about Mme de Maintenant. His incomprehensible attachment to a woman of forty, three years older than Louis and so much unlike the usual run of his fancies, was explained in various ways by the courtiers. Some thought she was helping him to write his memoirs, some that she was a confidante and some that she procured young girls for him. It never occurred to anybody for a single minute that he might be falling in love with her.

In the winter of 1678-9 an incomparable flower appeared in Madame's nursery garden, her new lady-in-waiting, Mlle de Fontanges. This physically gorgeous but mentally pathetic creature saw herself as the heroine of a romantic tale; the King was her knight and she was determined to be his lady-love. As she was the greatest beauty to have appeared at Court within living memory she had no difficulty at

80

The great sun (*Helianthus annuus* Linnaeus) painted by Nicolas Robert for the collection of *Vélins du Roi*.

Corona Solis
Tabern. Icon.
763.

MADAME DE MONTESPAN

MAD.lle LA VALLIERE

all in realizing her ambition. The King slept with her almost at once, keeping the affair a deadly secret, chiefly on account of Mesdames de Maintenon and de Montespan. He encouraged Athénaïs to spend her time and his money at a new game called Bassette, so that she would not notice what he was up to. Mlle de Fontanges was lodged in a little room near his own and during the day he pretended not to know her. This state of affairs did not last. Like Mlle de La Vallière, whom she resembled in many ways (they both came from comparatively humble country families) she was a first class rider; she went out with the King's pack of hounds and then it was soon noticed that he never left her side. When her hat was swept off one day by the branch of a tree, she tied up her golden locks with a ribbon and thus set a fashion in hairdressing for many years to come. The King was completely enslaved. Very soon she was ordering him about in a way no other woman had ever dared to. She went to Mass in a dress of the same stuff as his coat, both wearing turquoise ribbons; in church she and Mme de Montespan sat one on each side of the altar, vying with each other in the fervour of their prayers, their four huge blue eyes rolling towards heaven. Mlle de Fontanges was made a duchess and declared mistress in record time.

To begin with, Athénaïs took the whole thing rather well; such a stupid little girl could never be a serious rival; she helped her to dress up for parties; and she was loving Mme de Maintenon's disgust at this new infatuation. She wrote to Maréchal de Noailles, asking for some green velvet to line her coach and saying, casually, that the King was only visiting her twice a day but that it was better to see him less often in a friendly manner than all the time with quarrels. When Fontanges became a duchess, however, the rage of Athénaïs knew no bounds. She herself had never been able to receive that particular perquisite of the royal mistress because her husband, in order to tease her, had firmly refused to be made a duke. To keep her in a good temper, the King appointed her Intendant of the Queen's Household, the most important Court job there was, for a woman.

On 13 March 1679 Mme Voisin was arrested in Paris as she came out of church. Athénaïs de Montespan precipitately left the Court.

She was only away for a day or two and seems to have gone in order to see Mme Filastre, a particularly horrible witch who, having dedicated her own child to the Devil, murdered it herself. Filastre procured some more of Galet's powders for Athénaïs who presumably wanted to lay in a store of them before the supply was cut off forever.

(a) Miniature of Mme de Montespan thought to be by Louis de Chatillon
     or perhaps Pierre Mignard.
(b) Miniature by J. L. Petitot, set in the lid of a gold snuff box of Louis XIV.
(c) Miniature of Louise de La Vallière by Pierre Mignard (perhaps a copy).

Louis' state barge. A water colour by Jean I. Berain.

VI

POISON

Le voilà donc connu, ce secret plein d'horreur

VOLTAIRE

The years which immediately preceded the King's official announcement, in 1682, that Versailles was henceforth to be the seat of government, were laden with events which were to influence his reign. Although he was having a last fling, Mme de Maintenon was slowly strengthening her hold on him. He was beginning to 'convert', in other words persecute, the French Protestants. A sinister connection between the lowest and the highest in the land was being brought to light.

Poison was in the air. When the first Madame, Henrietta, had died in terrible pain, many people, rightly or wrongly, thought she had been poisoned. Then Daubray, chief of the Paris police, was poisoned by his wife; soon after that another policeman of high rank died mysteriously. In those days it was difficult to be certain that poison had been administered since there was no means of analysing it. A powder or liquid produced as evidence would be given to a dog and pronounced to be poisonous or not according to whether the dog died or lived. Doctors were always trying to invent reliable antidotes. These were sometimes tried out on prisoners under the death sentence; the experiment was only made with their consent and they were offered their freedom if they survived. They generally died in such appalling agony that even the doctors were sorry for them. In spite of the proved inefficiency of counter-poison everybody believed in it firmly and quite often it seemed to work – probably because the patient had not really been poisoned at all. The fashionable poisons were arsenic and antimony; they were often administered in enemas, a form of hygiene in general use to counteract gargantuan meals. Discontented wives were fond of impregnating their husbands' clothes with arsenic, to produce the same symptoms as those of syphilis, sometimes, but not always, fatal. The man was then discredited whether he died or not. An object treated with arsenic could kill but only if the victim put his fingers in his mouth after touching it.

In 1676 the Marquise de Brinvilliers, a gentle, mousey little person much given

The Marquise de Brinvilliers after torture and
on the way to execution, by Charles Le Brun.

The Hôtel Brinvilliers.

to good works, was brought to justice. As everybody in society knew her, the affair received enormous publicity. She had poisoned and killed her father over a period of eight agonizing months during which she nursed him devotedly; then she had done the same for her two brothers and had tried to polish off her husband. Luckily for him, her lover and accomplice had no wish to marry somebody as evil as he was himself, so every time the Marquis was given a dose by his wife the lover gave him an antidote; the result was that he survived, with a greatly impaired digestion. Mme de Brinvilliers had also killed people in hospitals, whom she used sweetly to visit and on whom she tried out various poisons. She confessed everything, repented and made a good end after suffering appalling tortures – probably no worse, however, than those she had inflicted. The whole of high society attended her trial and the execution; she was beheaded and then burnt 'so that,' said Mme de Sévigné, 'we are all breathing her now'. Almost her last words were to say that it seemed rather unfair that she should be the only one to suffer considering that most people of quality did as she had done, when it suited them.

Daubray was succeeded as chief of police by La Reynie, the right person in the right place, one of those men, brilliant, rich, urbane, who were a feature of Louis XIV's administration. Such was the total confidence placed in him by the King that he turned the Lieutenancy of the Police into a sort of extra ministry; he was in a position to do an infinite amount of good or evil to the highest in the land, while humble folk were in his power. He did as little harm as possible to anybody and instead of being loathed, as policemen generally are, he was universally esteemed. During the thirty years of his office he wrought miracles in Paris, cleaning it physically and morally; he found a filthy medieval town, a cesspool of vice and left the best administered city in the world. He took the part of sad people such as beggars and vagabonds and did what he could to help them; he made arrangements

Nicolas Gabriel de La Reynie. An engraving by Van
Schuppen after Mignard.

for the numerous foundlings who were dumped in churches, or in open spaces,
and had often hitherto been left to die of exposure. Before the Revocation he
protected Protestants and their churches against the persecution of their Catholic
neighbours; even after the Revocation of the Edict of Nantes he went as far as he
dared to save them from the worst. He was a bibliophile, he collected and collated
Greek and Latin manuscripts.

Before the Brinvilliers case, La Reynie had been warned by a priest at Notre
Dame that people were confessing, in greater and greater numbers, to murder by
poison. The priest had hesitated before disclosing secrets of the confessional, even
though he named nobody; but he was worried by this state of affairs – it preyed on
his mind. La Reynie tried in vain to find out more; the last words of Mme de
Brinvilliers seemed to confirm what the priest had told him and he was beginning to
suspect that a lot of sinister things were going on. He arrested one or two suspicious
sort of people but made no headway until a young lawyer, by chance, went to
dinner with a certain Mme Vigoureux. It has never been explained why a presumably respectable man was keeping such company – it must have been pretty
obvious, even on the slightest acquaintanceship, that Mme Vigoureux was the scum
of the earth. One of the party, Mme Bosse, got drunk during the evening and in
her cups she suddenly declared: 'What a lovely trade! What customers! Duchesses
and Princes! Only three more poisonings and my fortune will be made – I shall be
able to retire'. The lawyer might have thought she was joking had he not observed
an expression of alarm on the face of his hostess. He went to La Reynie with the
interesting story; a stool pigeon, sent to Mme Bosse, easily obtained a bottle of
poison with which to despatch a cruel husband. Mme Bosse, Mme Vigoureux, the
latter's son and two daughters were arrested as they slept, all in the same bed, and
sent to the prison of Vincennes.

Pandora's box was opened. Vigoureux and Bosse were most loquacious, anxious to help the police in any way they could. They said they were fortune-tellers and that there were at least four hundred members of this profession in Paris, or lurking in the shadow of the Court – lodging with people such as game-keepers and washer-women, of easy access to the King's various residences. When asked for names they made no difficulties and among many others they mentioned Mme Voisin. They said she had joined them in experimenting with chemicals. A client of theirs, whose fortune they had often told, was Mme de Poulaillon. These two names sufficed to warn La Reynie that he was now on the track of a complicated and sinister business which might have embarrassing ramifications. Everybody knew about Mme Voisin and her circle of highly placed clients; pretty Mme de Poulaillon was of a noble Bordelais family; she had been shut up in a convent by a rich old husband who suspected her of trying to murder him in several different ways.

La Reynie told Louvois where he had got to in his investigations and Louvois went to the King. The three of them held a consultation. They decided that it would be better not to have this affair dealt with by Parlement (the supreme judicial assembly), for two reasons. One, from every point of view the less publicity there was the better. Two, Parlement, while ready to pursue humble citizens with the utmost rigour, had recently shown itself loth to punish people, especially women, of quality. If the practice of poisoning was really as widespread in Paris high society as La Reynie was beginning to think, it must be wiped out at whatever cost to the nobility, not only that of the sword (the ancient landed families) but that of the robe, or magistrature, to which the Parliamentarians themselves belonged. The two classes had become so much intermarried since, as old and disapproving people often remarked, the French had stopped putting birth before money, that they were beginning to be inextricably mixed up. Society was small and there were few people belonging to it who were not connected in some way with the Parlement. So a special tribunal, called the Chambre Ardente, was set up under the presidence of the respected M. de Boucherat, a future Chancellor. He chose the magistrates who were to help him; they included such well-known names as Breteuil and d'Ormesson.

The Chambre Ardente assembled on 10 April 1679 and decided to sit in secret so that the details of devilish practices and the composition of poisons should not be publicised. The procedure was, that those whom La Reynie thought suspect should be arrested and their interrogation submitted to the procurer general. He would decide if they were to be confronted with other accused – if so, a detailed report of the confrontation would be sent to the judges of the tribunal who would then decree either the liberation of the suspects or their continued questioning. If the latter, the interrogation, carried to its conclusion, would go once more to the judges who would decide either to acquit or to continue the examination. Those not acquitted were to be heard again, under torture, and on the result of that hearing the judges would judge and pass a sentence which would be final, with no possibility of appeal. It may be imagined that Parlement was displeased by this arrangement; the King, however, disregarded the complaints of its President. He was probably right. That very few criminals were in fact brought to judgment was not the fault of the Chambre, as we shall see.

The Chambre Ardente went to work without delay. Bosse's house was searched and quantities of arsenic, cantharides, nail cuttings, crayfish powder and other things too filthy to mention (supposed to be aphrodisiacs) were found there. Mme Voisin was arrested and her interrogation began. She said she was a harmless fortune-teller which she had been since the age of nine when she realized that she had second sight. She advised the police to concentrate on real criminals like Bosse. When the two women were confronted with each other Bosse declared that Voisin had poisoned her own husband as well as those of Mesdames Dreux and Leféron. Sensation! Mme Dreux was a cousin of M. d'Ormesson, one of the judges, while Mme Leféron was the widow of a President of the Parlement and was now married to the man who had been her lover. Mme Dreux, according to Bosse, was crazily in love with the Marquis de Richelieu and had not only tried to poison Dreux but also Richelieu's wife and all his many mistresses. She, Mme de Poulaillon and Mme Leféron were arrested, to the horror of the Paris bourgeoisie, and sent to join the other prisoners at Vincennes.

More and more interesting names were coming out every day at the interrogations: Comtesse du Roure, Vicomtesse de Polignac, Duchesse d'Angoulême, Duchesse de Vitry, Princesse de Tingry, Comtesse de Gramont, Comte de Cessac, Comte de Clermont. Most horrifying of all, the witches spoke of Mme de Montespan's own maid Mlle des Oeillets who was known to have a child by the King, the Duchesse de Vivonne, Athénaïs's sister-in-law, and two members of the King's intimate circle, nieces of Mazarin, Marie-Anne Duchesse de Bouillon and Olympe Comtesse de Soissons. The Soissons were members of the French (Bourbon-Condé) and the Savoy royal families – the only surviving Comte de Soissons having been killed in action, his sister was allowed to take the title; she married a cadet of Savoy and their son married Olympe Mancini. The head of this family was known at Court as M. le Comte. The present Mme la Comtesse was an old love of the King's; she was an intellectual, had a salon, and had done much in his youth to civilize him, encourage his taste for works of art and teach him manners. They had remained on the sort of terms, an amorous intimacy, which led people to suppose that the affair had never quite come to an end. The Comtesse de Soissons had a young son, Prince Eugène, who was supposed to be a very bad hat indeed; he never came to Court but lived with a gang of other young reprobates who spent half their time dressed as women.

In spite of the fact that all the members of the nobility who were mentioned by the prisoners at Vincennes were his friends, the King firmly told the tribunal to proceed with its enquiries. Poisoning, he said, must be stopped. When Voisin's interrogation was complete, La Reynie, horrified, said he had lost all faith in human nature. 'Men's lives are up for sale as a matter of everyday bargaining; murder is the only remedy when a family is in difficulties. Abominations are being practised everywhere – in Paris, in the suburbs and in the provinces.' All those who knew, by the rumours flying round Paris or through acquaintances on the tribunal, what had been going on, were appalled. A friend of Bussy-Rabutin's wrote to him: 'In spite of the worldly life I have led I can't get over the horror of what you tell me.'

Among her other crimes Voisin seemed to have performed at least two thousand abortions and to have done away with many unwanted babies. Live babies had been sacrificed to the Devil, having been kidnapped from poor districts (indeed disappearances of small children had often of late been registered by the police). Voisin's daughter had kept her baby hidden away for fear of what might happen to it. Voisin mentioned many names, but never, even under torture, that of Mme de Montespan. This omission has been explained in two ways. Either Mme de Montespan was involved in nothing worse than a few harmless spells or Mme Voisin, terrified of the appalling death reserved for whoever even made an attempt on the King's life, did not want to seem to have been involved with anybody so close to him.

The three witches, Voisin, Bosse and Vigoureux, were condemned to death. Vigoureux died under torture; the other two survived it and were burnt alive. Mesdames de Poulaillon, Dreux and Leféron got off, but not scot free; these pretty ladies were sent to end their days repenting in convents in the Low Countries. The tribunal of the Chambre Ardente had proved to be quite as weak-minded, when it came to its own kith and kin, as Parlement would have been.

La Reynie's enquiries had been proceeding for about a year when (1680) the real bombshell burst in Court circles and the unbelievable news went round that there was a warrant out for the arrest of the Comtesse de Soissons for the murder of her husband; the Duchesse de Bouillon for poisoning a valet who knew about her loves and for trying to poison her husband; the Marquise d'Alluye for poisoning her father-in-law; the Princesse de Tingry (one of the Queen's ladies), said to have murdered her own baby; the powerful and popular Maréchal de Luxembourg and several others of the same sort. When the police came for the Comtesse de Soissons she was nowhere to be found. The King, against his own better judgement, had sent her a message. He told her that she could choose between going to the Bastille and standing her trial, or permanent exile from France. She did not hesitate, she fled to Brussels, taking with her Mme d'Alluye. Safely on foreign soil she began to bargain. She said she would come back, if she need not await her trial in prison and if it could take place at once. The King replied that she would have to go to prison like

The orange trees in their tubs at Versailles.

Overleaf: The Cour de Marbre.

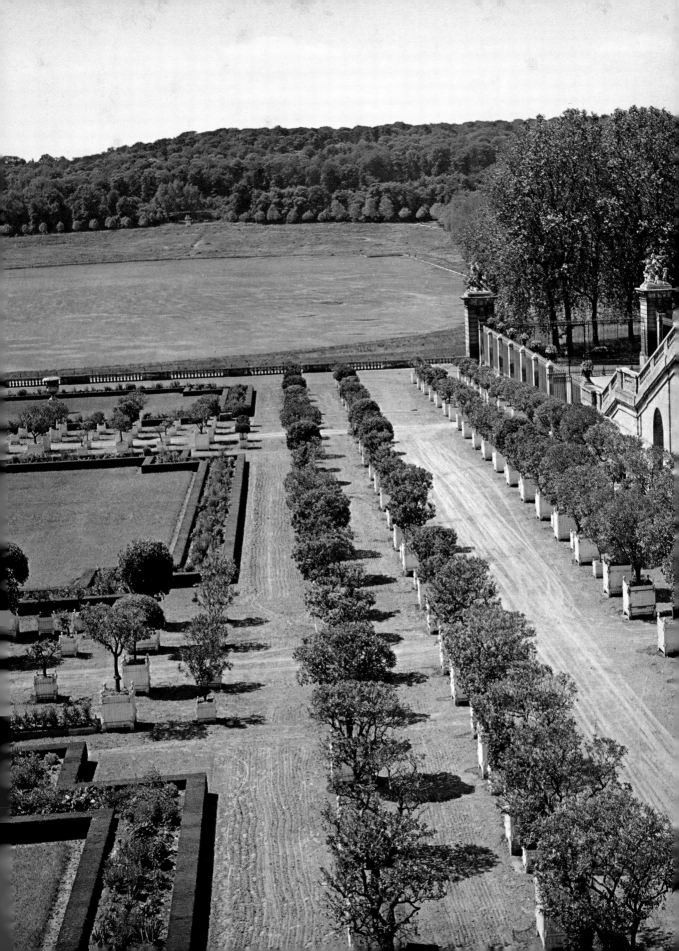

everybody else and he could not guarantee speed. She was never seen in France again and there is little doubt that she was guilty. The King told her mother-in-law that, for allowing her to escape from justice, he would have to account to God and to his people. Two more of those on La Reynie's list, M. de Cessac and Mme de Polignac also managed to fly, the others were duly arrested.

The trials were dramatic. The Duchesse de Bouillon arrived at the court room lovely, rosy, smiling, surrounded by adoring relations, hand in hand with her husband and the lover, the Duc de Vendôme (a cousin of the King's) for whose sake it was alleged that she had tried to murder him. The Duc de Bouillon worshipped his wife. His brothers were always urging him to shut her up because of the scandal she made with all her love affairs – he said that he didn't mind in the least so long as he had his share. She freely admitted that she and Vendôme had often been to Mme Voisin's together 'to see the Sibyls'. When the judge suggested that she had tried to murder Bouillon she laughed and said 'Ask him!' Boucherat enquired whether she had seen the Devil and if so what was he like? She replied 'Small, dark and ugly, just like you.' There was no proof against her and she was acquitted. She then sat down to invent many other witticisms, with which she was supposed to have floored the judges, and had them privately printed for her friends. The King had no intention of putting up with that sort of nonsense – he banished her for contempt of court and her *esprit de l'escalier* cost her several weary years in the provinces.

Maréchal de Luxembourg's trial lasted fourteen months. He was accused, not of poisoning but of using spells in order to get rid of the guardian of a widow whom he wanted to marry; to cause the death of his own wife; to make his sister-in-law, the Princesse de Tingry, fall in love with him and to give him victories in the field. He was not a clever witness and talked too much, but was finally exonerated on every count, though his secretary was sent to the galleys. Luxembourg then retired to the country for a week. When he came back to Court the King never mentioned the trial; he gave him great commands with which he won great victories for France.

The other society people involved were acquitted. They all said quite frankly that they had been customers of Mme Voisin but there was no proof that any of them were poisoners – the horrible crew of criminals at Vincennes could not be regarded as reliable witnesses. The unpopular Chambre Ardente was thought by the world in general to have covered itself with ridicule.

There was a rumour in Paris that the King wanted a general clean-up of morals and to put an end to sodomy, a vice he was known to abhor and which was punishable by the stake. Several times during his reign he was on the verge of taking steps against it; but his advisers seem to have pointed out that it would be difficult to do so, since in that matter all roads led to Monsieur. Indeed, the little man, mincing between Court and Camp and the lowest of the Paris underworld, with his rouge and his scent, and the diamond brooches he gave to boys provided wonderful protection for others of his sort. There was certainly an uncomfortable feeling abroad and many people, not only perverts, slept uneasily at this time. The great Racine himself was under suspicion. He had been a customer of Voisin's and his mistress had died suddenly (perhaps of an abortion). An order for his arrest was actually written out but never put into effect.

Suddenly the whole investigation collapsed. The reason for this was that the low-down criminals, who had lived together at Vincennes for many months, had all begun to name Mme de Montespan. Since the death of Mme Voisin and her companions, about a hundred and fifty fortune-tellers, kidnappers, alchemists, counterfeiters, unfrocked priests, abortionists, merchants of poison and love philtres and other sinister creatures of the underworld had been arrested. Among them was a man called Lesage who had been liberated from the galleys by one of Mme Voisin's powerful friends. Very much against the advice of La Reynie, Louvois offered Lesage his liberty if he would talk, and talk he did. He was the first person to bring Mme de Montespan into the affair, saying he knew that Voisin had taken powders to her at Saint-Germain. The next time her name was mentioned was when Mme Filastre, under torture, said that Mme de Montespan used to buy love philtres and other powders; but when the torturing was over, Filastre took this back. Then, as though by common consent, accusations against Mme de Montespan began to pour in from the prisoners. They affirmed, with a wealth of detail, that Mme Voisin had often been to see Athénaïs both at the Court and at Clagny. The two women had conspired in all sorts of sinister plots. Athénaïs had given the King love philtres over a period of years, and had taken part in one Black Mass. When Mme Voisin recommended two more, Mme de Montespan is supposed to have said (and this gives a certain verisimilitude to the accusation; one can almost hear her high, quavering voice) that she really had not got time. So the others were said in her absence, but on her behalf, and involved the sacrifice of babies. The accusations became more and more lurid. Mme Voisin was to have handed the King a poisoned petition the very day she was arrested and she was said to have given Mlle de Fontanges a pair of poisoned gloves.

Deeply embarrassed, La Reynie was obliged to report this turn of events to the King, after which the council of ministers, presided over by the King, sat almost continuously for days, trying to decide what had better be done. Mme de Montespan had been like a second wife to Louis; she was the mother of his favourite child; in spite of all her tiresomeness he was still fond of her and she lived in his house. There could be no question of her going before the tribunal. If she did so, however innocent she might be, she would be branded for evermore as a probable murderess and black magician. Nor was it pleasant to think of the jokes there would be in Paris if the story of the love philtres got about. So, supported by the ministers, he said the case must be stopped and the existing dossiers burnt. Single handed, La Reynie stood out against this decision on the grounds that poisoning must be put an end to in France and also that to pack up the tribunal at this point was unfair. 'Different punishment for the same crimes would tarnish the King's glory and dishonour his justice.' Besides, some of the depositions which would be lost if the dossiers were destroyed contained statements exonerating certain prisoners. The King said the trials could go on so long as all evidence relative to Mme de Montespan was suppressed. But as the dossiers were full of such evidence that would be a travesty of justice. La Reynie then said there was only one thing they could do in the circumstances. A *lettre de cachet* (a letter sealed by the King directing detention, without trial, of the person named in it) must be taken out against all the prisoners. This meant that a hundred and forty seven people who mostly seemed to have committed atrocious crimes, and who, if found guilty, would have been tortured and then burnt to death, would escape all punishment except imprisonment; and that those few who may have been innocent, would be unable to prove it and also be shut up for life. Guibourg, the unfrocked priest who pretended to have said Black Masses for Mme de Montespan and who may have helped her with sacrilegious prayers, Trianon, abominable poisoner, Chapelin who taught Filastre her dreadful art (abortion), Galet himself, would all benefit from this amazing stroke of luck. If Voisin, Bosse and Vigoureux were not already dead, they too would have escaped. However, there seemed to be no other solution.

The Chambre Ardente closed its doors in 1682. The total results of its judgments were: thirty-six burnt to death after torture; four sent to the galleys; thirty-six banished or fined (mostly gentlefolk) and thirty acquitted. All the others who, so luckily for them, benefited by *lettres de cachet*, were chained up in dungeons all over France for the rest of their lives, in solitary confinement. If they spoke to their gaolers they were whipped – Mme de Montespan's name must not be bandied about the French prisons. Thirty-seven years later some of these people were still alive.

The Affair of the Poisons had various repercussions, the most serious of which was that the King, furious with Olympe de Soissons, refused to take Prince Eugène into the French army. He had no use for the boy, who looked at him, he thought, like an insolent cock sparrow; and he suspected him of being a sodomite; in any case his bad reputation was undoubtedly justified. But as Eugène was the King's own relation and the child of such a great friend, it would have been difficult for the King to have refused if Madame la Comtesse had been there to support her son. Throwing Eugène into the enemy camp proved to be one of Louis XIV's greatest mistakes. The prestige of Colbert suffered from the Affair, as all the gentlefolk involved, including Mme de Montespan, were his special friends. He died in 1683, harassed, overworked and sad. In spite of the precautions against publicity, the whole case had been so widely discussed (indeed there was a time when nothing else was talked about in France) that people became more suspicious of poison than ever, and mysterious deaths were all put down to it. However, there was one good result: henceforward the sale of poison in France was strictly controlled (31 August 1682). Private laboratories were forbidden, and so were all the occult arts and superstitious practices.

And Mme de Montespan – was she guilty? M. Georges Mongrédien whose book on the Affair is by far the best (most of the foregoing facts, which are only like the visible part of the iceberg, have been shamelessly culled from it) thinks she was innocent of the criminal charges, that is, of attempting to poison the King and Mlle Fontanges and conniving at the sacrifice of infants during Black Mass. La Reynie seems on the whole to have been of this opinion; the King and Mme de Maintenon, who knew her by heart, certainly were. The witnesses against her were men and women of the vilest sort; they had unwisely been allowed to foregather while at Vincennes and had most probably leagued together there to accuse her, with the idea that, if she was thought to be involved they would never be brought to trial – and indeed this was the case. M. Mongrédien also points out that Mme de Montespan was never given the chance of defending herself. But there was no doubt she had played with fire. All the poisoners and unfrocked priests who were the most vociferous in accusing her said they had had dealings with her maid, Mlle des Oeillets. Interrogated by La Reynie, des Oeillets denied ever having seen any of them and demanded to be confronted with them. However, when La Reynie took her down to Vincennes they all, most disconcertingly, recognized and named her. So she remained under a shadow of suspicion, though nothing happened to her. Athénaïs had certainly tried spells, with the excellent results we have noted; and the King still remembered the awful headaches he had had at the time when he now knew that she had been giving him Galet's powders.

All this was bad enough, but it was not criminal. Luckily for her, the King found it easy to forgive women, whom he regarded as charming, irresponsible, inferior creatures. Mme de Montespan was not only the mother of his children but an ornament of his court. She dazzled the ambassadors. When she did not exasperate she amused him. He burnt all the papers relevant to the affair, not realizing that La Reynie's notes were kept in the police archives (they are to this day at the Bibliothèque Nationale) and put the whole thing behind him. He may well have thought that, had Athénaïs been a poisoner, at least one of her rivals would have died or been taken ill in a mysterious way, and that she would long since have poisoned Mme de Maintenon, whom she loathed from the bottom of her soul. Mme de Maintenon, indeed, wrote jokingly to a friend 'I am just off to Clagny which Nanon thinks *very dangerous*'. The proof of the King's belief in Athénaïs's innocence is that he kept her on at Versailles for another ten years. Nothing could have been easier than for him to have sent her to a convent, the usual fate of the discarded mistress. Those historians who attribute the end of their love affair to the part she played in the poison case have not examined the evidence; he had completely cooled after the birth of Toulouse, nearly a year before the arrest of Mme Voisin. Voltaire, with his great knowledge of human nature, put the matter in a nutshell: 'the King had reproached himself for his liaison with a married woman and when he was no longer in love, his conscience made itself felt more keenly'.

Poor little Fontanges's day was soon done; Athénaïs had been right in thinking that she was too stupid to hold a man who only liked intelligent people, after his physical desire for her had gone. This happened sooner than might have been expected because she lost her health. A year after the liaison began, she had a baby which died. She was messed about by the doctors; never stopped losing blood; became sickly and plaintive and cried all the time. The King, who could not bear ill people, packed her off to a convent where her sister, appointed by him, was abbess. She took no possessions except a little Venetian lace to remind her of her few months of glory. The King visited her, when hunting in the neighbourhood; and when he saw what he had done to her, he had the grace to cry. Soon after that, in March 1681, she died, saying she was happy to go since she had seen her King in tears on her account. She was twenty. Perhaps rumours of poison had reached the convent for her sister said there must be a post-mortem, and though the King was not anxious for one, it was finally held by seven doctors. It showed that her death was natural: her liver was diseased and her lungs in a bad way but the intestines, stomach and womb were quite healthy. The doctors said she had died of pneumonia brought on by loss of blood. She was the last of the King's pretty ladies from the household of Madame.

VII

A CITY OF THE RICH

Cette ville de riches aurait beaucoup d'éclat et de pompe mais elle serait sans force et sans fondement assuré . . . et cette ville pompeuse, sans avoir besoin d'autres ennemis tomberait enfin par elle-même, ruinée par son opulence.

BOSSUET

While the terrible events described in the last chapter were happening, the King, outwardly calm and unruffled, was settling into his new home. On 6 May 1682 he made the official announcement that from now on the seat of the French government would be at Versailles, and arrived there with some pomp, accompanied by his family, his ministers and the whole Court. The Court of France for ever in the country! The fashionable world was filled with dismay now that the long-expected blow had fallen. Not all the criticism was frivolous, however. For years Colbert had begged his master to abandon the project, for the obvious administrative reasons; Bossuet said that a City of the Rich needed no enemy – it carried the seeds of its own destruction. Versailles was indeed a city and the forerunner of Le Corbusier's self-contained *Unité*.

The house was still far from being ready, but the King thought he would never get the workmen out unless he moved in himself. As he was always adding to it and improving it, he probably never saw it without any scaffolding at all. Vast additions had been made to Le Vau's envelope. He had died in 1670; for some years after that his work was carried on by subordinates, but in 1679, Mansart, who had made himself a solid reputation with Clagny, became the King's architect and took over Versailles. He was now finishing the Galerie des Glaces where Le Vau's first floor terrace had been – the proportions of that façade sacrificed to the King's need for a vast reception room. However, what the house lost outside it gained inside, for this gallery is still one of the beauties of the western world. Seen at night soon after its completion, the painting and the gilding fresh and new; lit by thousands of candles in silver chandeliers and candelabra, furnished with solid silver consoles and orange tubs; crowded with beauties of both sexes, dressed in satin and lace, embroidered, re-embroidered, over-embroidered with real gold thread, and covered with jewels, it must have been like Aladdin's Cave or some other fable of the Orient.

The iron balustrade outside the *chambre du roi* at Versailles with Louis' monogram.

By day it had a different aspect, serving as the main street or market place of that City of the Rich. It was packed with people; servants hurrying to and fro with messages, courtiers buttonholing each other for a chat, or dashing at top speed from one ceremony to the next; cows and asses on their way to provide fresh milk for little princes – all this was occasionally pushed aside so that some royal sedan chair could get by, like the ministers' motor cars in a modern capital. Here, too, could be seen foreign visitors and tourists, easily recognizable by their strange clothes and aimless gait, looking round them in wonder. Versailles was more truly open to the public then than nowadays; anybody could wander in at any hour. There were seldom fewer than two hundred *fiacres* waiting outside where the car-park is now. Hardly any of the rooms were banned to the ordinary citizen, but if by accident he should stray into one that was, a servant would quietly follow him, pretending that it was to draw a curtain or make up the fire, and point out his mistake in a low voice so that he would not feel humiliated. The Kings at Versailles, almost unguarded, lived in a perpetual crowd, and yet, in a hundred years there was only one half-hearted attempt at assassination.

The two vast wings which flank Le Vau's envelope were finished. The one to the south was for the Princes of the Blood, the King's illegitimate children and their households; it contained fifteen flats, with another fourteen in the attics complete with shops and offices. Between this Princes' wing and the town there was a building (now a military hospital) with kitchen, pantries and lodging for fifteen hundred servants. The stables which so beautifully join the château to the town were being built. They housed the King's horses, his Master of the Horse and the pages, and were a sort of public school for the sons of the nobility. These pages, generally out of hand, plagued the Versailles bourgeoisie for a hundred years. Stables, kennels and other dependencies of the hunt occupied more space than the accommodation of the ministries. In 1701 there were six packs of hounds at Versailles, altogether five hundred couples, belonging to the King, his sons, the Dauphin, the Duc du Maine and the Comte de Toulouse and his cousin the Duc de Bourbon – they hunted the stag, the boar and the wolf. The King always kept a few hounds in his own rooms, and fed them himself, so that they would know him as their master – the hound-work interested him out hunting.

Hundreds of courtiers were crammed into the Nobles' or north wing of the château. It was a maze of corridors, where strangers lost their way hopelessly. People could live here for years, forgotten by everybody. Madame was once in need of a lady-in-waiting who had to be a single duchess, either a widow or deserted by her husband. This sad duchess seemed not to exist until somebody remembered that Mme de Brancas, separated from the brutal, spendthrift Duke, was quietly starving to death in a garret of the Nobles' wing. Madame liked her, engaged her and treated her respectfully; the courtiers followed suit and she had a happy life thereafter.

View of the stables from the middle of the *chambre du roi*
by Jean-Baptiste Martin, about 1690.

The sedan chairs which carried people from one part of the château to another belonged to a company, like hackney cabs; none but the royal family were allowed to have their own. They were not allowed to go further into the King's part of the house than the guard-rooms and never allowed in the Cour de Marbre. They made tremendous traffic blocks in the Nobles' wing. One of the corridors there was called the rue de Noailles, as its whole length gave onto flats occupied by that powerful but unpopular family. Such as they lived in splendour, but more humble folk could not be said to be well or comfortably lodged – in many cases the rooms they lived in had been chopped into tiny units with no regard for the façade – some had no windows at all, or gave on to dismal little interior wells. All the same, a lodging, however squalid, in the château, came to be more sought after than almost anything, as it was a sign of having succeeded in life. Those who could afford to also had houses or flats in the town of Versailles; and the very rich began building themselves seats in the surrounding country. The Ile de France is still dotted with wonderful houses built while the kings were at Versailles, although many disappeared during the Revolution and many others were destroyed by Germans.

Poorer members of the nobility were often ruined by life at Versailles. Everything there was expensive and appearances had to be kept up. The King liked to see his courtiers well turned out – elegant clothes in those days cost a fortune, although, since the fashions changed slowly, they could be worn for years. On special occasions, such as a royal marriage, he would let it be known that he would like everybody to appear in new clothes; and then there would be a scramble for tailors, dressmakers and embroiderers whom the courtiers shamelessly bribed away from each other. The best embroidery was done by men; and the masters of the craft, M. l'Herminot and the brothers Delobel, had grace and favour lodgings in the Louvre. When people felt they could no longer meet the expenses of life in the château they looked to the King for lucrative sinecures or even presents of cash. These benefits were generally obtained through the mistresses, who, in their turn, took a percentage. The King did not at all mind being importuned in this way, since the people concerned were thereafter in his power. Anyhow, the courtiers who lived on their wits were in the minority: most were decent, ambitious people drawn to Versailles by a desire to get on in the army, to find suitable husbands and wives for their children, and by a very natural love of fashionable society.

Those who think of the nobles at Versailles as hundreds of idle fellows, with nothing to do but gossip, take part in ceremonies, hunt, gamble and make love sometimes forget that the able-bodied men of military age there were all serving soldiers. It is true that they led an extremely agreeable life in the winter, but as soon as the days drew out they rode off to the front to vie with each other in deeds of valour; and Versailles was left to women, old men, and those whom the King thought unsuitable for army commands. In fact the château was a general head-

The Salon de la Guerre; Louis XIV as Mars, relief by Antoine Coysevox.   97

A fortification devised by
Vauban.

quarters, and the town as full of barracks as any garrison town. The Court was run
with military precision; the King himself was so punctual and so regular in his
habits that it was said that, in any part of the world, with a reliable watch, one would
know exactly what he was doing at any particular moment. The iron etiquette,
which has been made to seem so absurd, was a necessary discipline if an assembly
of between two and five thousand people were to live harmoniously under the same
roof. As Commander-in-Chief he liked to keep the officers under his eye; they were
the men to whom he entrusted his country's security and he wished to observe their
comportment, to know them and for them to know him. Many of the courtiers had
lost an arm, a leg or an eye at the wars; and were lucky to be alive, since a serious
wound in those days often led to an agonizing death by blood poisoning.

Superficially, it is true, the wars were fought in rather a civilized way. For one
thing, nobody ever thought of campaigning in the winter. Many of the operations
were sieges: the taking of fortified towns was brought to a fine art by Vauban,
the engineer who became Marshal of France. As soon as a town was in French hands
Vauban would set to work and re-design the ramparts, after which they were
supposed to be invulnerable. His fortifications were of a supreme elegance; when
the King wanted to be agreeable to Lord Portland he sent him to look at 'our
beautiful strong-places in the north'.

When Louis XIV was besieging Lille in 1667, the Comte de Brouais, the enemy
commander defending the city, heard that the French had no ice, so he sent some
over for the King every morning. After a while, the King asked to see the officer
who brought it and told him he could do with a little more. (At Versailles the
courtiers required five pounds of ice a day each, in the summer.) Brouais sent a
message back to say that the siege was going to last many months and as he would
not like to think of the King without ice he was economizing the supply. The Duc de

Sebastien Le Prestre, seigneur de Vauban.
French school.

Charost who was there shouted out 'Yes and tell Brouais not to surrender like the Governor of Douai'. The King said, laughing, 'Duc de Charost, are you mad?' 'No, Sire, I'm thinking of my family honour – Brouais is my cousin.'

But, for all this bonhomie, the wars were bloody and many families were wiped out in them. M. de Saint-Abré who lay with his son beside him, both dying on the field, wrote to the King: 'Sire, my son and I have lost our lives in the same battle. This is an end according to the rules and I believe that Your Majesty will be satisfied with both of us.' Nobody who had witnessed them was likely to forget the heart-rending scenes when news came of Condé's successful crossing of the Rhine under enemy fire in 1672. Half the *jeunesse dorée* had been drowned or shot down in that engagement.

The King was regarded as the Viceroy of the Almighty. In his chapel he worshipped God; and the courtiers, their backs turned to the altar, worshipped him. They treated him like a God, a father, a mistress – the mistress element was very strong. The King has not looked at one for two days. This is bad, but might be due to an exterior circumstance – if the two days are extended to eight there must be some sinister reason. One then asked for an audience in the hopes of finding out what was wrong (though of course in the heart of hearts one generally knew). If the quarrel was made up, the repentant lover embraced the King's knees. The *look*, out of half-shut eyes, was bestowed every day on hundreds of people all of whom the King knew all about. He knew their genealogies by heart. Absentees were noticed at once; it was most unwise to play truant and leave the château without asking permission, which was granted fairly readily to those who wanted to go and see to their estates but not often granted to those who thought of having two or three day's jollity at Paris. He hated the courtiers to go to Paris. In order to keep them at Versailles he arranged a constant flow of entertainments, amusing in themselves

and absence from which would be social death. Events in the King's own family, births and marriages and even deaths rated high as entertainment and in the ceremonies which marked these occasions most of the courtiers had some part to play. The great nobles were tied down by the daily ceremonies, the King's *lever, coucher* and *débotter* (when he changed after hunting), his dinner, always in public and the procession to the Chapel, which took a long time as then petitions and also outside people who wanted to pay their court were presented. Once a week the foreign ambassadors, who lived in Paris, came to visit him, using the beautiful staircase which Louis XV was to destroy.

In 1682 the King's day at Versailles was as follows. He got up in the presence of Princes of the Blood and certain courtiers, with a good deal of ceremony, between eight and nine; and when he was dressed he went straight to the room next to his bedroom, where he worked with his ministers. They were few in number, never more than three or four. This was to prevent leakages of information and to exclude the Princes of the Blood. Monsieur was only allowed to attend an unimportant council which took place every other week. The Dauphin was kept out of everything. At twelve-thirty, the King went to Mass in a temporary chapel with the Queen and the whole Court. This took an hour and when it was over he visited Athénaïs de Montespan and stayed with her until dinner time at about two o'clock. He dined alone with the Queen, eating a meal composed of four plates of different soups, a whole pheasant and a whole partridge or chicken or duck, (according to what game or poultry was in season) stuffed with truffles, a huge quantity of salad, some mutton, two good slices of ham, a dish of pastry, raw fruit, compotes and preserves. His appetite astounded the onlookers and frightened the doctors. Mme de Maintenon said if she ate half as much as he did she would be dead in a week. (At his autopsy, he was found to have a vast stomach and bowels twice the usual length.)

Louis XIV receiving the Doge of Genoa in the Galerie des Glaces, 15 May 1685, by Claude Hallé. Monsieur, the Grand Dauphin and the royal princes surround the throne.

The Grotte de Thétis; an engraving by Le Pautre, 1676. The statues, by François Girardon, are in the park by the Bains d'Apollon.

On hunting days he either heard Mass early and went out afterwards, or hunted after dinner until sundown – he hunted more in summer than in winter and in warm weather was out of doors nearly all day. When he came in he went to Mme de Maintenon, spending more and more time with her as years went on. He supped with the Queen at about ten-thirty and then went back to Athénaïs where he stayed until midnight or later, but was never alone with her after the birth of Toulouse. When there was *Appartement*, which began at seven, he spent about two hours there and then went to Mme de Maintenon. On Good Friday and Easter Day the royal family were all day in church.

In writing about the Versailles of Louis XIV it seems impossible not to speak of the destructions and alterations which have so greatly spoilt his beautiful creation. Apart from the lifelessness in a place intended to be occupied by an elegant, bustling crowd, which makes it seem like a house which has been too long to let, with the tourists and their guides in the rôle of prospective buyers being shown round by knowledgeable housekeepers, the material damage through the ages has been incalculable. What we see today is but the shadow of what has been. For instance there are only three hundred jets of water in the gardens now, as compared to fifteen hundred in the time of Louis XIV. The King himself very soon sent his silver furniture to be melted down to pay for national defence. It was not an economically sound thing to do: the furniture, having cost ten million *livres* in the first place, only fetched three for the metal and many people thought he would have done better to sell his diamonds. But he never would do that; he liked to see the women of his family covered with them, more covered as the financial situation deteriorated, as a sort of defiance to the foreign visitors and the ambassadors. The King also destroyed the Grotte de Thétis, an exquisite folly which he had built in the very early days and whose place was needed for the North wing.

Louis XV, though most respectful of his great-grandfather's house – surprisingly so for somebody whose chief interest and pleasure was building – did not leave it entirely alone. He put a flat for his daughter Mme Adélaïde where the Ambassador's staircase had been and gutted Louis XIV's private suite on the Cour de Marbre to make rooms in the new taste for himself and his family. These *petits appartements* are so exquisite that he must be forgiven, but his architect, Gabriel, made unfortunate additions to the east front, and would have completely altered it if money had not been short. Little harm was done by Marie-Antoinette, also mercifully short of cash. But at the Revolution all the furniture and furnishings were sold, and dispersed to the four corners of Europe, in a public sale in the château which lasted a year. Worse was to come. Louis-Philippe saved the house from being pulled down, and that is to his honour, but then what dreadful work ensued! The bedevilment of the view from the town, first impression of most visitors, begun by Gabriel, is completed by a horrible nineteenth-century equestrian statue in the Cour Royale; by a lowering of the level in the Cour de Marbre so that the marble columns of Louis XIII's château are suspended in mid-air instead of having their feet on the ground; and by the removal of the railings between the two courtyards. Inside the château, wherever the stodgy monogram LP appears instead of the lovely Ls, it means that the Citizen King has passed that way. He gutted the flats of the princes and the nobles, who had vied with each other in the beauty of their decoration; he destroyed the Dauphin's and Mme de Pompadour's apartments, tearing down the walls to make huge, boring picture galleries. He had intended to make a museum in Paris for the *boiseries* which he ripped out but after the revolution of 1848 many were sold; the rest were eventually burnt in stoves by German soldiers billeted at Versailles in 1871. Louis-Philippe put a vile staircase where there used to be a courtyard, making nonsense of the windows which look over it. He tried to reconstitute the furnishings of Louis XIV's bedroom from memory. These had been piously kept by Louis XV and Louis XVI so that, as a young prince at the Court of Louis XVI, Louis-Philippe had known them well. But he had no eye whatever and the result was a joke.

The Galerie des Glaces at the time of Louis XIV. Engraving by Leclerc.

VIII

THE GRAND DAUPHIN

*C'est un terrible avantage de n'avoir rien fait
mais il ne faut pas en abuser.*

RIVAROL

When the King moved into Versailles for good he was in his early forties and the pattern of his life was changing; he was soon to be a grandfather. Louis XIV's only legitimate child, his first-born, was known as the Grand Dauphin and addressed as Monseigneur. Grand meant tall, not Great as in the case of the Grand Condé. He was more like an Austrian archduke than a French prince, fair, handsome until he got fat and naturally good. His servants adored him but he was shy with the upper classes and therefore not well known to or appreciated by them. After a dreadful childhood, the Grand Dauphin probably led the most agreeable life of any human being since the world began. Although, once he had escaped from his cruel masters, he never opened a book or read anything but the births and deaths in the Gazette, he was by no means a fool, and was quick to notice absurdities including his own. His philosophical attitude was remarkable and he was exactly the son to suit Louis XIV. He knew quite well that his father would never allow him any say in public affairs, so he was careful not to show the slightest interest in them – he arranged his existence to suit himself. He loved and patronized music; all novelties were played first to him. He had a passion for works of art and collected them with taste and knowledge; when he went to Paris, which he did two or three times a week, it was to attend the Opéra and rummage in what were then called the curiosity shops. The King's present to him on his twentieth birthday in 1681 was fifty thousand *écus* with which to buy pictures. Very soon his collection of *bibelots,* furniture (especially Boulle) and old masters became one of the attractions at Versailles and nobody could pretend to have seen all the glories there unless he had visited the *cabinets* of the Dauphin. Indeed they became so popular that he was obliged, for the sake of privacy, to arrange other rooms for himself, giving onto an interior courtyard. One of these, where he used to play cards, was called his *caveau*; it communicated with his father's room by a little secret stair in the wall dating from the time of Louis XIII.

The Grand Dauphin by Nicolas de Largillière.

The Dauphin's apartment, on the ground floor facing south and west, was the most desirable of any in the château. His prospect was all light and air and pleasure, decorative vases, orange trees, sky reflected in water, woodland in every direction as far as the eye could see. Elegant people strolled about in front of his windows, their gossip and laughter mingled with country noises: the fountains, the frogs, the cuckoo, owl and nightingale and gardeners grunting over their work. The rooms were a marvel of decoration; one of them was entirely by Boulle, including the parquet which was designed round the Dauphin's monogram; the walls and ceiling were of looking-glass, framed in ebony and gold. His bedroom was gold, white and blue, with Poussin's *Triomphe de Flore* over the chimney-piece. Mme de Montespan gave him curtains for it, specially embroidered at the Convent of St Joseph, in which she took an interest.

The Grand Dauphin liked campaigning in his youth and the soldiers loved him – he was brave and generous, truly interested in their well-being. He gave money, whenever he could, to improve their condition. It was known that when he wrote to the King he expressed concern at the wretched state of the foot-sloggers and that he never forgot to mention those officers who had distinguished themselves in action.

Best of all he liked riding to hounds. He went out after the wolf, accompanied as often as not by his aunt, Madame, every day as soon as Mass was over; sometimes he would stay out long after nightfall and ride home in the early hours. He killed all the wolves in the Ile de France so that before his own death the species was extinct there – he once accounted for six in a single day. One famous old wolf, however, was too cunning for him – he went after it at least nine times but it always escaped. So, in these pleasant, enviable ways he passed his existence, while tranquilly waiting to become the greatest king on earth.

The Grand Dauphin had his eccentricities, one of which was his preference for ugly women. His father naturally wanted him to marry as soon as possible, but there was no obviously suitable princess available – luckily for his posterity no female Spaniard, which was what the King would have liked, since genetic considerations seldom influenced royal alliances. The Spanish royal family was now in full decadence; Queen Marie-Thérèse of France and her sister the Archduchess of Austria were really its last sane members. Philip IV, their father, had not been exactly normal. When Louis XIV went to Saint-Jean de Luz to fetch Marie-Thérèse away, the news had gone round that the Spanish King could only digest human milk. The French courtiers, who never could take anything very seriously, flocked to his dinner table pretending to hope that they would find him struggling with his wet-nurse. It was a miracle that the Dauphin, whose mother and grandmother were both of that stock, turned out quite all right.

The King was obliged to look to Germany for a daughter-in-law. He had a treaty with the Elector of Bavaria, whose daughter, Princess Victoire was of a

Marie-Anne Christine-Victoire of Bavaria,
Dauphine of France; French school, seventeenth century.

Overleaf: The *Triomphe de Flore* by Nicolas Poussin.
This painting hung in the Dauphin's room at Versailles.

marriageable age. Her mother was a Savoy and she descended from Henri IV in the same degree as the Dauphin; she seemed eligible. Colbert de Croissy, a clever, worldly man, at one time ambassador to the English King, was sent off to have a look at her. As Louis XIV needed heirs, it was essential that the Dauphine should not repel her husband; he particularly enjoined upon Croissy to tell the truth about the girl and her looks. Croissy's report was a masterpiece of tact. He began his letter to the King by saying that there was nothing absolutely shocking in her appearance. Her skin was rather sallow, with brown stains on the forehead, but no doubt she was not yet very clever at making up her face. Her eyes were not a salient feature – they were neither large nor small, neither sparkling nor languorous. Her hands were red, but her lips were not; her teeth fairly regular but rotten. The fatness of her nose, which was bulbous at the tip, was not exactly a deformity. On receipt of this letter, the King sent his painter, de Troy, to Munich with instructions to make a truthful portrait of the young lady. In due course the picture arrived; the whole of the royal family gathered to look at it; the verdict was, "not bad at all'. Unfortunately there was also a letter from Croissy saying that the portrait was absurdly flattering. The nose, he repeated, was *fat*.

The King was now inclined to get out of the marriage. But the more the Dauphin heard about the fat nose, the brown stains and the red hands the more determined did he become to marry Princess Victoire. Last month, says Madame, he had no wish to marry; now he thinks of nothing else, it is very strange. Probably he wanted his own establishment, to get away from his tutors. At last he overcame his father's hesitations and the Princess was duly sent for (1680). When she arrived word went round that the King wished her to be admired, so no more was heard about the fat nose. She was certainly very ugly and this was bad luck on her, in a Court where nearly all the women were beauties, but there were some admirable qualities. She was well-educated, spoke perfect French and Italian, was a good, graceful dancer and a clean eater. The King appointed Mme de Maintenon to be one of her ladies – an unfortunate choice because, as Germans always are, the new Dauphine was implacable on the subject of birth. She leagued together with her cousin, Madame, to make the lives of various courtiers who had an insufficiency of ancestors a misery to them; and they both firmly refused to be civil to Mme de Maintenon.

The Dauphin liked his ugly wife very much at first; and the longed-for heir was born soon after the Court had definitely moved into Versailles – indeed this birth was the first excitement there. The Dauphine was delicate; she had already had at least two miscarriages; so it was arranged that a surgeon, named Clément, should deliver her, instead of a midwife. The King himself saw to every detail, even to choosing the baby's wet-nurse who, he said, must be dark, healthy and intelligent and above all, must smell delicious. Such a one was duly found. When the Dauphine's pains began the atmosphere at the château soon became that of a party. The court-

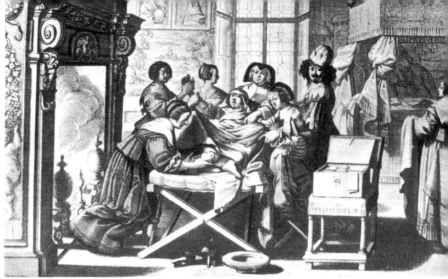

A childbirth scene from a Dutch seventeenth-century engraving by Abraham Bosse.

yard was illuminated; messengers were at the ready to carry the news all over France; those who had not got the *entrée* to the Dauphine's room crowded as near it as they could. It was August and a grilling heat-wave was in progress. The King had been woken at five, but told there was no great hurry; so he heard Mass before going to his daughter-in-law. The delivery seemed difficult and promised to be slow. At nine the King went to his council. The Queen sent for the relics of St Margaret, and they were exposed where the Dauphine could see them. The King came back; he thought her very weak and gave her food and wine with his own hands. Clément was calm and told him not to worry. Then Louis went to his dinner. The bed in which Marie de Médicis and Anne of Austria had had their babies was brought into the room – it had special bars for hanging on to and a foot-rest.

The crowd, by now, was indescribable. Ambassadors and foreign princes had come hot-foot from Paris; they, of course, had to be allowed at the bedside. Time went on. The Dauphine suffered horribly and became weaker and weaker. Clément was admirable. The King came back for good and stayed in her room all night. She said he was so kind to her she could hardly bear to leave such a dear father; for now she and everybody else thought she must die. The King said he would be glad even if the baby was a girl, if only the Dauphine's torment could come to an end. The Dauphin sat with his head in his hands, sunk in misery. Hour after hour dragged by. Dawn broke. Everybody was very tired (specially the Dauphine) except Clément who was as fresh as a daisy and never once lost his head; from time to time he bled her, saying that everything would be all right. The pains got worse and worse but there was still no sign of a baby. By ten-thirty a.m. on the second day the pains were excruciating. Then, just as it seemed as if she was at the end of her tether and must expire, the King's loud, clear voice was heard above the din of the onlookers: 'We have got a Duc de Bourgogne'.

The crowds all over the château and outside, in the courtyard, went berserk. They gave such a shout of joy that it was heard the other end of the town. Those who could get at the King hugged and kissed and cheered and clapped him. They pulled down the scaffolding in the Galerie des Glaces and pulled up the parquet everywhere and piled it all, with any other wood they could find including sedan chairs, topped by their own and other people's clothes, to make a huge bonfire in the courtyard. The King laughed, saying to let them be: 'I only hope they won't burn the house down!' He was transported with joy. The Dauphin forged himself a way through the mob, went out hunting and was seen no more that day.

But the Dauphine was still in agony. The excellent Clément went on keeping his head. He had a sheep flayed alive in her room (to the horror of her ladies – she was probably past caring) and wrapped her up in the skin. Naturally this cured her at once. Then she only longed to go to sleep. But Clément could not allow it. Sleep, after such a lengthy and precarious delivery would have been most dangerous, so she was forcibly kept awake for several hours. After that her room was hermetically sealed up and she had to stay in bed there, in the heat-wave, without even the light of a candle, for another nine days.

A fine binding with Louis' arms.

IX

THE QUEEN'S STAIRCASE

*Le roi ne manquera ni une station, ni une abstinence mais
il ne comprendra pas qu'il faille s'humilier, ni se repentir
et aimer Dieu plutôt que le craindre.*

MME DE MAINTENON

It is said that the Marquise de Maintenon, meeting the Marquise de Montespan on the Queen's staircase, remarked in her dry way, 'You are going down, Madame? I am going up'. The King had allotted her a flat at the top of the staircase, opposite the entrance to that of the Queen; so he had all three women on his own floor. What is now the *Oeil de Boeuf* was still two rooms, *le salon des Bassan* where the King hung his Bassanos, and a guard room; he had to cross these and the top of the staircase when he visited Mme de Maintenon. He could not go in unobserved as he could to Mme de Montespan on the other side; but his relationship with Mme de Maintenon was nothing if not above-board. Her rooms, so long the very centre of life at the Court, have been torn to pieces and reshaped and are now used as lumber-rooms. After the disappearance of Mlle de Fontanges, Louis had a short-lived affair with a Mlle Doré which gave Athénaïs the vapours and made Mme de Maintenon choke. When that was over, he resolved to sin no more and to dedicate his old age to God.

The King's religious outlook was that of a clever child. He was well up in theology, never failed to observe the outward forms and tried not to sin; but humility, self-criticism, true repentance and the love of God were beyond his ken. Certain things in the Gospels definitely displeased him; for instance he did not think it right that Christ should speak the language of poor people. He seems to have felt unfriendly towards the poor and never wanted to hear about the sad and often desperate condition of the majority of his subjects. Many, many people came to grief for trying to tell him of it: Mme de Maintenon used to say they discouraged him and did no good. Possibly he felt powerless to do anything for those in want and therefore could not bear the distressing truth; possibly he did not care. In this as in other matters he kept his own counsel. There was no excuse for indifference, if indifference it was. Enlightened men abounded in the seventeenth century; La Reynie, for instance, was truly charitable. St Vincent de Paul had seen to it that everybody knew

A detail from a Savonnerie carpet made for
the Grande Galerie of the Louvre.

about the horrible life of the galley slave. After the death of Louis XIV Madame, who was neither specially religious nor morbidly sensitive, begged the Regent to do away with galleys, which shows that they were considered a perfect scandal; but the King allowed Colbert to increase their numbers and to stick at no injustice to obtain the slaves that he required for them. Sunday after Sunday Louis sat under Bourdaloue who, among other things, was for ever trying to get reform in the prisons. Prisoners may well deserve their fate, he said, in one famous sermon, but are not they less miserable for that – indeed the innocent who are condemned unjustly are happier than the guilty: at least their conscience is clear. But consider the despair of a man awaiting judgment during endless days and nights, with nobody to talk to, in the horror of darkness – what must his lonely thoughts be as he anticipates an ignominious and agonizing death? To add to his spiritual torments, there are physical sufferings: a filthy dungeon to live in, just enough rotten bread to keep him alive, straw for his bed. Bourdaloue urged his congregation to go to the prisons and see how they could help those whom Christ had so often commended to them. The King listened attentively to such exhortations; nothing was ever done. He seems to have thought that one night of adultery was more displeasing to God than any amount of suffering inflicted on his fellow-men; in short, the spirit of Christianity was a closed book to him.

His confessor, Père de La Chaise, does not seem to have tried to enlighten him. He was a Jesuit; the King thought they were the best earthly servants of God and that all other orders were apt to have republican leanings. The director of a Catholic king's conscience in those days was almost like an extra minister (James II made Father Petre a Privy Councillor) and Père de La Chaise's anteroom was as crowded as if he had been one. The King took his advice about all the religious appointments, from Archbishop to Canon, so that the Father was very powerful. He was a delightful person, a gentleman, supple, polite, exquisitely cultivated and with a sweet nature, incapable of severity: in fact Mme de Montespan used to call him the *chaise à commodité*. He and Bossuet both encouraged the King to regard God as the only person to whom he was responsible. Remembering the famous *mot de Ramillies*, when, after that resounding defeat, Louis XIV said: 'God seems to have forgotten all I have done for him,' one cannot escape the suspicion, possibly unfair, that, having reached the pinnacle of success in spite of having led such an unchaste life, he thought that God would refuse him nothing should he become really reformed.

Louis XIV now renounced the sins of the flesh and devoted himself to the Queen. He had never abandoned her or left her bed, in which he habitually slept, although not always in a way that she, with her Spanish temperament, would have liked. Nevertheless he made love with her at least twice a month. Everybody knew when this had happened because she went to Communion the next day. She also liked to be teased about it, and would rub her little hands and wink with her large blue eyes.

Père de La Chaise. French school,
seventeenth century.

She was very unattractive. After twenty-two years in France, she still spent most of her time between a Spanish maid and a Spanish confessor, looking out for the courier from Spain. The Prussian ambassador Ezekiel Spanheim, a reliable witness, says the Court was never really gay because neither the Queen, nor the Dauphine, nor Madame (who only liked hunting), and least of all Mme de Maintenon, had the necessary high spirits.

When the Queen realized that she had got her husband to herself at last, her joy knew no bounds. She was not jealous of Mme de Maintenon: on the contrary she was grateful to her and attributed this turn of affairs to her influence. She gave her a portrait of herself framed in diamonds. Although Mme de Maintenon was attached to the Dauphine's household, it was noticed that when the Court went for the annual visit to Fontainebleau she went too, in spite of the fact that her mistress the Dauphine, still unwell from her lying-in, stayed at Versailles. The Queen's happiness only lasted about a year. In May 1683 the King went to the eastern frontier; France was at peace for once but he wanted to visit his regiments and inspect his fortresses. The Dauphine was again left behind but again Mme de Maintenon accompanied the Queen. All Louis XIV's women hated these journeys (the only thing they hated more was not to be of them) because of the wretchedness of the lodgings and the long, exhausting days in coaches or, worse still, on horseback, at the manoeuvres. This time they were away from 26 May to 30 July.

The Queen seemed very tired; and as soon as they were back at Versailles she developed an abcess under her arm. Fagon, the King's doctor, insisted on bleeding her although the surgeon implored him not to and even wept. Then, at midday, Fagon gave her a huge dose of emetic. Suddenly, those courtiers who happened to be in the Galerie des Glaces saw the King, distracted and in tears, running to the temporary Chapel to fetch the viaticum. Such a scene was extraordinary and those present were deeply embarrassed by it. The Queen died about an hour later, in the arms of Mme de Maintenon; she was forty-five. 'Poor woman', the King said, 'it's the only time she has ever given me any trouble.'

There was a rule that the royal family never stayed on in a house where death had occurred (ordinary people were forbidden to die in royal residences for this reason). The King went straight to Monsieur at Saint-Cloud for a few days while Fontaine-bleau was got ready to receive him. The Dauphine awaited him there, with Mme de Maintenon. Always soberly dressed, either in black or very dark colours, Mme de Maintenon had got herself up for this occasion in such deep, such exaggerated, such Earnest-like mourning that the King burst out laughing when he saw her and could not resist teasing her about it. He himself had quite recovered from whatever grief he may have felt and, having taken a momentous decision, was in an excellent mood. Mme de Maintenon found that she had been given rooms in the Queen's suite.

Obviously, if the King was really going to lead a life according to the rules of Christian sexual morality, in other words either monogamy, sanctioned by the Church, or abstinence, he would have to marry again very soon. He was only forty-five; he needed a woman. The choice available to him was not enormous – he had no desire to bring some foreign princess whom he had not seen, possibly with a fat nose, to Versailles. The Dauphin now had two healthy sons, the Duc d'Anjou, future King of Spain, having followed hard on Bourgogne; there seemed no need for more Children of France. If the King married, even morganatically, a member of the French high nobility, he would cause dreadful, possibly dangerous jealousies; if such a wife produced children the complications would be endless as, fruits of matrimony, they would have to take precedence of the adored du Maine. He never felt truly comfortable except with those he knew well. Mme de Montespan, had the circumstances been different, might have been granted her wish; as it was, what with the scandals in which she had recently been involved, her dreadful temper, her *embonpoint*, her husband and the fact that the King was no longer in love with her, she was out of the running. All his other women friends were married. Remained Mme de Maintenon. She was beautiful and attractive, with brilliantly bright eyes; too old to have children and yet young for her forty-eight years; she amused him and indeed she could be very funny as her letters show – her discretion was absolute, and that was vital; she was a widow and almost certainly a virgin; she was pious; she was the most correct and ladylike person at the Court; she used the French language so that it was a pleasure every time she opened her mouth; finally, he loved her. 'He loved me, it is true' she said, in later years, 'but only as much as he was capable of loving, for unless a man is touched by passion he is not tender.' Nevertheless he loved her more as time went on, more, perhaps, than she ever knew and certainly more than she loved him.

Nobody knows when they were married; Mme de Maintenon burnt all the

Queen Marie-Thérèse. French school, seventeenth century.

Mme de Maintenon. Engraving.

relevant documents after the King's death, saying she wished to remain an enigma to posterity; and the secret was well kept by the few witnesses of the ceremony, which must have taken place at Versailles in a little oratory in the King's apartment. It is thought that there were three people present, Père de La Chaise, the fascinating, wicked Monseigneur Harlay, Archbishop of Paris, who married them, and Bontemps, the King's body servant. Everything points to this wedding having been celebrated in the autumn of 1683, soon after the Court returned to Versailles from Fontainebleau. The Pope sent his blessing to the King and the relics of St Candida, done up in several different parcels, to Mme de Maintenon in August. Early in September she wrote to her dreadful brother (whom she loved but who was a proper thorn in her flesh) telling him on no account to join her at Fontainebleau. 'The reason which prevents me from seeing you', she said, 'is so valuable and so marvellous that it ought to bring you nothing but joy.' As she could never write him an entirely agreeable letter, she had to finish with: 'You are old [he was forty-nine], you have no children, you are unhealthy; what do you need but rest, liberty and piety?' Her young cousin, Mme de Caylus, who now lived with Mme de Maintenon says she never saw her in such a nervous state as during that Fontainebleau visit. On 20 September she wrote to her confessor, Abbé Gobelin, to say that her agitation was over; she was looking forward to telling him of her new-found peace of mind and her happiness and meanwhile begged him to pray that she might put them to good account.

Their contemporaries never knew for certain that a marriage between the King and Mme de Maintenon had in fact taken place, though, for those who could read them, there were unmistakable indications that it must have. The King, whose custom it was to address his subjects by their name and title and who had hitherto called her Marquise de Maintenon, now said Madame as he had done to the Queen.

Mme de Maintenon by Pierre Mignard.

She sat in the little, draught-proof box constructed for the Queen in the Chapel and took the head of the table at family dinner parties in the King's country houses, though not at Versailles where she dined alone. After her marriage she hardly ever left her own apartment to mingle with society, but when she did she took her former rank which was mediocre, a long way behind the duchesses; the few people who were received in her room found themselves as though in the presence of the Queen. The same, slightly false, humility obtained in her way of dressing. Her unfashionable clothes were richly embroidered and her underclothes were luxurious. She prided herself on wearing no jewels; but the cross which dangled from a necklace of huge, perfectly matched, pearls, was made from the finest diamonds in the King's collection.

The King from now on half lived in her flat, where he spent all his leisure time, saw his children and worked with his ministers. Given his nature and the fact that he was known to have no mistress, it was most unlikely that he could have been for hours every day with a beautiful woman without making love to her. In fact there is proof that he did so; and more often than Mme de Maintenon would have wished. Unthinkable in that case that they should both go regularly to Holy Communion unless they were married. Madame for one knew quite well that they were: 'In another world it will be decided whether she belongs to the King or to the paralytic Scarron; but when the King finds out the truth about her, there is no doubt he will return her to Scarron.' Madame said the King was so changed one would hardly know him. He no longer treated her as an intimate – not surprising in view of the libels and lies about his wife she was daily posting off to various foreign Courts.

Who was this Mme Scarron who took the centre of the stage at Versailles only fourteen years after her début in a walking-on part? Françoise d'Aubigné's life had already been full of contradictions; nobody would have thought that she was born under a lucky star – misfortune seemed to be her birthright. The d'Aubignés were an old, noble, provincial family; Mme de Maintenon's grandfather, Agrippa, an admirable person, was a friend of Henri IV and a Protestant; his son, her father, was a scamp, a rolling stone, in and out of prison for debt. When she was very small, d'Aubigné dragged her mother, her brother and herself across the Atlantic to Martinique, and dying there, left them to struggle back to France as best they could. Then the mother died. Françoise, who had not a penny in the world, became a poor relation in the houses of various aunts and cousins. At the age of sixteen she was converted to Catholicism, not an easy process in the case of this serious, clever girl, intensely religious and versed in theology. Finally two doctors of divinity argued the question with each other, in front of her; their propositions seeming valid, she at last consented to turn. Fervent Roman Catholic as she became, she retained certain prejudices and practices from her Protestant youth; she never could get used to saying a rosary; never cared for the Virgin or mentioned the saints; always preferred

A view of the south parterre.

Overleaf: The Queen's staircase.

Vespers to Mass. So she grew up, from hand to mouth, beautiful and clever but with the bleakest prospects that could be imagined. There seemed nothing for it but the convent, and against that she resolutely set her face. In spite of her piety she loved the world. She went out in it, in Paris, and had many admirers but not a single suitor on account of her poverty. At last Scarron (always called the poet Scarron, though anything less poetic than himself and his works can hardly be imagined) proposed marriage. He had long been a feature of the literary world; was old (forty-two), paralysed, shaped like a Z and poor, but people flocked to his house because of his naughty wit.

Françoise d'Aubigné would have snatched at any straw which rescued her from the nunnery; she accepted the poet's offer. She was a perfect wife to him and was spared what she was later to call 'those painful moments,' as Scarron was both impotent and helpless. She kept his house well; and there they entertained all that was most amusing, if not most edifying, in Paris society. The old fellow had a touching side, which other people felt, but she never did: she was never fond of him and always spoke in later years as if he had merely been a burden she was obliged to shoulder. Like her father and her brother, he was hopeless about money and no doubt she minded this; hers was an orderly soul. They were married for eight years; he died when she was twenty-five. The Widow Scarron inherited nothing but debts; all the furniture of her husband's lodging had to be sold to pay them, including her portrait by Mignard and *The Ecstasy of St Paul* by Poussin which had been painted specially for Paul Scarron. This picture, now in the Louvre, was before her eyes every day in later life; the Duc de Richelieu, who had bought it from her, had sold it to the King and it hung in one of the rooms of the Grand Appartement. Mme Scarron was only saved from actual starvation by Anne of Austria who gave her a tiny allowance on which she struggled along, lodging in a convent, until Mme de Montespan opened new horizons for her.

Her brother was even more of a ne'er-do-well than her father had been. As soon as she was recognized as a powerful figure in the King's entourage she set about finding an heiress for him. Many rich families would have liked the alliance for their daughters in return for various benefits she could have obtained for them through the King and her friend Louvois. But the wretched brother always made difficulties and finally, it really seemed in order to annoy her, he married a poor little doctor's daughter with no money, no brains and no connections. Mme de Maintenon was devoted to d'Aubigné; they laughed together; to her dying day she could never resist a joke. He did not like her nearly as much as she liked him. He hated the lectures which she thought it her duty to deliver when she saw or wrote to him; and although he accepted everything she did for him as a matter of course, he was for ever tormenting and teasing her.

It was d'Aubigné who put it about that she had had lovers while married to

The Ecstacy of St Paul painted by Nicolas Poussin for Paul Scarron.

Scarron. He said she had once been found, dressed as a page, in bed with the Marquis de Villarceau. Now beautiful young women generally do have lovers, but in her case one may doubt it. Mme Scarron was careful of her reputation to an unattractive degree, saying over and over again that it mattered to her more than anything else: 'Irreproachable behaviour is the cleverest policy' (*meilleure habileté*) was her motto. Whereas all the unchaste old beauties of her generation were tormented by fear of hell-fire, there is never a word in the letters she wrote to her spiritual directors which suggests that she felt remorse for any sins of the flesh committed when she was young. Since that particular temptation is practically irresistible, the greatest proof of her virtue is that she seems not to have understood the language of love. Mlle de Fontanges once said, exasperated, that Mme Scarron had advised her to divest herself of her passion for the King, exactly as if it were a garment that could be put on or off at will. Ninon de L'Enclos, the famous courtesan, with whom she was most friendly, said she was too awkward for love. She had the gifts of a mother as opposed to those of wife or mistress; she was perfect with children, though she generally lost interest in them when they grew up.

Mme de Maintenon's letters are not read as much as they deserve to be. At their best they are as witty as those of Mme de Sévigné. (She wrote to the Duc de Noailles one month of May: 'The chapter of the green peas goes on. Looking forward to eating them, the pleasure of having eaten them, and the joyful hope of soon eating more have been the sole topics of conversation the last four days. Certain ladies, having supped with the King find peas in their own rooms which they eat before going to bed'.) Her letters provide the key to her curious nature. She was worldly and religious, both to an unusual degree. This combination, which is far from rare, needs to be fully understood if it is not to look like hypocrisy. She herself truly thought that she hated the world. She never had words hard enough to condemn Versailles and the life at the Court, appearing to forget what a long, difficult and relentless struggle she had sustained in order to arrive at her great position there. She said, speaking of herself and Athénaïs, who made no bones about adoring the Court: 'What does God do? He binds it to the one who hates it and sends away the one who loves it, for the salvation of both'. And again: 'I am filled with sadness and horror at the very sight of Versailles. That is what is called the World; that is where all passions are at work: love of money, ambition, envy, dissipation. How happy are those who have put the World behind them!'

She was for ever telling her sister-in-law Mme d'Aubigné, hardly out of the nursery and naturally all agog for high life, that she was lucky to lead an anonymous existence, and be able to spend hours alone in her room, quietly reading. 'I wouldn't place you here for anything. Love your husband and don't make new friends.'

There was another contradiction. From her outward appearance, sober, quiet, self-controlled and dignified, and the fact that the King used to call her Your

Solidity, it has often been assumed that she had a strong and reliable character. Nothing could be further from the truth. She was easily influenced, a poor judge of human beings and, as will be seen, a far from loyal friend. She took people up with enthusiasm and dropped them again ruthlessly when it suited her to do so. She had an underlying melancholy, perhaps caused by the curious conflicts of her nature; and often said she wished she were dead. D'Aubigné once riposted to this 'I hope you've made sure of marrying God the Father'.

Mme de Maintenon was tormented by migraines, as people sometimes are when they live with a dominating personality. Athénaïs, too, suffered from them, more than ever now. In December 1684 the King turned her out of her flat next to his and gave her the Appartement des Bains, with all its memories of happy days when first she lived at Versailles. Furious and miserable she went down the Queen's staircase.

Sunburst from the Ambassador's staircase.

Victoire
of Bavaria

MARRIED 1st

Grand Dauphin,
Monseigneur

MARRIED 2nd

Marie-Thérèse
Joly de Choin

Louis-Armand
de Bourbon,
Prince de
Conti

MARRIED

Marie-Anne,
daughter of
Louis and
Louise de la
Vallière

François-Louis
de Bourbon,
Prince de la
Roche-sur-Yon,
becomes Prince
de Conti

MARRIED

Marie-Thérèse,
daughter of
Prince de Condé
grand-daughter
of the Grand Condé

Louis III
de Bourbon,
Prince de Condé,
'M. le Duc'

MARRIED

BROTHER TO

Louise-Françoise,
daughter of
Louis and Athénaïs,
'Mme la Duchesse'

Louis-Auguste
de Bourbon,
Duc du Maine.
Son of Louis
and Athénaïs

MARRIED

BROTHER TO

Louise-Bénédicte
de Bourbon,
grand-daughter
of the Grand
Condé

Philip II
d'Orléans,
Duc de Chartres.
Son of Monsieur
and Palatine

MARRIED

Françoise-Marie
de Bourbon,
daughter of
Louis and
Athénaïs

The younger generation.

X

THE YOUNG GENERATION

*I shall cheerfully bear the reproach of having
descended below the dignity of history.*

LORD MACAULAY

In 1685 the Dauphine had a third son, the Duc de Berri. 'Ah my little Berri, I love you dearly, but you have killed me' she used to say. Indeed, she was never well again – Madame told her correspondents that Mme de Maintenon had made the doctors see to it that she never would be; which is the kind of wild statement in which Madame specialized. The Dauphine appeared less and less at the Court and shut herself up in a dark little back room, with her Italian maid, a prey to melancholia. The doctors said that her illness was imaginary, so she got scant sympathy from the King, who naturally wanted her to play her part in public. She used to say she would have to die in order to prove that she had not been shamming; and in 1690 she did die and it was proved. Her lungs were ulcerated, her stomach gangrened and there were several abcesses in her intestine. The Dauphin had loved her at first but she showed her indifference to him too plainly, in spite of friendly warnings from Mme de Maintenon. By the time she died he had made other dispositions. He fell in love first with one and then another of his wife's maids-of-honour. They were hastily married off, one to a Polignac, the other to a du Roure, and were never seen again at Versailles. Mme de Maintenon was certainly relieved by the death of this princess who was so disagreeable to her; the King hunted and gambled as if nothing had happened; and the only person who mourned her was Madame, who used to talk German to her and said that she had been somebody you could laugh with. She had a ready wit. One day the King's exquisite daughter Marie-Anne de Conti seeing her asleep, said to one of the ladies-in-waiting that the Dauphine was as ugly as when she was awake. The Dauphine then woke up and observed that *she* had not the advantage of being a love child. Madame wept copiously at the funeral; and extra tears were jerked because the Palatinate and Bavarian coats of arms were practically the same, so that they reminded her of other deceased dear ones. But in later years she discovered that the Dauphine had repeated to the King various disagreeable jokes they had had together, about Mme de Maintenon. The three little boys were taken over by the King – the Dauphin never showed much interest in them. He called them by their full titles: M. le Duc de Bourgogne and so on, and they called him Monseigneur.

As the Dauphine never would appear in society, the young fashionables of the rising generation centred round the Dauphin, his half-sister Marie-Anne de Conti and her husband, and Conti's younger brother, Prince de La Roche-sur-Yon. Now that Louise de La Vallière's daughter Marie-Anne was grown up, the most beautiful women at Versailles were nothing to her. Mme de Sévigné says she was above humanity, you could see she was a daughter of the Gods; her scented bedroom was the very shrine of Venus. She had been married since she was thirteen to the Prince de Conti and was the first of Louis XIV's bastards to marry into the royal family. The Conti brothers, like their cousins the Condés, were Princes of the Blood but not Children of France, since they were not descended from a Bourbon king but only from an uncle of Henri IV. They were nephews of the Grand Condé and great-nephews, through their mother, of Cardinal Mazarin – first cousins of Mary of Modena. So they had the same blood on both sides as Prince Eugène whom the younger brother resembled in his nature and his gifts. Their father was dead; he had been a most fascinating man, the model for Molière's Don Juan. Little Marie-Anne cried when she heard that she was engaged. Louis XIV, always very fond of her, asked why, but she was too timid to say that she preferred the younger brother. She was not too timid, however, after a few days of marriage, to pronounce that her husband was no good at making love – which, coming from such a baby, surprised even the sophisticated courtiers at Versailles. The King sent for her, gave her a wigging and reduced her to tears; and after that the young couple got on quite well, but there were no children.

Marie-Anne was right in preferring the younger Conti to her husband, who was a nonentity. The brother was very different: valiant, brilliant and ambitious, adored by those who knew him, with all the gifts of a leader, he was often likened to Germanicus. He was just as charming to the butcher, the baker and the candlestick-maker as he was to the highest in the land, could be as frivolous as anybody and yet had as many friends in intellectual circles as among the playboys of the Court. He could discuss their special problems with magistrates and scientists; had read immensely and remembered what he read; knew where to find the sources of information; was versed in astronomy and mathematics; had the genealogy of all the nobles by heart (a polite accomplishment in those days) and possessed a marvellous clarity of thought. With a gift for friendship, he chose his intimates well and then made their relationship truly profitable; he was courteous and never hurt anybody's feelings. He was fond of making love and it was said of him that, like Caesar, he was every woman's husband and every man's wife. In warfare he was a

François Louis de Bourbon, Prince de Conti. French school, seventeenth century.

hero. He attached the soldiers to him by his goodness and the officers by his affability: all ranks felt total confidence in him. He distinguished himself at the battles of Steinkirk and Neerwinden, and was known throughout Europe as a chivalrous adversary. He had been brought up with the Dauphin and was his greatest friend – their tutor, Bossuet, loved him more than a son. Even Mme de Maintenon was charmed by him.

But this splendid Prince was born under an unlucky star. For one thing his fortune was not great enough to support his rank. This would not have signified if he had pleased the King, but unluckily for him the King soon realized that he was worth a hundred of the Duc du Maine and was jealous on his son's behalf. He blighted the young man's career, so that with all his brilliant gifts he was able to make nothing of his existence. Now he is forgotten. However, while the princes were in their early manhood, it was taken as a matter of course that whenever the Dauphin should be called to the throne his cousin would be at his right hand. Life seemed to be full of promise then.

In 1683 the Turks were surging into Europe. The King of France, whose chief enemy had always been the Emperor, was not displeased to see him in difficulties and refused to join an alliance against the Infidel; although Pope Innocent XI offered him Constantinople if he would do so. The Conti brothers and various other young bloods at Versailles, bored with peace at home, begged permission to go and fight the barbarians. The King consented; they went off; he had second thoughts and ordered them to come back; they turned the deaf ear. They joined up with their cousin Eugène, performed prodigies of valour and no doubt enjoyed themselves very much indeed. Unfortunately they had urged their friends at Versailles to keep in touch and letters passed to and fro. Now the King was fond of reading other people's letters; it was one of the ways by which he knew what was happening under his enormous roof. The post was censored and the meatiest morsels were brought to him. He had a shock when he saw himself referred to by the younger Conti as a Monarch of the Stage. After that there was a whole bag of letters from Versailles to the French volunteers in Hungary, none of which was relished by the said monarch. Some of them made fun of him and Mme de Maintenon and complained that the dullness of Versailles now beggared description; there were several homosexual love-letters and, in the same fatal packet, one from Marie-Anne de Conti saying that she was obliged to drive out with Mme de Maintenon and an old freak called the Princesse d'Harcourt, day after day. 'Judge what fun this must be for me.' The King sent for Marie-Anne and blasted her with his terrifying tongue. Three fashionable young men were exiled on account of this mail-bag. Another of the writers was the grandson of Maréchal de Villeroy, the King's greatest friend – who said how lucky it was that the boy had only blasphemed in his letter: '*God* forgives'. Mme de Maintenon never forgave Marie-Anne de Conti.

The courtiers noticed that the King was in a difficult mood altogether at this time, 1685, the year of the Revocation of the Edict of Nantes. He suddenly exiled Cardinal de Bouillon, Grand Aumônier de France, and the Duke, his brother; some thought for an affair of sodomy, others that the Bouillons were altogether too grand and pretentious. They were furious; the Duke said 'the King is only an old gentleman in his château who has got one tooth left which he keeps to bite me with'. The brothers were hated at the Court, so nobody minded their departure. Then the King, for some reason, sent beautiful, thin Mlle de Crenan to the Bastille.

One evening there was a party at Marly; the Maréchal de Villeroy, the Duc de Roquelaure and the Marquis d'Antin, all intimate friends of the King's, asked the Duc de Luxembourg to tell him that they were at the door. Louis XIV in his new, curmudgeonly mood, said 'All right – they can go away'.

News now came of the death of Charles II; Milord Arran fell in a dead swoon in the Galerie des Glaces, which showed that he was nicer than most English people who were generally thought to hate their kings. 'Now,' said Mme de Sévigné, 'the stage is set for some great acting, between the Prince of Orange, M. de Monmouth and that infinite quantity of Lutherans there are in England. It seems that Charles died more as a philosopher and an Englishman than as a Christian.' This death was politically a serious blow to Louis XIV.

When the two Conti brothers got back from the war Marie-Anne almost immediately fell ill with smallpox - she recovered but gave it to her husband. He seemed to be getting better and was sitting up in bed, joking with her, when he fell back, dead, leaving her a childless widow at nineteen. So her brother-in-law was now head of the family and Prince de Conti. The King, who had never liked him, and, since the famous letters, could not bear the sight of him, exiled him from Versailles and he went to live at Chantilly with his uncle, the Grand Condé, who loved him more than his own children and married him to his grand-daughter.

Exquisite as she was, the Dowager, or, as she was more often called, to distinguish her from her sister-in-law, the Beautiful Princesse de Conti, never had much luck in love and never married again. The King of Morocco asked for her hand, and she could have married the Duc de Chartres, the son of Monsieur, but she preferred to be free. She was a good-natured soul, most kind and attentive to her mother, Louise de La Vallière, whom she visited regularly in her convent. Like her, she was dull. She always behaved decently, and Spanheim says that the fashion for virtue at Versailles was set by the piety of the late Queen, the goodness of the Dauphine, the indifference (to men) of Madame and the excellent behaviour of the lovely Princesse de Conti. She and the Grand Dauphin now became inseparable - he could hardly bear her out of his sight - but they never created an agreeable society, as they might have done. The Dauphin had no social gifts, he was too shy. When the day's hunting was over he either took his sister to the Opéra in Paris or played cards with her and a few close friends. People thought that when he came to the throne he would live in Paris and abandon Versailles – also that he would never go to war since he was lazy and not in the least ambitious.

Soon after his wife's death, the Dauphin fell in love with one of the Princesse de Conti's ladies, called Mlle de Choin. Ugly, like all his women, she was a fat, squashy girl with a snub nose, an enormous mouth and huge breasts on which he would beat a tattoo with his fingers. She became mixed up in the intrigues which always surrounded him, since nobody could forget that from one day to another he might be the King of France. At this time, Marie-Anne de Conti was rather in love with a good-looking member of the Duc de Luxembourg's staff called M. de Clermont. Luxembourg, always full of schemes, suggested to Clermont that if he married Mlle de Choin they could rule the Dauphin between them; so Clermont, in the best traditions of French classical comedy, proceeded to court both mistress and maid. While this was going on he left for the front. Marie-Anne was certainly unlucky where the post was concerned: Clermont's mail was opened and given to the King; it contained the love letters of this three-cornered affair. The King sent for the Princess who arrived trembling as all his children did, except du Maine, when summoned to the dread presence; he then read out loud Clermont's letters to Mlle de Choin. Marie-Anne fainted away. He revived her and made her read out loud her own letters to Clermont. After that, and having pulled her out of another fainting fit, he spoke rather kindly to her and sent her off in a tremendous rage. She dismissed Mlle de Choin; but the Dauphin went on seeing her and eventually married her. He did so for exactly the same reasons as those for which his father had married Mme de Maintenon. As in their case total secrecy was observed; no details of the ceremony are known, but a letter from the Dauphin to Mme de Maintenon (19 July 1694) leaves no doubt that it took place. 'I was amazed that you spoke to me of my wife – amazed and taken aback. I am delighted that I am in favour; my only thought is how to please the King.' Mlle de Choin behaved well, living very quietly at Meudon and never putting herself forward. Clermont, many years later, married the Dowager Countess of Jersey, widow of the English ambassador to Paris.

Athénaïs de Montespan's daughters were much more amusing than the Princesse de Conti. The frivolous Mortemart strain was powerful and came out in her children. In 1685 her eldest daughter married M. le Duc (de Bourbon), grandson and heir of the Grand Condé. She was thereafter known at Versailles as Mme la Duchesse. Some people thought it strange that the rich, powerful, famous Condé should allow his heir to marry a bastard. But Condé's life was complicated by the part he had played in the Fronde, when he had fought against the Queen Mother and Mazarin. He was ashamed, now, of his behaviour and was for ever trying to make amends to his cousin the King whom he both loved and feared. The bride was only twelve and Mme de Montespan showed her hard heart with a vengeance on this

Marie-Anne de Bourbon, Princesse de Conti, attributed to Pierre Gobert.

LOUIS DUC DE BOURBO

occasion, insisting that she should be put to bed at once with her seventeen-year-old husband, for fear that otherwise he might have second thoughts and seek an annulment of the marriage. The King was more humane and would not allow it. M. le Duc was intelligent and well-educated but most unattractive; large for a pigmy, small for a man, with a bright yellow face and a head too big for his body. His appearance was thought to be due to his mother's having intercepted a sexy look from her dwarf when she was pregnant; but his sisters were little black beetles, and the Condé family was to be strange, physically and mentally, for several generations.

Mme la Duchesse was a darling. Her plump little body could not compete with that of the swan-like Princesse de Conti for beauty, but she had the face of a real love child. Madame said of her (and Madame hated bastards) 'She ridicules everything in such a droll manner that one can't help laughing . . . in all her life she has never had a bad-tempered moment'. This may have been due to the fact that she always had the best food in France. The Grand Condé was subjugated by her and she adored him; they were a touching pair, never apart. The year after her marriage she caught smallpox while the Court was at Fontainebleau. Condé nursed her devotedly and stayed with her there after everybody else had left for Versailles. She recovered; but he had worn himself out; this great captain suddenly died, at the age of sixty-five, as the result of his fond attachment to a little girl of thirteen. On his death bed he wrote a letter to the King, begging him to take the Prince de Conti back into favour.

After all the services Condé had rendered him, the King could not do otherwise and Conti reappeared at Versailles. He and Mme la Duchesse were in love and their liaison, though it did not prevent Conti from loving his pages as well, was cloudlessly happy and romantic and lasted until death parted them, many years later. The affair was conducted with the greatest discretion, their only confidants and go-betweens were the Dauphin and Marie-Anne de Conti. For twenty years Conti never visited Mme la Duchesse in her own flat; when he was ill or absent she never asked for news of him. M. le Duc was dangerously jealous, not only of his wife's love for Conti but of his brother-in-law's irresistible charm, ever before his eyes, and of the fact that the Grand Condé had been so fond of him. However, Mme la Duchesse was always on the best of terms with her husband, as was Conti with his wife; M. le Duc and his sister, the Princesse de Conti, were thus kept under control.

Conti became more popular every year; he was adored by the Parisians – his town house was where the Monnaie is now – and by the army. It was more and more obvious that he must play a great part as soon as the Dauphin became King. Meanwhile the Duc du Maine was showing himself to be a figure of cardboard. Louis XIV's dislike of his cousin grew. In 1696 he saw a chance of getting rid of him at

Louis III de Bourbon, M. le Duc. School of Rigaud.

Françoise-Marie de Bourbon and Louise-Françoise de Bourbon, daughters of Louis XIV and Athénaïs de Montespan, by Philippe Vignon.

which he eagerly snatched. The throne of Poland fell vacant; it was offered to Conti by a section of the Polish aristocracy and accepted for him by the King. Never has a prospective monarch been more reluctant. Like most Frenchmen, Conti loathed the idea of living anywhere but in France; in spite of the King's unkindness, his eventual prospects were brilliant; but above all it would break his heart to leave Mme la Duchesse. However, the King would not hear of a refusal and Conti was obliged to do as he was told. He begged the King not to publish the news and not to treat the Princesse de Conti as a Queen until he had been to Poland and found out how the land lay. To no avail. 'Here we have the King of Poland!'

Louis XIV greatly enjoyed the farcical pretence that he was conferring a benefit on his dear cousin. The dear cousin was obliged to play the game. There were sad scenes of adieu – heartrending in the case of Mme la Duchesse; it seemed probable that the lovers would never meet again and they could not hide their despair. Conti went off by sea, with Jean Bart, the celebrated sailor who alone, it was thought, could circumvent English and Dutch pirates and get him safely to his new kingdom. The story has a happy ending. At Danzig, the only noble of any importance to come on board Conti's ship and pay his homage was Prince Sapieha; the Elector of Saxony, backed by a powerful army, had stolen a march on the French and was preferred. In wild spirits Conti returned to Versailles and the arms of Mme la Duchesse. But the King's attitude to him was in no way modified. He was the only royal prince with no governorship of a province, no job at Court, not even a regiment of his own. The result was that, as the years dragged on uselessly and his hopeful youth was succeeded by a disillusioned middle age, the Prince de Conti became embittered and gave himself up to debauchery.

The Duc du Maine was Conti's brother-in-law, having married another tiny sister of M. le Duc's. He brought more gaiety to the King's life than all his other

Françoise-Marie de Bourbon, Duchesse de Chartres, as Thetis.
French school, seventeenth century.

children put together, partly because he was the only one whom the King did not terrify; he breezed in and out of his father's apartment with all the gossip and jokes of the Court. He was noted for his wonderful imitations (when the King lay on his death-bed du Maine was imitating old Dr Fagon, in the next room). As nobody else had much use for him, he spent his life insinuating himself into the good graces of his father and Mme de Maintenon and was rewarded for his assiduity. The Grande Mademoiselle was blackmailed by her cousin the King into leaving whole provinces to du Maine; and he was given the governorship of Languedoc. When he married his father bought Sceaux for him from Colbert's children. Du Maine had that high command in the army which was denied to Conti; and here he proved himself not only incompetent but also cowardly, a fault, perhaps the only one, that the French nobility could never forgive.

The King found it out almost by accident. He flew into a violent temper which he worked off on his servants; but he could not live without du Maine, who was his beloved son; so he always turned a blind eye to his faults, of which he was only too well aware.

The letters the Duke wrote to Mme de Maintenon from the front are as deplorable as his seven-year-old letters are charming. He boasts of his courage, saying she need not keep his exploits to herself – she may pass them on to the King; he begs her to be most severe with anybody who speaks ill of him. 'Brought up by you, how could I be found wanting?' he adds cunningly, and signs himself the *poor cripple*. Belle Madame was nothing to him now that she had lost her hold over the King. (The only one of Athénaïs's children who was faithful to her as her star waned was her son by Montespan, the Duc d'Antin.)

Another member of the young set at Versailles was the Duc de Chartres, future Regent of France. He was the only surviving son of Monsieur and the German

Madame. Though less brilliant than Conti, he had solid gifts – was a first class soldier and loved science and all the arts. As·with Conti, the King was prejudiced against him and never gave him a chance to be useful; and he, too, was driven to drink and sex for consolation. He was forced to marry the youngest daughter of Athénaïs de Montespan (1692). Monsieur did not care for this alliance of his heir with a bastard but was bribed into allowing it by the promise of an enormous dowry, and the order of the Saint-Esprit for the Chevalier de Lorraine. Madame, with her German ideas about genealogy, became hysterical. According to Saint-Simon, when she heard that Chartres had consented to the marriage (the boy was too much intimidated by his uncle to do otherwise) she boxed his ears in front of the whole Court. Neither Madame herself, nor Dangeau nor any other memorialist speak of this famous *gifle*; nevertheless there is no doubt that her rage and distress over the misalliance were great.

The Duc and Duchesse de Chartres were married by Cardinal de Bouillon, in a chastened mood after seven years of exile, and the King gave a series of amazing fêtes and entertainments to celebrate the wedding. All Chartres's suits for these fêtes were designed by Bérain – his wedding clothes were solid with pearls and diamonds, which followed the pattern of the Spanish needlepoint lace with which his coat was trimmed. The bride's wedding dress was gold and silver with tiny black flowers woven in the gold. The skirt was silver stripes edged with ruffles of gold Spanish needlepoint. This dress took several months to make. Her beautiful hair was done up with diamonds and rubies. Their marriage did not turn out badly. The Duchess was droll and pretty like all the Mortemarts; she amused her husband and did not reproach him for his mistresses; she was too lazy to have lovers so she herself was never an object of scandal. But their many children were a sad failure.

It is a bad mark to Mme de Maintenon that she not only took no interest in these attractive young people who were beginning their lives under the same roof as herself, but definitely disliked nearly all of them. She was, or pretended to be, fond of the Dauphin and was always kind and understanding about his second marriage. He called on her every day to recount the hunt, leaving out the kill, which she thought too sad. Her feelings for du Maine never altered; he was the person she loved the most. But the others found no favour with her, even her own nursling, Mme la Duchesse. The Princesse de Conti never lived down her unlucky letter. Mme de Maintenon made the stupid observations about present-day youth which always have been and always will be heard. Her great complaint was that the young set at Versailles thought of nothing but pleasure – Satan findeth mischief still and so on – though, given the existence forced on them by the King, it is hard to see how else they could have passed their time. Indeed when, years later, Marie-Anne de Conti turned to religion, Mme de Maintenon most unfairly complained that she had become dowdy and dreary and was not pulling her weight at the Court.

Philippe d'Orléans, Duc de Chartres. French school, seventeenth century.

XI

THE NEW RÉGIME

S'il est ordinaire d'être vivement touché des choses rares,
pourquoi le sommes nous si peu de la vertu?

LA BRUYÈRE

No doubt the new régime, imposed by the King and attributed to the influence of Mme de Maintenon, cast a gloom at Versailles. There were a lot of horrid new rules. No plays or operas were allowed during Lent; there was even a question of doing away with the theatre altogether; but Père de La Chaise very sensibly said that if that happened young people, who must have amusements, would find more equivocal ones. Chatting and giggling at Mass were now severely looked upon – the King, from his little box above the heads of the congregation, was not so busy with his own prayers that he did not see exactly what was happening. He also noticed when people did not go to their Easter duties; sent for them; and spoke. He sent Père de La Chaise to tell Madame she had been talking too freely – she had been heard shouting to the Dauphin that even if she saw him stark naked it would not tempt her – and that she would do well to be stricter with her ladies! Piety was in fashion, though it was noticed that the saints of Versailles often became sinners when they got to Paris. The King himself was trying to set an example of holy moderation. When some bishops went to see him and said he was getting to be too much like Henry VIII, with his claim to be head of the French church, instead of freezing them up, as they had expected, he merely replied: 'What I have just heard is *considérable.*' All this underlined the fact that the King and his contemporaries were now middle-aged. It was over twenty years since they had first disported themselves in the bosquets and gardens of his father's little house; and the band of special friends was scattered. Henrietta, the first Madame, had been dead some fifteen years. She was still remembered at the Court and the Dauphin once saw her ghost. He was sitting on the *chaise percée* by his bed when the door opened and she came into the room, wearing a beautiful yellow dress with blue ribbons. He was so frightened that he leapt back into bed, waking up the Dauphine, and put his head under the bed-clothes until the poor ghost had vanished.

Mme Maintenon and her niece, afterwards the Duchesse de Noaïlles,
by Ferdinand Elle, about 1687.

Louis being wheeled round the gardens with his courtiers, by Jean-Baptiste Martin, 1688.

A real ghost appeared at Court in the form of the Marquis de Vardes, a friend of the King's young days who had been mouldering in exile for twenty years. Louvois met him in the south of France and spoke of him to the King who summoned him. Vardes appeared, looking very odd, in the same clothes as those in which he had gone away, saying, 'When one is wretched enough to be far from Your Majesty one is not only unhappy but ridiculous'. The King presented the Dauphin to him, pretending that he was a courtier, but Vardes was not taken in. He bowed. 'What are you doing, Marquis de Vardes, you know very well one does not bow to people when I am there!' 'Sire, I know nothing any more – I have forgotten it all.' The King forgave him the palace intrigue for which he had been exiled and he ended his days at Versailles.

Louise de La Vallière was ageing in her convent, so ugly now as to be unrecognizable; the King never gave her a thought. She was recalled to his memory for a moment when their son Vermandois died in a garrison town at the age of sixteen (1683). When a little boy he had been mixed up in a homosexual scandal; this had brought down the dreadful wrath of his father who had taken no interest in him thereafter. The King spared himself the painful experience of going to condole with Louise by saying that he longed to go but thought himself too sinful to disturb the devotions of such a holy nun. She said she was still weeping for the birth of her son when she found herself weeping for his death. Other early friends were dead, and yet others, such as the Comtesse de Soissons and her sister, disgraced. Lauzun had come out of prison much less amusing than when he went in.

Very different were the people who henceforward were to surround the King. Mme de Maintenon ruthlessly cleared the decks of her brother and his unpresentable wife. She kidnapped their child, whom she brought up as her own daughter – finally marrying her to the heir of the Duc de Noailles; she forced Mme d'Aubigné into a nunnery and d'Aubigné into a home for pious gentlemen at St Sulpice. She heard that he sometimes escaped and made his way to a brothel, or, worse still, would sit on a bench in the Tuileries gardens and talk to anybody who would listen about his 'brother-in-law'. So she paid a lay brother to follow wherever he went. Fond as she was of him, she really could not have him wandering in and out of her sanctum at Versailles, embarrassing the King and upsetting her own little group of friends with his dreadful jokes.

This group centred round the two daughters of Colbert, the Duchesses of Beauvilliers and Chevreuse and their husbands; four people who were never happy when they were apart and who spent their lives together. Chevreuse is summed up by Spanheim as devout, a gentleman, weak, ruled by women, to whom nobody pays any attention; but Beauvilliers was more of a person and he became indispensable to the King. His father, the Duc de Saint-Aignan, a jolly, worldly fellow, member of Mme de Sévigné's circle had been a boon companion of Louis XIV when he was young. Molière portrayed him as Oronte in *Le Misanthrope* and Racine dedicated his first play, *La Thébaïde* to him – he was a member of the Académie Française, an arbiter of elegance, director of the King's fêtes and a repository of all the Court gossip; the King used to find out what was going on from him. He got through an enormous fortune. Beauvilliers, his second son, was the exact opposite. He was intended for the Church; his parents took no interest in him whatever and he was kept in their concierge's lodge until he was seven. Then he was sent to live with a poor priest who was to educate him – there was not a room for him in the priest's house and he shared a bed with the maid. When he was fourteen his luck turned; his elder brother died and he became his father's heir. He was removed from the maid's bed, given the command of a regiment and for several years lived a life of violent debauchery. When he was twenty-three and she fourteen, he married Colbert's third daughter, heiress to a huge fortune. She soon converted him, and between them they converted Louise de La Vallière, a work which Beauvilliers undertook in order to atone for his father having encouraged the King's adultery. The Beauvilliers had thirteen children of whom nine were daughters. Saint-Simon wanted to marry one of them, he did not mind which, in order to have Beauvilliers for a father-in-law. He admired him more than anybody at the Court. But they were all hunchbacks with vocations except one and she, most unsuitably, married the Duc de Mortemart, the raffish nephew of Mme de Montespan. The others became nuns.

Beauvilliers was called the Good Duke. He was always on the side of the poor and one of the few people who could speak to the King about their condition with impunity. He was politeness itself – he would beg his coachman's pardon if he kept him waiting a few minutes. As he grew older he became more and more devout, with an underlying silliness which shows in a curious letter he wrote to God when

Paul, Duc de Beauvilliers; an engraving.

he was sixty. 'I am old, . . . my end is at hand and I am about to enter the darkness of death.' He then proceeds to a sort of self-analysis. He wishes Versailles were more like Bethlehem and reproaches himself for loving jokes and gossip, for talking too much about his own ancestors, for not bringing God into every conversation, for eating more than he required, for fussing about cleanliness and for praying to be made a minister of state. His prayer was answered (1692); he was the only member of the old nobility to be admitted to the King's *Conseil* during the whole reign. Beauvilliers gave the orders at Versailles when the King was away.

The Beauvilliers introduced the Abbé de Fénelon into Mme de Maintenon's little set. This fascinating, ambitious, vain, aristocratic, holy man, disciple of Bossuet, was like a brother to Beauvilliers; they seemed to have but a single soul, so perfectly did they agree on every subject. Fénelon wrote a Treatise on the Education of Girls for Mme de Beauvilliers, to help her with her nine daughters. Mme de Maintenon soon made friends with Fénelon and saw a great deal of him. She met him with the Beauvilliers in their flat at Versailles or at the Hôtel de Saint-Aignan in Paris where, after dinners at which they helped themselves, to avoid being disturbed by the servants, Fénelon would stand by the fire, one beautiful white hand on the chimney-piece, talking and talking about God.

Other friends of Mme de Maintenon were the beautiful, pious Marquise de Dangeau, born Löwenstein; Monseigneur, later Cardinal, de Noaïlles, whom the King appointed Archbishop of Paris only in order to please her (1695); Mme de Montchevreuil, a horrid old person with long, yellow teeth who was the terror of pretty ladies because she used to tell the King what they were up to; and Chamillart, almost the only courtier who could give the King a decent game of billiards. He was a gentleman, a charming fellow who presently became a disastrous minister. These good people were not very stimulating company for Louis XIV who liked *les gens d'esprit*, In fact, hardly had he assembled his most interesting and important subjects under his roof, than he retired into almost private life with an ageing spouse and her circle of excellent nonentities.

In 1685 the King committed one of his mistakes: he revoked the Edict of Nantes by which his grandfather Henri IV had ensured freedom of conscience for the Protestant minority in France. For some years Louis XIV had quietly been tormenting them. They were excluded from holding any office under the crown, and from the liberal professions; mixed marriages were forbidden and the children of existing ones declared illegitimate; a Protestant woman could not employ a Roman Catholic midwife; when Protestants were ill they were forcibly taken from their homes and put into state hospitals so that their last moments could be surveyed by a priest. A hardship of a minor but extremely annoying kind was that they were forbidden to employ Roman Catholic servants. (The Protestants were nearly all of the well-to-do bourgeois class, and servants were hard to come by among their co-religionists.) Finally the rich towns of southern France, where the reformed religion thrived, were subjected to the *dragonnades*; regiments were moved in and the soldiers billeted on Protestant households with permission to make as much of a mess as they liked. Rape and looting, if not exactly encouraged, were never punished.

All these measures led to a good number of real or pretended conversions; but a hard core of sincere men and women was left and this the King decided to crack. It must be said that he was encouraged to do so by practically every responsible person in the land; by all the great preachers and the bishops, the ministers of state, all the members of the Paris and provincial Parlements, not to speak of society people like Mme de Sévigné. Bossuet, whose opinion the King valued, perhaps, more than any, called him: 'This Constantine, this Theodore, this Charlemagne' when he heard of the Revocation; the holy and respected Rancé, founder of the Trappists, said 'What the King has done is prodigious'. Père de La Chaise, says Spanheim, was very responsible, which seemed odd for such a sweet person, but then he was a Jesuit. Spanheim himself was Protestant, (Brandenburg at this time led the Protestant German States) and it was thought that he was actively engaged in smuggling his co-religionists to Prussia. His daughter married a French refugee.

The Protestants were deeply unpopular with all sections of the French – for the same reasons as the Jews were unpopular in pre-war Germany. They were too rich, successful and clannish. The King had never been particularly intolerant or bigoted; in fact he once said, when talking about a Catholic mission to Siam, that God had coloured the leaves on the trees in many different shades of green, and perhaps He wanted to be worshipped differently by the various peoples of the world. The Revocation had nothing to do with Roman influence; Louis XIV differed with Pope Innocent XI over practically everything, including the Revocation which the

Pope regarded as a pointless act of folly. The King's attitude to the Protestants was above all political; he saw them as an obstacle to his cherished ambition of creating a truly united state; the fact that their religion was the same as that of his enemies the Dutch made it seem all the more dangerous. Unfortunately Louvois, whose power and importance depended upon the army, chose to treat the 'conversions' as a military operation. The *dragonnades* became more and more terrifying, the soldiers were soon encouraged to maltreat their unlucky hosts in every possible way; murder and torture became the rule. Those who were caught trying to emigrate went to the galleys.

Mme de Maintenon has been freely blamed for the Revocation, but never by responsible writers. Voltaire realized that it had nothing to do with her and said so in his *Louis XIV*, long before her letters on the subject became available to him. When they appeared, he read them anxiously since, if they had proved her to be accountable, his estimate of her would have fallen to pieces; on the contrary they showed how right he had been. From the very beginning she reproved the excesses committed by Louvois, but she was too cowardly to speak up to the King. Indeed it is very likely true, as many French historians have stated, that Louis knew little or nothing of what was going on in the provinces. He thought that thousands of Protestants were being converted and a few villains, who were probably criminals in any case, were being punished. Mme de Maintenon told Fénelon that she groaned at the thought of the vexations the Protestants were enduring, but that if she so much as opened her mouth on the subject her enemies would say that she herself was still a Protestant at heart and all the good she might be able to do would be undone; as it was, the King thought her too tender and wondered whether she had not got leanings towards her old Church. She had converted too many people herself to believe for a single moment in 'conversions' by force or by bribery. Mme de Maintenon was a truly religious woman and she could distinguish the truth from falsehood in such matters. Oddly enough, she had several unconverted Protestants in her own household who were never interfered with and who lived quietly with her all through the persecutions.

At Versailles the King decided to make an example for all to see. Most Protestants belonged to the middle classes. (Indeed one of the reasons why Charles II could never wholeheartedly accept that religion was that, during his young days in Paris, the fashionable world had regarded it as too dowdy and dreary for words.) But one of the great nobles was a Protestant, the fifty-seven year old Duc de La Force. The King sent for him and they had a long talk during which the Duke promised to do his best to be converted. So he was sent to a seminary; but when he had been there some time and the reports on his progress remained decidedly pessimistic, the King, worried about the state of his soul, sent him to the Bastille (where he arrived on a curious date, 14 July 1689). He was provided with various Catholic books and urged to read them. The old man cried a great deal; he suffered from dropsy brought on by lack of exercise. He sent a petition to the King begging to be allowed to go to the Oratorians, or better still Versailles. In the margin of this document somebody has written: *Pères de l'Oratoire, non. Versailles, encore moins*. Then he disloyally told a visitor that his wife was a far more bigoted Protestant than he was. So the Duchess, also dropsical, was arrested and sent to a fortress. Four years later the La Forces were allowed to go home on condition that they had a priest to live with them. 'Whenever Père Bordes thinks it better that the Duke should not see the Duchess, this lady must be told to stay in her own room, not for hours but for days on end.' In 1699 the Duke died, and the Duchess managed to make her way to London, travelling in the suite of the English ambassadress, Lady Jersey. King William gave her a flat in St James's Palace, but her troubles were not yet over. When she had lived for a while on such jewels as she had managed to bring with her, she ran out of money. So she wrote to Louis XIV asking if it was not shameful that a French duchess should be reduced to beggary in a foreign town? This struck a clever note; the King sent her four thousand livres. She never went back to France. After Louis XIV's death the more easy-going Regent allowed her to have her fortune. When she died she left it to Greenwich Hospital, with a clause in her will requesting that if any Protestant La Force should ever be exiled to England he should be provided for. The contingency has not arisen. A Duc de La Force did emigrate to England during the French Revolution but he was not a Protestant.

The results of the Revocation were, as might have been foreseen, a disaster. The thousands of Protestants who managed to get away, to England, Holland and Germany, were valuable citizens whom France could ill spare (William of Orange had over a thousand French officers in his army at the battle of the Boyne), but perhaps the greatest damage was caused by the propaganda which they disseminated, presenting the French as ogres, dangerous to all countries which practised the Reformed faith. Sweden, Holland and various German states banded together to form the League of Augsburg (1686) against Louis XIV, and were soon joined by Spain and the Catholic Empire, his traditional foe.

A word must be said about the Jansenists who have had so much attention, caused such rivers of ink to flow and bedevilled French religious life for a hundred and fifty years. The doctrine of this gloomy sect, founded by the Dutchman Jansenius, was that of a return to the simplicity and discipline of the early Christians. Jansenism was made fashionable in France by Mère Angélique d'Arnauld and had its headquarters in two convents, Port-Royal in Paris and Port-Royal-des-Champs which was situated in a romantic valley not far from Versailles. Those of the courtiers who had relations in Port-Royal-des-Champs used often to visit them, and there was much coming and going between the two establishments. The austere Jansenists always managed to seem holier than the Jesuits, the supple, adroit

An engraving showing Louis signing the Revocation of the Edict of Nantes.

men of the world who ruled the King's conscience, and there was little love lost between them. As usual in those days, politics played their part in the matter; many Jansenists had been Frondeurs; the King hated them more than he hated the Protestants and much more than atheists. His nephew Chartres wanted to take a friend of his campaigning. The King said he could not allow it because he had been told that the friend was a Jansenist. 'Fonpertuis a Jansenist?' said the Duke, astonished. 'I very much doubt if he believes in God!' The King said in that case he would make no objections. Port-Royal, greatly as the King disliked it and its proximity to Versailles, was tolerated during the life-time of Père de La Chaise.

The Court is now that described by the Duc de Saint-Simon, who arrived there himself in 1691, in time to note that the King seemed relieved by the death of Louvois. From now on the little Duke peoples the stage for us so that we should not only recognize almost every courtier of note if he should suddenly appear in flesh and blood, but also know what, in Saint-Simon's opinion, he would be thinking. Saint-Simon's prejudices were violent. He worshipped the King in spite of himself, while detesting his policy of governing through the bourgeois ministers and of abasing the ancient aristocracy. But with all his genius he never fully understood what a secret man the King was, or his capacity for drawing a smoke-cloud over his real feelings. Saint-Simon took him too much at his face value. He hated Mme de Maintenon and all her works. He regarded du Maine as Satan, thus doing that insignificant fellow too much honour, and execrated the royal bastards for no better reason than that they were given precedence over dukes. He took the very lowest view of human nature, and had no aesthetic sense whatever. He loathed the château of Versailles. Ezekiel Spanheim speaks of 'Saint-Simon: to whom nobody pays any attention'. He made as little impression on his contemporaries as a duke could make – attention has been paid to him since his death, however.

146   The Revocation of the Edict of Nantes.

Louis par la grace de Dieu Roy de France
et de Navarre. A touz presens et avenir Salut. Le Roy
Henry le grand n're ayeul de glorieuse memoire voulant empescher
que la paix quil avoit procurée a ses subjectz, aprez les grandes
pertes quils avoient soufferte par la durée des guerres civiles
et estrangeres, ne fust troublée a l'occasion de la Religion pretendue
reformée, comme il estoit arrivé soubz les regnes des Roys ses
predecesseurs, auroit par son Edict donné a Nantes au moys
d'Avril mil cinq cens quatre vingtz dix huict, reglé la conduitte
qui devoit a tenir a l'esgard de ceux de lad. religion, les lieux
dans lesquelz ilz en pourroient faire l'exercice, estably des
juges extraordinaires pour leur administrer la justice, et a fin pourveu
mesme par des articles particuliers a tout ce quil auroit jugé
necessaire pour maintenir la tranquillité dans son Royaume,
et pour diminuer l'aversion qui estoit entre ceux de l'une et
l'autre religion, affin d'estre plus en estat de travailler comme
il avoit resolu de faire a reunir a l'Eglise ceux qui s'en estoient
si facilement esloignez. Et comme l'intention du Roy nostred.
ayeul ne peut estre effectué a cause de sa mort precipitée, et que
l'execution dud. Edict fut mesme interrompue pendant la minorité
du feu Roy n're tres honoré seigneur et pere de glorieuse

SANCTIORIBUS CONSILIIS ARCHIATRORUM COMES CRESCENTIUS LUDO GUIDO FACON REGI A

Hyacinte Rigaud Pinxit.   Edelinck Sculpsit CPR.

XII

THE FACULTY

*Presque tous les hommes meurent de leurs
remèdes et non de leurs maladies*
                                    Molière

Illness and death were very dreadful at Versailles. As soon as the breath had left the body of a member of the royal family, his or her gilded bed-chamber was turned into a butcher's shop. Lords or ladies-in-waiting, who had spent their lives with the deceased and were often in a sad state of grief, were obliged to stand by the bed while the body was chopped to pieces. The head was sawn open and examined; the liver and lights laid aside, the heart, on a silver salver, was given to one duchess and the entrails, in a big silver bowl, to another. Seven or eight doctors made notes of their gruesome findings and pronounced the causes of death; the only cause which invariably escaped their notice was their own incompetence.

It is not a very reassuring reflection that in another two hundred and fifty years present day doctors may seem to our descendants as barbarous as Fagon and his colleagues seem to us. The fashionable doctors, as different from the general practitioner as an *Abbé de Cour* from a *Curé de Campagne*, stood then as they do now, in admiration of their own science. As now, they talked as if illness and death were mastered. Molière has presented that sort of doctor once and for all; a consultation of big-wigs is ever a scene from one of his plays. The learned, magic, meaningless words, the grave looks at each other, the artful hesitation between one worthless formula and another – all are there. In those days, terrifying in black robes and bonnets, they bled the patient; now, terrifying in white robes and masks, they pump blood into him. The result is the same; the strong live; the weak, after much suffering and expense, both of spirit and of money, die. The ferocious blood-letting which was the fashion killed in two ways – exhaustion from want of blood and blood poisoning. Smallpox patients were regularly bled; they generally died. One doctor got so tired of seeing this happen that he exclaimed 'Smallpox, I intend to get you used to bleeding'. After being bled the patient always felt much worse, and this was considered an excellent sign. The Comte de Toulouse, having bravely

Guy-Crescent Fagon, one of the King's doctors. An engraving.

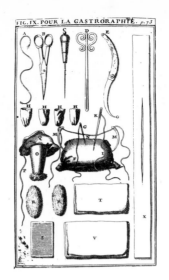

Sutures for sewing up wounds and instruments and vessels for bleeding from *Cours d'opérations de chirurgie*, Paris, 1714.

endured the operation for stone, was bled four times in twenty-four hours. Strong and young, he recovered. Twenty-six years later he received the same treatment for the same complaint, and died.

Laymen were divided on the subject of doctors; those who believed in them disapproved of those who did not – they thought them, as Molière put it, 'impious in medicine'. But, alas, then as now, the most ardently impious when in pain and terror, were apt to change their minds, deliver themselves up to the self-styled experts, and die according to the rules. Mme de Maintenon and the King were rigidly pious in medicine and insisted on piety among those in their power; the King took it very much amiss if the courtiers did not submit entirely to the orders of Fagon when they were ill. Madame was impenitently impious.

Descriptions of seventeenth-century diseases read strangely to us. Racine's twelve-year-old daughter, Fanchon, went to bed with a headache. Presently Racine, who adored his children, went to see how she was getting on. He found her with her head on the floor and her throat full of water, drowning. He picked her up; she was like a wet sack. He and his wife forced salt down her throat and rubbed her with spirits of wine; it still seemed that she must smother. They sent frantically for doctors but all were away from home. Finally she vomited an appalling quantity of water which seemed to have come into her chest from her brain; then she was perfectly all right. Mareschal the surgeon arrived and bled her; Fagon arrived and diagnosed suffocating catarrh; he said it came from not blowing her nose enough. After this she drove everybody mad by blowing her nose noisily all day long.

The hazards to human life in those days were childbirth for women, battle for men, babyhood and smallpox for everybody. Old age was not particularly danger-ous or disagreeable; people lived to enormous ages and never seem to have become senile. Lauzun rode to hounds every day at eighty-nine. Mme de Ventadour

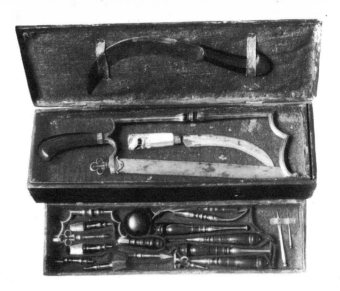

Surgical instruments of the early seventeenth century.

danced a minuet at ninety. Mme de Maintenon, at over seventy, complained bitterly to her confessor that the King insisted on his conjugal rights every day and sometimes twice. She died at eighty-four, but only of boredom. Mme de Cléram-bault was the best of company at ninety. Le Nôtre was in perfect health at eighty-eight. Isaac Bartet, one of the King's secretaries, died at a hundred and five, and the Spanish Marquis de Mansera at a hundred and seven, having practically lived on chocolate for years. Octogenarians abound in the pages of the memorialists, as lively as larks.

Infant mortality was appalling; and the doctors were responsible. When a child was ailing, first they bled it, then purged it and then administered an emetic which generally did the trick. They never noticed that this treatment left anything to be desired, and though of course the mothers and nurses knew, they could do nothing, since pious public opinion would have accused them of murder had they refused to let the doctors have their way. As soon as the faculty was called in, the mothers were left to say their prayers, and find what consolation they could in the thought that their darlings would soon be with God. Ten of the seventeen children the King had with his wife and principal mistresses died in infancy - a perfectly normal percentage for a rich person. The poor, whose lives were in many ways so wretched, were at least spared the attentions of such as Fagon; had his methods prevailed in country districts the population of France would certainly not have been twenty millions.

The surgeons did a better job than the physicians. They tied the patient to a board with linen bands and paid no attention to his screams; but they honestly tried to hurt as little as possible. The profession of surgery was inferior to that of medicine, the doctors liking to think that they were intellectuals while the saw-boneses were mere craftsmen. This attitude came from the middle ages when doctors were always priests who were forbidden to shed blood; when people had to be cut up or bled, it was done by the barbers. The status of surgeon was raised in the seventeenth century. Félix, the Court surgeon and his successor Mareschal de Bièvre were remarkable men; the King was fond of them, they became influential figures at the school of medicine in Paris. Both achieved some spectacular cures, notably of the stone, a disease which was prevalent at that time and many of whose victims were little boys under ten years old. The operation for it as performed by them was horrible enough (Bossuet preferred to die in agony sooner than submit to it) but there was a fashionable quack in Paris called Frère Jacques who inflicted worse tortures than they did. Martin Lister, visiting Paris, went to watch him operate and was appalled by what he saw. Nearly all his patients died, but that did not prevent high society from flocking to him. Finally he killed Maréchal de Lorges in circumstances of such horrifying butchery that the number of his patients fell off and he was ruined. Félix and Mareschal lost far fewer patients than most surgeons of the day – possibly their instruments were cleaner.

The King's first doctor was M. de L'Orme (1584–1678) who had attended Louis XIII and was the fashionable doctor for fifty years. De L'Orme swore by hygiene and applied his theories to himself, with the result that he lived to be ninety-four. 'Why do fish live to such a great age? Because', said he, 'they are never subjected to draughts.' So he spent his days in a sedan chair draped with blankets and lined with hares' fur to ensure that no air could percolate. When obliged to go out, he covered himself with a morocco robe and mask and wore six pairs of stockings and several fur hats. He always kept a bit of garlic in his mouth, incense in his ears and a stalk of rue sticking out of each nostril. He slept in a sort of brick oven, surrounded by hot water bottles, and lived on sheep's tongues and syrup of greengages – he never touched vegetables, raw fruit, jam or pastry. At eighty-seven he married a young wife and wore her out; she died within the year. M. de L'Orme discovered the excellent properties of the waters at Bourbon, which he made into a fashionable spa.

Louis XIV's most famous doctor was Guy-Crescent Fagon who managed, in the course of about twenty years, to see most of the royal family into their graves. He is first heard of looking after Mme de Maintenon's little charges when they lived in the rue de Vaugirard and he owed his career to her. She obtained the post of Doctor to the Queen for him. He killed Marie-Thérèse almost at once, but stayed on at Versailles; on All Souls' Day (*le jour des morts*) 1693 he was named *Premier Médecin du Roi*, one of the most important offices of the Court. The First Doctor had a flat in the château, a house in the town of Versailles, and a huge income; he was a member of the Conseil and was ennobled. He had every interest in keeping his master alive since his was the only appointment that automatically ended with the King's death. Fagon's fame extended all over Europe. William III, when he was dying, sent him an account of his symptoms, pretending to be a simple parish priest, and asked for an

Christ at the column; from Louis' collection of jewellery.

Overleaf: The Grand Dauphin with his wife and their children;
the Duc de Bourgogne is standing, the Duc d'Anjou is seated holding a dog
and the Duc de Berry is beside his mother; by Pierre Mignard, 1687.

opinion. Fagon sent word that he had better make his peace with God, since he had not long to live – after which William resigned himself and died. Many of his contemporaries describe Fagon as a good, honest man. He had charm, wit, an excellent bedside manner, knowledge of the world and of all the subjects to do with his profession such as botany and chemistry. If he liked somebody he could be very kind – as he always was, for example, with Mary of Modena. But he was hated by some, notably by Madame, who roundly accuses him of murdering his patients. There was no love lost between them and Fagon certainly did not cover himself with glory when he pretended that her son had poisoned practically all the King's heirs. Fagon was ugly, even frightening to look at, with long thin legs like a bird, a shock of black hair, rotten teeth and hanging lips. He suffered from asthma, and never went to bed but always slept in a chair.

The King had excellent health. Like almost everybody he suffered from his teeth; part of his upper jaw-bone had been removed while one of them was being torn out so that he had difficulty in masticating his food, bits of which sometimes came down his nose. He took medicine regularly once a month, a tremendous purge which worked six or seven times. On these days he never left his room. He had gout. But he was not regarded as liable to real illness. So it came as a great shock to the courtiers, on the morning of 18 November 1686, to learn that the King had undergone a severe operation at seven a.m. Unbeknown to the public he had been suffering for many months from an anal fistula (which probably accounted for his notable bad temper during the past year or so) and at last he had decided that the surgeons must see what they could do for him. This disease had hitherto baffled them; and Cardinal de Richelieu had died of the treatment they gave him for it. Félix, the King's surgeon at this time, got hold of several poor men suffering from the complaint and sent them to take the waters at Barèges which were said to cure it. When none were cured he began operating on fistulas in all the Paris hospitals; he perfected an instrument which was supposed to lessen the pain.

Nobody knew that the King was to undergo the operation except Mme de Maintenon, Louvois, Père de La Chaise and the doctors – they kept the secret for six weeks. The King endured it heroically. If he was hard on other people he was not indulgent to himself; his control was extraordinary. He had been in particularly good spirits the day before, walking round the gardens at Versailles and inspecting the Reservoir. On the operating table he was cut eight times with scissors and twice with lancet – not only did he make no sound or movement but his breathing never altered its rhythm. The news was only released when all was over. A messenger was sent to find the Dauphin who was, of course, out hunting. He galloped home hell-for-leather, in tears, and rushed distractedly to his father's room, too much upset to speak. At Paris, the churches were filled in a quarter of an hour after the news arrived. Although the King never went there and was not exactly popular, the

Louis' inkstand in red jasper and gilt. Cup in lapis lazuli surmounted by Neptune in silver. From Louis' collection of jewels.

Parisians were proud of him. They told each other that whatever might be thought of Louis XIV, he had raised the name of France above all other nations.

The Grand Condé and Mme de Montespan were at Fontainebleau nursing Mme la Duchesse who was recovering from her smallpox; a messenger was sent, telling them on no account to come to Versailles. The story that Athénaïs stormed into the King's bedroom only to find Mme de Maintenon quietly sewing by his bed, that she stormed out again and had hysterics in her own room, is quite untrue. Condé obeyed the King's injunction not to come, because he did not want to bring infection to Versailles and also because he felt unwell. He sent his son and his beloved nephew Conti, begging the King to see him. The King said drily that he was not forbidden the Court; he spoke to him quite amiably.

Although Félix begged the King to rest, he insisted on holding a council that very evening, in such agony that the sweat was pouring down his face. The next day he received the ambassadors, as he wanted them to take note that he was not dying; the pain altered his face so that he was unrecognizable. As the days went on he seemed to make a remarkable recovery, singing to himself and suffering from gout, considered to be a good sign. He had to live on soup and felt very hungry. People in the château began talking of other things; such as the Grand Condé, who seemed far from well; but the topic of the day was that the Dauphin had cut off his hair, saying that it was a bore out hunting. Hitherto he had worn his own beautiful, long, golden curls; from now on he had a wig which was not nearly so pretty.

The King's state became less satisfactory and on 6 December Félix thought it necessary to give him a few more jabs to prevent the wound from healing unevenly. On the 8th it was not in a very good state and he cut it again. On the 10th there was another long, serious operation during which, Mme de Maintenon said, the King suffered for six hours as much as if he had been broken on the wheel. It was infinitely more terrible than the first. But the very next day he was much better, though distressed by the news that Condé had died. For the next week or so he suffered a great deal of pain; after that he made a complete recovery.

Louis II, Prince de Condé, known as the Grand Condé, by Antoine Coysevox, 1688.

156 Saint-Cyr; an engraving.

XIII

SAINT-CYR, THE SCHOOL

Jeunes et tendres fleurs, par le sort agitées
Sous un ciel étranger comme moi transplantées
Dans un lieu séparé de profanes témoins
Je mets à les former mon étude et mes soins

RACINE

Some years before her marriage to Louis XIV, Mme de Maintenon, with a great
friend of hers, Mme de Brinon, had started a tiny school for girls. Having had such a
difficult youth herself, she always felt sorry for the children of *hobereaux* – the minor
provincial nobility to which she belonged. With the peasants, they were the worst
sufferers from the King's wars. Fénelon said a well-born youth of twenty who had
not already served in several campaigns was hardly to be found in the whole of
France. Recruiting was supposed to be voluntary, and of course many young men
went off filled with the spirit of adventure and the love of battle, but there was not
much choice; the nobles were allowed no profession except the army and the
Church; the peasants were bribed away from their fields with specious words or, if
these did not lure them, they were subjected to a sort of press-gang. Townsfolk,
richer and more resourceful, could often get out of serving if they wanted to. The
hobereaux could not hope for much advancement; the higher commands all went to
the King's friends at Versailles; and the prospects of 'a man I never see' were dim.
Towards the end of the reign, when the great captains were dead and their successors
incompetent, somebody suggested to the King that there might be better soldiers for
him to choose from in the provinces. 'Very possibly' he replied 'but how am I to
find them? It would mean taking other people's protégés – I'd rather have the men
I know.'

The daughters of country gentlemen had very miserable lives. They were unedu-
cated for the most part. Those who did not marry often became the servants of
their sisters-in-law, or went, without a vocation, into nunneries. Mme de Maintenon
thought it would be a good work to rescue some of them from a fate she had so
narrowly escaped herself.

Mme de Brinon was a woman of character and intelligence, an Ursuline nun
whose convent had been obliged to shut for lack of funds. Her school began at

Girls of the first and second classes at Saint-Cyr.

Rueil. Mme de Maintenon interested the King in it; they decided to enlarge it and bring it to the neighbourhood of Versailles where Mme de Maintenon could keep an eye on it. At the bottom of the park there was a little hamlet called Saint-Cyr, clustering round an ancient convent of Benedictines. The King sent for the Mother Superior and asked whether she and her nuns would not like to move to Paris. But she respectfully begged that they might be allowed to stay where Good King Dagobert had placed them. The King told Mme de Maintenon that he could dislodge them with a *lettre de cachet*, but she thought that would be an unfortunate beginning for her scheme. So new premises had to be built and Mansart got to work, with the assistance of the army, which in times of peace, always provided builders for the King. Mme de Maintenon told him to design her a large plain house like a barracks; neither luxury nor beauty were required. She herself saw to every detail of the interior decoration and plain but pretty furnishings – the linen she bought was of such excellent quality that it lasted fifty years. There was room for two hundred and fifty girls between the ages of six and nineteen; thirty-six lady professors (known as the Dames) of the same social category as the girls and very little older than they were, and twenty-four lay sisters. The Dames were to be called Madame and their surname.

The whole point of the scheme was that Saint-Cyr should not be a convent. Mme de Maintenon had married the Z-shaped Scarron sooner than enter one; and the King was against religious establishments, especially for women who, he thought, became dour and stultified in them. His wish was to improve the education of the womenfolk of his *race guerrière*, not to shut them up and condemn them to sterility. Père de La Chaise agreed, saying there were plenty of good nuns in the world and not enough good mothers. So it was arranged that the Dames and the sisters would take simple, not perpetual, vows; the girls were to be brought up with a view to

Girls of the third and fourth classes at Saint-Cyr.

living in the world; and the whole atmosphere was to be one of civilized piety. Saint-Cyr would provide a good general education. The young ladies must converse and write in excellent French, giving the proper value to each word and constructing solid phrases. They would learn poetry by heart and do a great deal of decorative needlework. (One of their first achievements was an altar cloth for the cathedral at Strasbourg, a recent French conquest). The girls and the Dames were to be on friendly terms with each other and the lessons must be given in an easy, smiling, natural way; there was to be no strict and painful holiness, and no unnecessary rules.

The constitution of Saint-Cyr was drawn up by Mme de Maintenon, Mme de Brinon and the King, approved by Père de La Chaise and Mme de Maintenon's confessor; the language was corrected by Racine and Boileau, and the final document sent to the Pope. Innocent XI was asked to approve a transfer of funds from the rich Abbey of Saint-Denis, but, on bad terms with the King, he most unsportingly made difficulties which were only resolved after his death. Mme de Brinon was to be Superior for life and Mme de Maintenon to enjoy pre-eminence, honours, prerogatives and entire authority. She was also to have a flat for herself and her household (kept up at the expense of the school) which she could occupy whenever she pleased. Indeed many of the courtiers thought her main object in founding this institution was to get away from all the fresh air at Versailles. Whenever the King went to her room the first thing he did was to fling open the windows, only allowing them to be shut when he left. Mme de Maintenon sat shivering in a *tonneau* or hooded chair, covered with rugs and shawls, but he never took the hint. At Saint-Cyr she used to get into a warm bed on arrival and often stay there all day.

The girls were chosen by the King, after d'Hozier, his genealogist, had looked at their pedigrees (four degrees of nobility on the father's side were required). The list of their names and birthplaces makes amusing reading for anybody who knows

159

France. They were never allowed to forget that they were the daughters of warriors. The King and his generals used to go and worship the God of battles among these innocent souls before leaving for the front. The girls were told to pray, not for victory but for peace, which in those days of French supremacy came to the same thing.

The King took a great interest in the uniform, saying that it must be unlike that of nuns, with plenty of white muslin and ribbons. Mme de Maintenon's maid put on various models, to show him. A lightly woven brown woollen stuff was chosen, to be lined with fur in winter and striped cotton in summer. An apron to match was edged with ribbon showing to which form the wearer belonged. The girls were enjoined to care for their looks since beauty is a gift from God, and told to do their hair well, indeed fashionably, and cover it with a prettier version of a nun's veil. The Dames had the same dress with no apron. They wore a gold cross, inscribed with words by Racine:

> *Elle est notre guide fidèle*
> *Notre félicité vient d'elle*

One was not quite sure whether *elle* referred to the cross or Mme de Maintenon.

The house was ready in 1686; the women were brought there in royal coaches, preceded by the relics of St Candida. Crowds from Versailles and the neighbourhood lined the road to see them go by; Mme de Maintenon was at the door, to greet them with the words: 'These walls are my retreat and my tomb; may this establishment live as long as France, and France as long as the world!' One of the first visitors was Athénaïs de Montespan, bringing her youngest daughter, Mlle de Blois, aged ten. Then all the princes and princesses came and by degrees most of the courtiers. Saint-Cyr was a nine days' wonder.

As this was the time of the King's operation he only came himself a few weeks later. He was greeted by three hundred fresh young voices chanting an anthem with words by Mme de Brinon and music by Lully:

> *Grand Dieu sauvez le roi*
> *Grand Dieu vengez le roi*
> *Vive le roi*
> *Qu'à jamais glorieux*
> *Louis victorieux*
> *Voie ses ennemis toujours soumis*
> *Vive le roi*

For Mme de Brinon was the author of 'God Save the King'. Lully's tune has been lost.

The King inspected everything. He talked to the girls, made a speech to the

View of the château from beyond the Orangery by Jean-Baptiste Martin.

Dames, attended Mass and ended by thanking Mme de Maintenon for the pleasure it had all given him. From now on Saint-Cyr was to be a life within a life for him as well as for her. The troubles he had brought on himself by the revocation of the Edict of Nantes were beginning to harass him and he liked to forget them for an hour or two among his wife's pretty little pupils. He was at his very best there; he shed his terrifying majesty and turned into a kind old uncle, taking little girls on his knee, chatting with them and hearing them recite their lessons. Never had he been so natural with his own family. His eagle eye saw everything, as it always did; he summed up the children's characters, knew who was happy, who had been crying, who was mutinous. As for Mme de Maintenon, she was there, in the beginning, two days out of every three, often arriving at 6 a.m. and only leaving ten or twelve hours later. She attended to every material detail, from brushing the hair of the very little ones to the composition of the meals. On summer evenings the King would join her there, go to Compline in the chapel and walk home with her. It could not have been foreseen, at this stage, what a source of worry Saint-Cyr was to become.

Since part of the curriculum consisted in learning and reciting poetry, Mme de Brinon, with the approval of Mme de Maintenon, thought it would be a good idea to let the girls act little plays. She wrote them herself and they were on the silly side; Mme de Maintenon, who was obliged to sit through the performances, found them insupportable. She said the children really must be given something better, so they were then put on to *Andromaque*. The love and loathing of which this play are compounded were so well interpreted that Mme de Maintenon took fright. She wrote to Racine and said she could never allow the girls to act in one of his plays again unless he wrote one with a religious subject specially for them. Would he not do this?

Racine was in high favour at the Court. He was Gentleman-in-Ordinary to the King who said that his handsome, rubicund, jolly face was one of those he liked best. When the King suffered from insomnia, Racine would read aloud to him, which he did incomparably; he could read from a Latin text putting it into exquisite French as he went along. He and his inseparable friend, Boileau, were appointed to be the King's historiographers, in which capacity they used to go to the front. Like journalists in modern wars, they were regarded as a perfect nuisance by the soldiers; unlike the modern journalists, however, they were very much against risking their skins. Racine told the King it was not surprising the soldiers were brave – their lives were so ghastly they must long for them to end; he had something to live for and had no wish to be carried off by a cannon ball. Indeed he loved the life at Versailles, he idolized the King and was under the glamour of high society. He said the secret of getting on with society people is never to speak of one's own work – let them think it is they who are brilliant. The King, seeing Racine out for a

A silver table given to Charles II of England in 1670
copied from French models of the time.

Jean Racine by Jean-Baptiste Santerre.

ESTHER
TRAGEDIE
Tirée de l'Escriture Sainte.

A PARIS,
Chez DENYS THIERRY, ruë Saint Jacques,
devant la ruë du Plâtre, à la Ville de Paris.
M. DC. LXXXIX.
AVEC PRIVILEGE DU ROY.

Title-page from *Esther*.

walk with the fascinating Marquis de Cavoye, said 'I often see those two together and I'm sure I know why. Cavoye likes to think he is an intellectual and Racine fancies himself as a courtier'.

Racine was a Jansenist at heart; he had been partly brought up at Port-Royal where his aunt was one of the nuns. After the shock of nearly being involved in the Affair of the Poisons he turned to religion. He married a holy person and four out of their five daughters became nuns. Mme Racine knew nothing about poetry and had never read, let alone seen, one of her husband's plays; to her, as to all simple folk of the day, there was something damnable about the theatre and everything to do with it. Racine grew more and more obsessed with Jansenism; he gave up writing plays altogether and composed little things for Louis XIV, inscriptions for medals, the captions underneath tapestries and so on. He divided his time between Versailles, Port-Royal and his happy family life in the street which is now called rue Visconti, at Paris.

When Mme de Maintenon asked Racine to write a religious play for her girls to act, he went off to consult Boileau who said the whole idea was ridiculous. Racine agreed with him. But then, as so often happens with writers, the proposition turned in his head until finally he conceived *Esther*, a play about the existing situation and characters at Versailles, dressed up in biblical garb. Mme de Maintenon, who was portrayed most flatteringly as holy Esther, triumphing over Mme de Montespan (*l'altière Vasthi dont j'occupe la place*) was delighted with the play; and the young actresses, choir and so on were put to work. She said it was good for them to have something on hand which kept them busy, filled their heads with beautiful words and stopped them gossiping.

They had good reason to gossip, for a crisis had arisen in the school. The girls, the Dames and Mme de Brinon herself would hardly have been human if all the fuss

162

that was made of them had not turned their heads. They began to assume an intolerably self-important air. The girls, most of whom came from dull little country homes, soon had visions of some Prince Charming who would carry them off to a glittering existence at the Court. In vain did Mme de Maintenon hold forth on the boredom of Versailles; they could hardly be expected to believe her. In the end, their hopes of marriage were seldom fulfilled; Mme de Maintenon was always to complain that there were not enough of what she called sons-in-law. 'Alas, my children, few men prefer your virtues to other people's dowries.' She consoled them by saying that marriage makes three-quarters of the human race miserable (it was one of her favourite observations); the woman has to submit to such dreadful things. 'When the young ladies find themselves faced with the ordeal of marriage they will see that it is no laughing matter.' However, at the beginning, when Saint-Cyr was so much in the news, a few excellent matches were made, notably that of the future Lady Bolingbroke who married an ancient, rich M. de Villette.

Mme de Brinon, thoroughly spoilt by Mme de Maintenon, began to see herself as a key personage of the realm, confidante of the King himself, a sort of female minister. She let it be understood that she could help people to obtain benefits at Versailles. She surrounded herself with favourites in the school, holding a little court of her own; her room there was absurdly luxurious and over-decorated. She went to take the cure at Bourbon and behaved in a mad way, like a reigning mistress, receiving delegations from local big-wigs; when she got back to Saint-Cyr she was bold enough to criticize and even to undo some changes made by Mme de Maintenon in her absence. Mme de Maintenon watched all this with growing disgust. Suddenly she took a high hand with Mme de Brinon and told her that everybody at Saint-Cyr, the Dames, the girls and not least the Superior had become impossible. She proposed to take away some of her friend's prerogatives, to punish her. Mme de Brinon hit back, pointing out that under the constitution of Saint-Cyr she was there for life. The girls and the Dames were on her side and let this be felt; there were mutinous faces everywhere.

Mme de Maintenon sat alone in her room, pondering the next move. It was nothing less than a *lettre de cachet*, signed by the King, digging out Mme de Brinon and ordering her to go at once to a convent. She left early in the morning, without saying goodbye to anybody, by the garden gate, where a hackney carriage awaited her. The Dames and the girls were thunderstruck and inconsolable when this departure became known. Mme de Maintenon assembled them and said that in spite of all she owed to Mme de Brinon, they differed too much on matters of policy; therefore it was best that they should part. In fact the two women remained on friendly terms and corresponded for years. Mme de Brinon also had the satisfaction of acting as go-between for Bossuet and Leibniz, who wrote to each other, through her, about possibly unifying the Catholic and Lutheran Churches. She was a clever person, but too masterful to be able to work with Mme de Maintenon for long.

The Saint-Cyr production of *Esther* in 1689 was a smashing success. Mme de Maintenon had always intended that it should be played to a small, intimate audience but the King, who went to the dress rehearsal with the Dauphin, thought the play so good that he wanted all the world to see it. He drew up a list of those to be invited; and came back early from hunting for the first night, which he attended with courtiers, ministers and members of the Paris Parlement. He stood with his stick across the door of the room which had been transformed into a theatre, only lowering it for those who had really been asked. After that, everybody who was anybody had to see *Esther*. On the second night the Dauphin went with various members of the royal family and his own friends; the third was for Père de La Chaise and the clergy; but the last night was the most brilliant when the King came again with his cousins, the exiled King James of England and Queen Mary, who had just arrived in France. Three crowned heads! Mme de Sévigné went down from Paris with other old friends of Mme de Maintenon's. Places had been kept for them just behind the duchesses. Mme de Sévigné thought the play sublime and touching. The King, who had an air of being the host which gave him an amiable sweetness, actually spoke to her:

'Madame, it seems you are satisfied.'

'Sire, I am charmed.'

'Racine is a man of parts.'

'Sire, indeed he is, but in truth the young ladies must take some credit.'

'Ah! That is a fact!'

Then he went off, having made her an object of envy. After that she talked for a second with Mme de Maintenon, off like lightning after the King, and had a word with Bossuet. At a supper party in Paris later that evening she recounted her 'little prosperities' to her friends.

Racine was covered with glory, and had to go and pray in the chapel that God would take away his pride. But of course, the French being what they are there was a good deal of irreverent joking about *Esther*. M. de Breteuil, the father of Voltaire's Mme du Châtelet, wrote satirical verses pointing out, what everybody had noticed, the identities of 'Assuerus' and the others. Mme de Lafayette thought the play lamentable, only written to flatter Mme de Maintenon and crush Athénaïs. Furthermore she thought it was folly to keep all these pretty girls within a stone's throw of the Versailles gallants. Public opinion, on the whole, was shocked by the idea of innocent and well-born young women on the stage. Hébert, the curé of Versailles, refused to attend the play, but Bossuet, Fénelon and the Jesuits were in favour of it. The Dutch gossip writers said that old Esther was establishing a seraglio at Saint-Cyr for Ahasuerus.

When the King got back to Versailles a particularly poignant piece of bad news awaited him. The Queen of Spain, charming, pretty daughter of Monsieur and the first Madame, had died after vomiting incessantly for two days. She was almost certainly poisoned, probably by the Comtesse de Soissons, in the interest of the Austrians, who wanted to remove a French influence at Madrid. The little Queen had longed very much to marry the Dauphin. When the King told her she was to be Queen of Spain he had added 'I couldn't do more for my own daughter'. 'But you could have done more for your niece', she remarked sadly. In 1679 she had left France, in floods of tears and had thereafter never known a happy moment. Her letters worried everybody, but there was nothing to be done. She was trapped in the ghastly etiquette of the Spanish court, not even allowed to speak to her old French groom, lonely and always frightened. She had duly informed the King of the one state secret entrusted to her, namely that King Charles II of Spain was impotent. All the same she had brought a ray of happiness into the life of that pathetic man. The Court went into deep mourning and there were no more performances of *Esther*.

XIV

SAINT-CYR, THE CONVENT

The woman is so hard upon the woman

LORD TENNYSON

The success of *Esther* had finished turning the heads of Mme de Maintenon's charges at Saint-Cyr. At the very first contact with the great world they had ceased to be simple little girls, and had become affected, ambitious women, all too reminiscent of everything she hated at Versailles. She blamed herself for her original conception of the place and decided she must begin again from the beginning, on an entirely new basis. Having envisaged Saint-Cyr as a sort of finishing school, where she would equip ardent young creatures to carry French civilization to the four corners of the provinces, the moment she came up against difficulties which were largely of her own making, she went into reverse. She began by forbidding literature lessons; there were to be no more poetry readings, dangerous for young women, and above all no more interesting conversation or the girls would be bored to death when they got back to their dull homes. Rather, let them love silence, suitable to the sex. Then she decided that it would be better not to educate them at all; women are too superficial; they never learn anything properly, and a little useless knowledge is apt to make them neglect their duties. So their books were taken away and intellectual studies replaced by household work. She told them that they had become absurdly coquettish and clean; a little dirt never did anybody any harm. Of course they were all furious and miserable at this new state of affairs, so much so that two of the girls tried to poison a Dame who had thrown away make-up which she found on their dressing-table. They were caught, given a punishment which made the others tremble (we don't know what it was) and expelled.

The King took the girls' side as much as he could. He was so sorry for them that he sent his band to play in their courtyard, hoping to cheer them up. When the curriculum was changed he insisted that they should go on with their music; and he literally forced Mme de Maintenon, against her will, to allow them to give a performance of *Athalie*, with which Racine had followed up the success of his

Mme de Maintenon by J.-B. Vanloo.

Esther. They did so, but it was not very amusing for them (if such a word could be used in the same breath as the horrifying *Athalie*) since they were allowed no costumes, no scenery and no audience, except the two old Kings, Louis and James.

All this was only the beginning – much worse things were in store. Mme de Maintenon talked a great deal to Fénelon about her problems, and he now set down some reflections for the young ladies. No other joys than our hopes of Eternal Bliss; no assemblies except to hear words of the Faith; no feast but that of the Lamb; no pleasure except the singing of psalms. Fénelon had taken Mme de Brinon's place as Mme de Maintenon's bosom friend, perfection in her eyes. It was a bad choice; Fénelon was not the man for her. In spite of a worldly appearance (his great charm, good looks and gentle manners making him seem almost like an *Abbé de Cour*) he never deviated from the teaching of Christ, so of course he was soon at odds with the temporal power, in other words the King, and finally, up to a point, with the Pope himself. But before the King grasped the intransigence of his nature, he had allowed himself to be persuaded by Mme de Maintenon to appoint the Abbé tutor of the precious grandsons, the Duc de Bourgogne and his brothers.

Mme de Maintenon was looking for a spiritual director. Fénelon would have liked the post; and she longed to have him but gave striking proof of how little she understood human beings (and nobody has ever understood them less than she) by deciding that he would line the path to heaven with too many flowers. She made overtures to Bourdaloue, but he was beginning to practise what he preached and to devote himself to poor people and those in prison. He had no time for Mme de Maintenon. Meanwhile Fénelon wrote her a letter, summing up her character. He said she was dry, cold and often tactless; she liked people too much at first, and when they turned out to be less than perfect she was cruel to them. Greater submission to God was needed, to make her more understanding of others. She was too proud and egotistic, though naturally good and confiding. As for the King, she must touch, instruct and open his heart but it was useless to tire him by returning to the charge and always bringing up the big guns. She should make him long for peace and to relieve his people, and also give him a horror of despotic actions, but above all she must choose the best moment to implant these truths.

Then Fénelon wrote a similar letter to the King, full of disagreeable observations – we are told every day that you are the delight of your people but an unjust war ruins the nation; you reward those who deserve to be punished; glory, which hardens your heart, is dearer to you than justice; you neither know or love God – whereupon Mme de Maintenon, in her turn, accused him of tactlessness and not choosing the best moment to implant home truths, which only irritated and discouraged the King. These two letters were the beginning of the end of Fénelon's career as a courtier.

Mme de Maintenon finally chose Godet de Marais Bishop of Chartres, to be her confessor. He was a strait-laced man, more like a monk than a Prince of the Church. He took over the lady and her school which, in double quick time, he turned into a convent. Six priests of the order of St Vincent de Paul, noted for their humility and obscurity, were installed at Saint-Cyr as regular confessors. Then the Bishop of Chartres sent for the Dames whom he interviewed in private, one by one. He told them they were at liberty to leave Saint-Cyr, either to go back to the world or to join other convents, but if they stayed there they must become nuns. There is a French proverb: 'Where the goat is tied up, there she must browse'; this was their situation. Most of them had been at the school, either at Rueil or at Saint-Cyr for years. Their homes were like a faraway dream and in many cases held no place for them any more. It would be pointless to go to an unknown convent. Only one of them left, to be married; the others, with great repugnance, decided to obey the Bishop. He made them sign a document accepting his direction and, begging them to tranquillize their souls, he took his leave.

The new nuns of the Community of St Augustine could hardly grasp the full horror of what had befallen them. They found themselves belonging to a particularly severe order; they were never again to leave Saint-Cyr, even in mortal illness (a little hut was built in the garden for smallpox patients, where twelve girls and Dames once died in a single week); they must never receive letters or visits, except from members of the royal family. Having taken the vow of poverty, they must live in miserable discomfort, with no warmth in winter, nightly vigils and not one moment, ever, to themselves. When food ran short, the children must have what there was; it did nobody any harm to fast, they were told, and they could live on vegetables, of which a delicious list was appended to the rules. The King greatly regretted this new state of affairs but was talked into accepting it by Mme de Maintenon and Bossuet. The Pope now, in 1692, gave Mme de Maintenon a signal honour, the right of visitation in all French convents.

Everything at Saint-Cyr appeared to be in order, but another storm was brewing. By far the most attractive of the Dames was Elise de La Maisonfort, described by Mme de Maintenon as devout, absent-minded, adorably giddy and brilliantly intelligent. She had brought a little sister to be a pupil; Mme de Maintenon talked to Elise, thought her charming and made her stay herself, as a Dame. She had come to Paris from her native Berry, hoping to obtain the post of lady-in-waiting to one of the princesses. Soon she was Mme de Maintenon's particular *protégée*; the King, too, had a great fancy for her, sought her company, and gave her a small estate and an income for life. Most of the girls were in love with her. 'It is my destiny to be loved', she used to say. But she had no religious vocation and had taken simple vows with the greatest reluctance. She suffered from doubts, which she could only overcome in moments of religious ecstasy; worse still, she loved (or thought she loved, for she had never sampled it) the World. She had a horror of being bored. She was the recipient of Mme de Maintenon's famous letter:

> How can I make you realize the boredom which devours the great of this world and the trouble they have in occupying their time? Can't you see that I am dying of grief in spite of my incredible destiny? And that only the love of God keeps me from going under? I was once young and pretty; I tasted the pleasures of this life and everybody loved me.' Later on I lived for years in a brilliant society; then I came into favour. I swear to you, my dear daughter, that all these conditions produce a fearful emptiness, an anxiety, a lassitude, a longing for a different existence because all are unsatisfactory. One is only at rest with God . . .

Mme de La Maisonfort was not convinced. At the age of twenty-three she no doubt thought it would be quite all right to be at rest with God when she was an old lady like Mme de Maintenon, meanwhile she had a passionate desire for the pleasures of this life. Mme de Maintenon, the Bishop of Chartres and Fénelon had the greatest trouble in persuading her to take perpetual vows. Finally they almost dragged her to the altar (1692). Mme de Maintenon was delighted with this outcome because she planned eventually to make Mme de La Maisonfort the superior of Saint-Cyr; she told her how lucky she was to belong only to herself and thus to be able to offer herself up as a sacrifice. Fénelon preached a moving sermon on the joys of monasticism. But the new nun seemed more dead than alive.

Now Mme de La Maisonfort had a cousin called Mme Guyon (who was also, oddly enough, related to Fénelon and the d'Arnaulds of Port-Royal). This widow woman was entirely given over to piety and when she heard of Mme de La Maisonfort's doubts she went to Saint-Cyr to try and help her resolve them. Mme de La Maisonfort, with her craving for religious stimulus, fell an easy victim to Quietism, the brand of poetic mysticism which Mme Guyon preached. The pure love of God, according to her, should be influenced neither by fear of hell nor by hope of heaven: deeds were nothing; love alone ought to count. Mary was a hundred times better than Martha.

As Mme Guyon's doctrine gained more and more hold over her imagination, Mme de La Maisonfort could not imagine why she had ever hesitated to take the veil; not only she but most of the other Dames became as radiantly happy as they had hitherto been discontented. Mme de Maintenon, too, fell under Mme Guyon's undoubted charm; she was grateful to her for what she had done at Saint-Cyr, which now seemed ready to fulfil all hopes. She singled out Mme Guyon for favours including a room of her own in the convent. A little set was soon formed there led by Mesdames Guyon and de La Maisonfort. Those few Dames who were not admitted to it felt left out in the cold; but they comforted themselves by mocking both Mme Guyon's doctrine and her neckline – which seemed low for such a saintly person. Her followers gave themselves airs and had all sorts of affectations,

Jeanne-Marie Bouvier de la Mothe, Mme Guyon.
Engraving.

for instance they never went to hear sermons which, they said, interrupted their thoughts of God. Mme de Maintenon, so incredulous of earthly love, approved; one must and should love God without reserve. All the same, Mme Guyon had the good sense not to speak to her, as she did to the Dames, of visions and ecstasies; she felt that such dangerous subjects might not be very well received. At Versailles, and at the Hôtel de Saint-Aignan, she was constantly with the 'holy flock', as the courtiers called the Beauvilliers, Chevreuses and Mme de Maintenon; and it was with them that she met Fénelon. In the words of Saint-Simon: *'leur sublime s'amalgama'*. Mme Guyon said: 'It seemed that Our Lord united me to him very intimately, more than to anyone else' – Fénelon himself said 'I am closely united to you beyond all that I can say or understand'. Fénelon, who had cleverly noticed that human beings love themselves to the point of idolatry, was always looking for means of transferring this love to God; there was much in Mme Guyon's doctrine that appealed to him.

Mme Guyon seems to have been truly dreadful, but opinions have been divided on her ever since she caused the breach between Fénelon and Bossuet. In our own century, Monsignor Knox was against her, and Abbé Brémond for. She was one of those excessive creatures, totally without sense of humour, who make an easy target for irreverent spirits. Writing of her mystical experiences, she described herself as a sort of reservoir through which grace flowed into the friends sitting round her – she became so filled with it that sometimes she had to ask one of the duchesses to undo her stays. She liked to roll in nettles, suck the wounds of poor people and so on. Having married Jesus Christ in one of her ecstasies she ceased to bother about the saints; the mistress does not ask favours of the employees. The effect that she had on many of her most respectable contemporaries was such that idle mockery is out of place; though one may feel thankful never to have met anybody like her. It seems strange that all these people so much interested in theology did not realize

at once that her doctrine was doubtful if not heretical: a reader of her books might well come away with the idea that a state of sin is permissible as long as God is loved. Mme de Maintenon, with all her gifts and her knowledge of the world really ought to have seen the red light but she found Mme Guyon irresistible. She liked new friends.

All might have been well had Mme Guyon not taken up her pen; unfortunately she was one of those people who must draw attention to themselves in every possible way. Her books, *Les Torrents* and *Le Moyen Court de Faire l'Oraison*, began to be widely read. Bossuet smelt error; Rome smelt Molinism. The Bishop of Chartres asked the resident priests at Saint-Cyr to find out what was going on there, and presently appeared in person to investigate. He told Mme de Maintenon that there was a dangerous atmosphere in her house and that she must get rid of Mme Guyon. Mme de Maintenon made no attempt to stand up for her friend. She put her hand in her apron pocket, drew out *Les Torrents*, threw it in the fire and went off to forbid Mme Guyon ever to set foot at Saint-Cyr again. Abbé Brémond thinks that she had become jealous of the intimacy between Mme Guyon and Fénelon. Probably, too, she foresaw the annoyance which a religious controversy so near home would cause the King, and wanted to be safely under shelter before the storm broke. She was never loyal to her friends if this was likely to make difficulties for her with him.

The Bishop of Chartres assembled the Dames, in 1693, exposed the errors of Quietism and begged them to forget such a dangerous doctrine. He merely drove it underground. Mme de La Maisonfort became the apostle of Mme Guyon, smuggled her letters into the convent, copied them out and passed them round. Mme de Maintenon asked for the books to be given up, but some copies were hidden away, to be read at times when the nuns were supposed to be busy.

Fénelon was not prepared to admit that Mme Guyon was in error; he bitterly reproached Mme de Maintenon for not having sent for him to come to Saint-Cyr and settle the affair. Mme de Maintenon who liked him much less since his letter to her, prepared to throw him overboard. She persuaded the King, who was by now the only person at Versailles unaware of what was going on, to appoint Fénelon to the vacant archbishopric of Cambrai. The King, who had just received and been annoyed by his own letter from Fénelon, thought (as she did) that this would be a way of seeing less of him at Court. He willingly agreed. Fénelon was consecrated by Bossuet at Saint-Cyr (1695) in the presence of his pupils, the King's grandsons, and of Mme de Maintenon. Mme Guyon was not there, nor any of the Dames.

The Bishop of Chartres had a feeling that all was still not well at Saint-Cyr; he went back there, searched the cells and the library himself and found a quantity of inflammable literature. He confiscated it all, including some pamphlets by Fénelon. The feeling in the convent was such that Mme de Maintenon begged Bossuet to come and talk to the Dames. He preached two sermons and then saw the young women separately. Mme de La Maisonfort was the only one brave enough to argue with him; and Bossuet, who thought her very attractive, was astounded by the brilliance of her theology. Sometimes even he found no means of putting her in the wrong and had to fall back on: 'One has to take all this with a grain of salt'. Certainly a grain of salt was needed to bring the rainbow theories of Quietism down to earth.

Mme Guyon went to Meaux to be examined by Bossuet. He was not the least charmed by her, and he found thirty-four articles in her works which he declared dangerous to the discipline of the Church. Fénelon energetically supported, if not all her doctrine, at least the purity of her life and her intentions, which had been put in question. His own writings now came under fire and the great controversy between him and Bossuet began, inflamed, it must be said, by Mme de Maintenon. If she saw any signs of its fizzling out, she would write to the Archbishop of Paris or whisper in the King's ear to make sure they were not losing interest. In 1698 the affair went to Rome and went against Fénelon, who was obliged to make a public act of submission in his own cathedral. The Pope, however, was heard to remark that if M. de Cambrai loved God too much, M. de Meaux loved his neighbour too little.

This affair broke up the holy set at Versailles. The Chevreuses and Beauvilliers remained faithful to Fénelon; they thought Mme de Maintenon had behaved badly to him; she was displeased with them for taking his side. But for all her influence with the King she was never able to bring about the disgrace of Beauvilliers. Twice he thought she had succeeded and that he would be obliged to go, but the King trusted and respected him too much; and he kept all his appointments and his place with the Duc de Bourgogne.

It is significant that the King had no idea that anything was amiss at Saint-Cyr until the quarrel between Fénelon and Bossuet made it impossible for Mme de Maintenon to keep him in the dark any longer. For a long time Quietism had been the burning topic among those very courtiers of whom he saw the most. From now until the end of his life one wonders how much he knew about any happenings in France. As Mme de Maintenon had foreseen, when at last he realized what had been going on under his nose for years, he was extremely angry. He looked into Mme Guyon's teachings and said they were the ravings of a madwoman. Mme de Maintenon tried reading to him some of the passages which had so charmed her; he shrugged his shoulders and said 'These are day-dreams'. But he saw the danger of these day-dreams, knowing too well the fatal fascination that new ideas always had for his subjects. Indeed, the Court, Paris and the provinces were now talking of nothing but Quietism. The Jansenists were gloating over the state to which, they said, the Jesuits had reduced religion in France. The King hated any form of religious enthusiasm; he had enough trouble as it was with the Protestants and the Jansenists; he very much disliked Rome meddling in French affairs. The Vatican was an inter-

François de Salignac de la Mothe Fénelon, Archbishop of Cambrai, by Joseph Vivien.

national body which he loathed. Furthermore this public quarrel between the tutors of his son and his grandsons was unseemly. He said of Fénelon: 'Of all the clever men in my kingdom he is the most unreal'; and he nearly had words with the thirteen-year-old Bourgogne who firmly supported his adored master.

The King vented his fury on Mme de La Maisonfort who was sent away from Saint-Cyr, as Mme de Brinon had been, secretly, by the garden gate, after crying all night. She went to a convent at Meaux; Bossuet was most good to her but her life was blighted. Mme Guyon spent the next eight years in the Bastille and was then allowed to go and live with her son. Fénelon was never seen at the Court again. He remained in his bishopric until his death seventeen years later, ageing under the dreadful weight of the hope, always postponed and finally extinguished, that Bourgogne would succeed to the throne.

At one moment Mme de Maintenon thought the end had come, for her. She took to her bed. The King did not go near her. Then he heard that she was really ill, went to her room and said, not unkindly, 'This business is killing you, Madame'. At last the Bishop of Chartres intervened, begging the King to take his excellent companion back into his confidence which, probably nothing loth, he did.

Finally the King paid a state visit to Saint-Cyr. He assembled the Dames and the elder children and told them he was sorry he had been obliged to be so strict but that unsound doctrine was too dangerous to be allowed to proliferate. Then he sat in their midst and chatted with them. After that, Quietism was extinguished for ever, at Saint-Cyr. It was now sixteen years since Mme de Brinon had founded a little school at Rueil. The house duly became a retreat and a tomb for Mme de Maintenon. The Dames were her adoring slaves; they wrote down every word she said to them; she destroyed all other documents relevant to her strange destiny before she died, well aware that a flattering memorial existed in their archives.

Most of the girls who did not marry – and they were in the majority – took the veil, on Mme de Maintenon's advice. She said it would be preferable to going home and there being obliged to look after infirm, widowed and probably eccentric parents. Saint-Cyr thus became a holy establishment for old maids; and Mme de Maintenon was satisfied. She thought that this was what she had always intended.

Boulle commode made for Louis' room at the Grand Trianon, 1701.

Marquetry chest, boulle.

XV

LORD PORTLAND'S EMBASSY

*Il y a une infinité de conduites qui paraissent
ridicules, et dont les raisons cachées sont très
sages et très solides.*

LA ROCHEFOUCAULD

During the last years of the seventeenth century the thoughts of statesmen were
almost entirely occupied with the question of who should succeed to the throne of
Spain. The Spanish King, Charles II (half-brother of Marie-Thérèse), was certainly
not long for this world. After the death of Monsieur's daughter he had married
again, a Bavarian princess; but, on account of the state secret sent back to Versailles
by his first wife, she had no children either and the huge Spanish empire was without
an heir. It consisted of Spain, most of Italy, the Catholic Netherlands, the Balearic
Islands, most of Morocco, all South America except Brazil, a great deal of North
America including Mexico, and the Antilles. The American possessions were
lumped together under the name of *Les Indes*. Nearest in blood to Charles II were
the Emperor, the Grand Dauphin and a Bavarian prince aged four; the Grand
Dauphin had a better right to succeed King Charles than the other two because his
mother was the eldest daughter of Philip IV and his grandmother had also been a
Spanish princess. True, they had both renounced their claim to the Spanish crown
on marrying Kings of France; but, with a little legal jiggery-pokery these renuncia-
tions could be declared void. Most Spaniards preferred an Austrian claimant, partly
because the two countries had already been united under a single Emperor and
partly because of an age-old hatred and distrust of their French neighbour. Neither
the Emperor Leopold nor Louis XIV was so mad as to contemplate putting his heir
on the Spanish throne; the other European countries would all have banded together
immediately to prevent such an agglomeration of power, but they both claimed it
for cadets of their families – the Emperor for Archduke Charles, his second son, and
Louis for the Duc d'Anjou, the second of his three grandsons. Even so there was the
danger of a European war. Nobody wanted this, Louis having exhausted not only
France but most of western Europe with twenty-five years of almost continual
conflict; and a serious effort was made to regulate the matter by diplomacy.

Hans William Bentinck, first Earl of Portland, by Hyacinthe Rigaud.

King William III of England by studio of Wissing.

Louis XIV by Hyacinthe Rigaud.

Old enemies as they were, Louis XIV and William of Orange recognized each other as the only statesmen of any importance in Europe. As Louis himself remarked, they had only to join forces in order to dictate to the universe. William's situation was very different from what it had been in the early days of their rivalry; he was King of England now as well as Stadholder of Holland; the acknowledged leader of the whole Protestant world. The two men were anxious to know each other's views and intentions in the Spanish affair; each chose his most brilliant diplomatist to send to the other.

Hans William Bentinck, Earl of Portland went to France. He had two objects in view, both delicate; he was to try and persuade Louis XIV to send James II further away from England than Saint-Germain-en-Laye, where, surrounded by English exiles and receiving all the malcontents from over the Channel, he was busily plotting the assassination of William and his own return to the throne. Portland was also to find out Louis XIV's plans for Spain. He had already negotiated the Peace of Ryswick (1697) ending the wars that had followed the persecution of the Protestants. He and Maréchal de Boufflers had thrashed out the terms walking up and down in an orchard together without any of the usual formalities. One of the clauses which Louis XIV had been obliged to accept, albeit reluctantly, as he knew how much it would hurt the feelings of his cousin King James, was that he must recognize William as King of England.

Portland was chosen for these delicate tasks for two reasons. First, he knew King William's thoughts and intentions as nobody else could, since he had been heart's brother of the King all their lives. William never confided the secrets of his foreign policy to Englishmen, who he thought cared nothing for foreign affairs and seemed to ignore the existence of other lands, beyond the sea. He was having a difficult time with his new subjects, now that the honeymoon was over. In so far as the English

Saint Germain-en-Laye; tapestry.

took account of foreigners, they felt that the best of a poor bunch were the Dutch. Though they had been at war with them so recently, they bore them no grudge and on the contrary respected them as honest Protestant sea-faring folks like themselves, and sworn enemies of the abhorred French. The idea of William the Silent has always appealed to the English; he may be said to be an honorary Englishman. So when the time came to get rid of the hopeless James, they were not displeased that the crown should go to Mary and her Dutch husband. What was their distress when this honest Dutchman turned out to be a product of *French* civilization – speaking, writing and thinking in French, obviously more at home with Frenchmen than with the native lords. Like the Prince Consort, William was appreciated by his English subjects only after his death when he was to become, in the eyes of more than one historian, our greatest king. As for his shadow, Hans William Bentinck, he spoke not a word of English and was frankly unpopular among his new countrymen: his brilliant social gifts were wasted on those of them who had no French and the money, lands and honours which William showered on him were a cause of much jealousy. He was known as The Wooden Man.

The second reason for the choice of Portland may seem frivolous but was in fact most cunning: he knew how to behave. William realized that it would be useless to send an English nobleman with the usual insular contempt for and ignorance of etiquette to Louis XIV: the ambassador to a dictator must be a man who can get on with him otherwise nothing is gained. Nobody without manners ever succeeded at Versailles; the lack of them was to be the only cause of Voltaire's failure in a domain where he would so much have liked to shine. The Duke of St Albans who had preceded Portland, to carry King William's congratulations on the marriage of the Duc de Bourgogne, had made the worst possible impression: civilized behaviour was a closed book to him and he had left debts everywhere. Indeed what British bulldog would ever have been conversant with the mysteries of the *Armchair*, the *Door* and the *Coach*, or aware that the English Ambassador must not give precedence to the President of the Paris Parlement? Portland knew.

His embassy was magnificent; the French, accustomed as they were to splendid and luxurious establishments, had never seen anything like his. He took the house of Prince d'Auvergne, situated in a large garden, where the Boulevard Raspail now cuts across the rue de Varenne. The dining-room was too small for his requirements, so he built one in the garden; it was ready in three weeks. Here he kept open house for any Englishmen who were in, or passing through Paris. Prince d'Auvergne only had ten horses; Portland had ninety and seven coaches, so stables had to be hired all over Paris for them. He was prepared to cut a dash out hunting as well as in other ways. In his train were Lords Cavendish, Hastings, Paston, Raby and Woodstock, who found houses for themselves and provided their own servants and carriages. Matthew Prior was Secretary to the Embassy; Portland's personal secretary,

Arnold Joost van Keppel, first Earl of Albemarle
by Sir Godfrey Kneller.

d'Allone, was a French Protestant refugee. He was never molested, but the chaplain
was taken off on one occasion by the police and accused of holding illegal services.
Portland soon got him back, however.

In spite of the glitter he showed the world, Portland came to France with death
in his heart. As he left London, Whitehall Palace was in flames, his own apartment
there collapsing; he may have thought this all too symbolical. The one person in
the world he cared for was William; and William's favourite now was Arnold van
Keppel, Lord Albemarle, a stupid, pretty, jolly young fellow of so little value that
nobody could have much doubt as to the nature of their relationship. The Englishmen who accompanied Portland told Madame all about it. When they found that
sodomy was fashionable in France they made no secret of their own predilection for
this form of amusement and were soon disporting themselves in Monsieur's set.
They said that King William was in love with Albemarle as with a woman, and
used to kiss his hands before the whole Court. Portland passionately minded leaving
these two together and his letters to William reveal a broken heart. William (so
like a man) replied with such phrases as 'I cannot explain myself more clearly on
this subject, at present, than by assuring you that I always entertain for you the same
affection'. 'Impossible to love you more heartily than I do – death alone can make
me change my feelings.' 'I hope that you no longer doubt the solemn oath I swore
you.' His letters were still signed with the little G (Guillaume) which he reserved for
Portland. Portland was unconvinced; and presently he learnt that Albemarle and
William were dining alone together twice a week. However, he may have been
slightly cheered to get a letter from King William saying that never had he been
more depressed.

Portland's state coaches were loaded on ships which were to bring them the whole
way to Paris; but when he arrived, in January 1698, the Seine was frozen over so

Queen Mary of Modena by William Wissing.

King James II. Artist unknown.

that it was some time before he could make his official *entrée*. He saw the King at once, however, going to Versailles in Maréchal de Boufflers's coach. He had an audience at 9 a.m. alone with the King and the foreign minister, who was now the Marquis de Torcy, son of Colbert de Croissy. Then he paid calls on all members of the royal family, dined with Torcy in his flat and returned to Paris. Not for another fortnight did he have a business interview with the King, when he immediately raised the question of King James's domicile. The King said that James was his near relation; that he was afflicted by his troubles and could not in honour send him away. Portland, who knew as everybody did that the penniless exiles were a great expense to Louis at a time when his finances were in a poor state, proposed that King William should pay Queen Mary of Modena her jointure of fifty thousand pounds a year on condition that she and her husband and family should leave Saint-Germain-en-Laye and live either at Modena or Avignon. The King replied that he would never oblige them to go unless they wished to.

Indeed his behaviour to King James was quixotic to the point of rashness; and no question of interest ever budged him from it. The exiles always cost him more money than he could afford; in the end they nearly cost him the fruits of his life's work. No doubt Louis had a weakness for Queen Mary, whose mother had been yet another niece of Mazarin's, and who, though not at all clever, was charming and beautiful. She became intimate with Mme de Maintenon and was a great addition to their little circle. As for James, he was, like Louis himself, the Lord's Anointed and this set them both apart from their fellow men. It was a comfort to the King to be sometimes with people of his own age and whom he could regard as equals. Everybody liked 'the poor Queen' and felt sorry for, while slightly despising 'the poor King', who was a tremendous bore and whose troubles were so obviously of his own making. William of Orange of course was regarded at Versailles as a usurper, and his late wife and her sister as worse than Goneril and Regan.

182

Meudon, the seat of the Dauphin, near Paris, by Pierre Denis Martin.

Portland then spoke of the assassins who he saw – to his horror and amazement he said – were quite at home at the Court. Assassins? The King had no idea whom he meant. Portland did not beat about the bush; he meant the Duke of Berwick (James's illegitimate son by the sister of Marlborough), Lord Middleton, Sir George Barclay and others, who had all been privy to a plot to ambush King William on his way out hunting and murder him. (Whereas Charles II in exile had refused to hear of his supporters killing Cromwell, his brother James was all in favour of doing away with his own son-in-law. Whether Louis XIV knew of this plot is a moot point.) The King raised an eyebrow when Portland brought out the names of the conspirators. He said he thought the Duke of Berwick may have been to England on his father's business, but was certainly not involved in any such plot. As for the others, he seemed not to know them and vaguely said he had no idea where they might be. Portland saw that it was no good pursuing this subject. He thought most probably the gentlemen in question would be told to make themselves scarce when he was about, and that this would be as much as he could hope for. (However, the very next time he went to Versailles there they were as usual.) The Spanish question had not yet been raised.

Portland now describes Versailles, as the King his master desired that he would. Dutch, Protestant and therefore prejudiced against Louis and all his works, he gives a truthful account of houses and gardens, but has no talent for describing people, or is perhaps too discreet; he says he will do it *viva voce* when he sees King William. Versailles itself he does not like, or will not admit to liking, though it is certainly very grand, must have cost money to build and be expensive to keep up. But the smaller houses, Meudon, Marly and Saint-Cloud can be praised unreservedly – Meudon the best of all: 'Your Majesty would love this place'. Most unluckily, since gardens are his greatest interest and he is Superintendent of King William's, the weather is abominable (and was to be so during his whole visit – a bitter winter followed by a cold, wet spring; it was freezing hard again on 4 May.) The reservoirs are frozen and the fountains put out of order by the frosts. He has not seen any of the thousands of flowers one hears so much about; not so much as a snowdrop; everything seems completely dead. He has been shown the orange trees and only gives them a fairly good mark – they are nothing to those in King William's palaces in Holland. It was a great favour to be allowed to see Marly as no other envoy has ever been there. He often goes wolf-hunting with the Dauphin and Madame, who keeps up wonderfully, also with the Chevalier de Lorraine at Royaumont, but is never invited to go out with the King's hounds in case at the last minute King James should wish to do so. Once, indeed, he was pulling on his boots to go with the Dauphin when there was a message asking him to stay away as the 'King of England' was going out that morning. Portland thinks it really rather foolish of King James not to want to see him.

He cannot obtain the fruit trees he requires – has had to send all the way to Orléans for them. He thinks he can persuade Le Nôtre to make designs for Windsor. He is also looking out for a good huntsman. All this can be managed, but as to the beds and furniture King William has told him to get, he doesn't truly think they will do, they are so over-decorated, fringed and embroidered with gold and silver. Better get them made in England. Living, here, is expensive; horses are three times what they cost in Holland. Commerce, as far as one can see, is not very prosperous and the French public finances are far from sound, though the King has a huge sum of money in his coffers. May Lord Portland give permission to Major Packmore to go home and put his affairs in order? He is engaged to one of Madame's maids of honour.

So far Portland, not having as yet been able to make his state entry, had not found himself at grips with the ferocious etiquette of the French Court. When he did he was more than equal to coping with it, though several times in his letters he said he had never understood ceremonial. At last his coaches arrived and he prepared for his entry. The first trap that was laid for him was in the matter of the procession. He heard that the Duchesse de Verneuil's carriage would precede his own with those of the royal family. Now the Duchesse de Verneuil, a daughter of Chancelier Séguier, was the widow of a bastard son of Henri IV. She had never in her life counted as royal, and Portland discovered that the Venetian ambassador in the same circumstances had recently refused to allow her to precede him. It was said that Louis XIV's idea in suddenly putting her forward like this was to give more consequence to his own bastards. Portland was quite firm. He said he did not mind du Maine and Toulouse, who had been legitimized, going before him but there could be no question of Mme de Verneuil's doing so. He won his point without difficulty and the state entry into Paris then took place. He was astounded by the

Marly; château, gardens and pavilions from the north, by Pierre Denis Martin.

Overleaf: The Galerie des Glaces.

vast crowds who had turned out to see him, not only poor people but the rich and important. Every window on the route was crammed and every roof covered with spectators. Portland was amused to hear some people on the Pont Neuf crying out 'This is worth seeing – the solemn entry of a King (William III) we have been burning on this bridge for years'. All went well until he arrived at the Hôtel des Ambassadeurs, a large and beautiful house in the rue de Tournon, which was kept for these occasions and where an ambassador after his state entry was entertained to supper.

Here the King sent his own first lord-in-waiting to call on Portland with his compliments. Of course this nobleman received the *Door* (greeted at it), the *Hand*, the *Armchair* and the *Coach* (taken to it, put in, and seen off), in fact the whole works. Then came the Marquis de Villacerf representing the little newly-married Duchesse de Bourgogne who, the Queen and the Dauphine being no more, was now the first lady in the land. M. de Boneuil, the *Introducteur des Ambassadeurs* (what is called now *Chef du Protocole*) wanted Portland to go half way down the stairs to meet Villacerf. Portland refused to budge further than the antechamber. Boneuil flew into a temper and hit the banisters with his cane. Portland took no notice. He and Villacerf then sent messengers to and fro. After a good long time Portland said he would go down two steps and no more. If this did not suit M. de Villacerf he had better withdraw. So up he came. However, there was more trouble when he left; Portland saw him downstairs (the *Door*) but did not wait to see him leave (the *Coach*). Boneuil, beside himself, seized Portland's coat-tails but Portland shook him off and went his way. 'The *Introducteur* made great complaints to me.' Then Monsieur's representative arrived and the same difference arose; and again with Madame's. 'Things may have been very different' he wrote to William 'when the English King [Charles II] was ruled by the French; but this is no longer the case.' Boneuil, 'confounded and irritated', left the house abruptly, though he was supposed to sup there with Portland. The next day Portland went to Versailles to inform Torcy of these incidents and to tell Monsieur and Madame how very sorry he was that they had occurred. However, Monsieur, 'who knows about these things', said that he had been quite right. Boneuil was reproved; and after that, Portland never had any more reason to protest, all was plain sailing.

At his first public audience with Louis XIV at Versailles the crowds in the château were so great that he could hardly get through them to the King's bedroom where he was received. Once there he made three deep reverences; the first on seeing the King, the second half-way across the room and the third when he was inside the balustrade surrounding the bed. Here the King awaited him, hat in hand, standing up and, signal mark of favour, spoke to him between the second and third reverences, saying he was glad to see so many French and English people together. He put on his hat; upon which Portland put on his and made his address, taking off the hat

Louis receiving the Papal Legate at Fontainebleau,
detail from Gobelins tapestry, 29 July 1664.

185

every time he mentioned his own or the French King. Louis then said 'many things extremely flattering to myself' and dismissed him with a gracious smile. The courtiers remarked that Portland had been received as if he had been a sort of divinity. (Oral tradition has it that on one occasion Louis took Portland in his coach, inviting him with a gesture to get in first. When Portland did so without the slightest hesitation, Louis is supposed to have said 'they told me that you were the most polite man in Europe and now I see that you are'.)

On receiving Portland's letter about the foregoing events, William replied 'I have always commended your firmness and shall continue to do so provided you do not put it into practice against me'. He wrote to the Pensionary Heinsius, in Holland, to say that it was perhaps a pity that Portland had begun with the question of King James as 'now he is perplexed as to how to proceed'. He told Portland not to mention it again but to get on with the Spanish succession.

However it was Louis XIV himself who broached this subject, through his ministers. They called on Portland and pointed out that King Charles might die at any minute: what did the King of England think should be done in that case to prevent war? Portland replied vaguely that this death would certainly plunge their two countries into another war: the French and English interests were so much opposed that it was difficult to see how it could be avoided. The hard bargaining then began. Nobody now envisaged the whole Spanish empire remaining under one king, so the main points at issue between William and Louis were Spain itself, the Spanish Netherlands and, of special interest to England, South America and the security of Mediterranean trade. Louis XIV proposed that the crown of Spain should go to one of his younger grandsons, Anjou or Berri (now aged fifteen and thirteen), who should finish his education in Spain without a single Frenchman in his household. The Low Countries should go to the Elector of Bavaria. There

186

Silver font by J.-M. Cousinet made in Stockholm 1696–1707.

Drawing for a silver table for the Grande Galerie by Nicodemus Tessin.

The Hôtel de Bretonvilliers, acquired by the Duc de Tallart after his exile. This house, said to have been the most beautiful of seventeenth-century Paris houses, was destroyed in 1840.

should be such treaties for the protection of English trade as would give full satisfaction to Portland. Louis XIV supposed that the English would not like to see Spain joined to the Empire? The answer to this was that the English would not mind at all, knowing the state of the Emperor's affairs and in view of the fact that their enemy was France. The negotiations thus begun went on for several months, like a game of poker. Portland saw the King continually and the two men evidently enjoyed each other's company, though Portland never wrote kindly about anything French and professed a deep distrust of the King's good faith. All the same he was gratified by his own personal success. One standing joke between him and Louis was the Duke of Savoy – the mere mention of his name – a suggestion, for instance, that he should be given Milan – was enough to send them into fits of laughter; and William, too, laughed sardonically on his side of the channel. This duke, a son-in-law of Monsieur's, turned his coat between France and the Empire and was renowned for never finishing a war in the same camp as that in which he began it, while always managing to be beaten – until Prince Eugène fought his battles for him, but this was not yet.

William told Portland to try and secure an interview with Mme de Maintenon; but she never saw the ambassadors, and as a firm friend of King James and Queen Mary was not likely to make an exception in favour of the usurper's. Portland was not invited to the very grand dinner party which Mme de Maintenon gave in April, when she married her niece to the Comte d'Ayen, son of the Duc de Noailles. Mme d'Aubigné, the despised sister-in-law and mother of the bride, was allowed to leave her convent for once in order to attend the festivities.

Louis XIV now sent the Comte de Tallart to represent him in London. Tallart was one of those Frenchmen who seem to be the nearest thing to perfection that humanity can produce. He was delightful and brilliant and was considered the best

Decorative motif from the Ambassador's staircase.

Cock from the labyrinth at Versailles.

company of anybody at Versailles. Portland had seen a good deal of him there and, while never denying that he was a good talker, described him as being too pleased with himself. If Portland had a fault, it was jealousy. King William, whose own ambassador had received so much courtesy from the French, wished to show all possible kindness to Tallart: he sent his yacht, the *William and Mary*, to bring him from Calais. Tallart soon became a great addition to London life, with his painted coaches, elegant clothes and charming personality; and King William liked him very much. He took the Duke of Ormonde's town house, in St James's Square, on to which he built a chapel, and here he kept one of those French embassies which to this day outshine all others. Lord Macaulay once remarked that French embassies to London, enjoying the advantages of good food, beautiful decoration and brilliant entertainment, have been the objects of degrading worship, and certainly the envoys from other lands are inclined to think so. In those days governments did not possess houses in foreign towns, as now; the ambassadors sometimes exchanged with each other (for instance, under Louis XV, the Dukes of Nivernais and Bedford exchanged not only houses but also servants and carriages) but more often they took some available house for the duration of their mission. The exception was the French ambassador to Rome who generally, but not always, lived in the Palazzo Farnese.

Louis XIV had drawn up a set of instructions for Tallart which show an extraordinarily acute knowledge of the English character and way of life. He was to find out which members of society were the leaders of public opinion – they would not necessarily be members of the government or aristocrats. There would be no harm in hobnobbing with the opposition; only of course he must have nothing to do with any Jacobite or he would be discredited. If the subject of King James were to be raised, Tallart was to say that Louis XIV would naturally like to see his cousin back on the throne but only if this was the unanimous desire of the English people.

As much as Portland distrusted Louis XIV, Tallart was convinced of the good faith of King William; but he wrote home saying that he was 'by no means as powerful as we thought'. Public finances, he added, were in a bad way and the only interest the average Englishman took in the Spanish succession was to know how it might affect trade. He said that Lord Albemarle rose every day in favour. William himself told Portland that he was having a good deal of trouble with the English, who 'don't care a fig for foreign affairs and only think of how one party can injure the other. Parliament does more harm than can be imagined by reducing the army estimates'. Presently he went to his beloved Holland, paying Tallart the compliment of taking him.

Towards the end of Portland's visit, on 22 April, Monsieur gave a dinner party for him at Saint-Cloud. There were twenty guests, including the Chevalier de Lorraine and the Marquis d'Effiat. Madame seems not to have been there. Portland sat between Monsieur's son the Duc de Chartres and the Duchesse de Foix – Monsieur had Chartres on his right and Mlle de Montauban on his left. The food was marvellous – all the early vegetables appearing for the first time. There was a splendid silver-gilt *surtout de table*, a new invention, much remarked upon, by M. de Launay who had made two for the King.

In June 1698 Portland took his leave of the French King, from whom no foreigner and few French people had ever received so many honours and marks of favour. But Portland's dreadful sorrow was not lightened thereby, and he went to· rejoin William knowing that things could never be the same between them again. Indeed when he had concluded the business with France, he resigned his charges at Court and retired into private life. One is glad to know that William sent for him on his deathbed and died in his arms, while Albemarle stood by. However it was Mary who had the last word: dangling over that strange man's heart, they found a locket containing her hair.

The Treaty of Loo was the outcome of Portland's and Tallart's embassies and it was a striking success for all concerned. The little Bavarian prince was to have Spain and her colonies, while the Dauphin and the Emperor were given various European territories as conpensation. Louis XIV seems to have signed the treaty in good faith, since he wrote to d'Harcourt, his ambassador at Madrid, telling him to explain to any Spaniards who might show preference for a French King that it was the only method by which peace could be preserved. This arrangement came to nought, and is now forgotten because the baby who was the lynchpin of it died – poisoned, his father thought, by some Austrian spy. So all was to begin again.

XVI

THE TURN OF THE CENTURY

Ce siècle est devenu immobile comme tous les grands siècles ; il
s'est fait le contemporain des ages qui l'ont suivi.

CHATEAUBRIAND

At the turn of the century the King had reigned for nearly sixty years, had governed by himself for forty and had been married to Mme de Maintenon for seventeen. He was now an old man. He no longer greeted the duchesses with a kiss: he said his face had become too horrid. His grandson was married; his elder children were middle-aged, the Grand Dauphin rising forty and the Princesse de Conti thirty-four. Her life had been disappointing for one so lovely and so romantic: she never had a faithful lover or even very devoted friends. Now she had become pious, rather ailing and as dry as a stick; and officers of the guard were no longer sent away for daring to gaze at her. As soon as the much more fascinating Mme la Duchesse was grown up, she took Marie-Anne's place as the Dauphin's favourite sister.

Mme de Montespan had left the Court in 1791; she had long been urged to do so by her own son, du Maine, who coveted her flat. He also appropriated her house at Clagny which was thought embarrassingly near Versailles for her to live there once she had parted from the King. Mme de Maintenon had seen to it that her position should become more and more difficult; her younger children were taken away from her, the Comte de Toulouse, aged thirteen, was sent to the wars and Mlle de Blois put in charge of dreadful old Mme de Montchevreuil. This was the last straw. Athénaïs flew into a rage and told Bossuet to tell the King that she wished to retire for ever. She was taken at her word, as perhaps she had not expected to be; and the very next day du Maine was supervising the removal of her furniture. Quick work, as she remarked ruefully. After the death of the Marquis de Montespan in 1701 she hoped that the King would turn against Mme de Maintenon and marry her. She always declared that she was the one he loved, and that he had only left her for fear of hell-fire. But in fact she never saw him again. Plunged in devotion and good works, she spent her last years trying to avoid her old colleague the Devil; she could not sleep alone or in the dark and was terrified of death. Saint-Simon describes her as

The ages of Louis by Antoine Benoist.

still perfectly beautiful at sixty, but Madame says her skin was like a piece of paper children had been playing with, her whole face covered with little lines and her hair snow white.

A few months after his mother's departure, du Maine married one of the midget Bourbons, a sister of M. le Duc. Athénaïs was not invited to the wedding. Du Maine was still the heart, the soul and the oracle of Mme de Maintenon, and the King loved his company; but everybody else much preferred his brother Toulouse who made an honourable career for himself in the Navy, married (for love) a member of the Noailles family and never had any royal pretentions. His country seat was Rambouillet – his town house the present Banque de France.

The King's family life had never been so sunny. It was transformed by the arrival, in 1696, of a bride for the Duc de Bourgogne: she was the twelve-year-old Marie-Adélaïde, the child of that Duke of Savoy who was considered so ridiculous by his fellow-rulers. Her mother was a daughter of Monsieur and Henrietta. There was such a to-do over the arrival of the little princess that Saint-Simon was able to play truant from the Court to achieve a long-cherished project; he took the painter Rigaud to La Trappe. The holy Abbé de Rancé would never allow himself to be painted – Rigaud had to pretend to be an ordinary visitor; but by dint of staring at Rancé for an hour or two he was able to go away and produce an excellent likeness from memory. That the King did not even notice the absence, without leave, of one of his dukes, was a measure of his interest in the new grand-daughter. He went all the way to Montargis to meet her, and wrote from there to give Mme de Maintenon his impressions of the infinitely important child, future Queen of France. This is the only letter (as opposed to little notes) from Louis to his wife that she did not burn after his death.

'I got here before five o'clock; the Princess arrived just before six. I went to receive her at her coach. She waited for me to speak first and then she answered very well, with a hint of shyness which would have pleased you. I led her through the crowd to her room, from time to time I had the torches brought nearer so that their light fell on her face and she could be seen. She endured this walk and these lights with graceful modesty. At length we got to her room where the crowd and the heat were enough to kill one. From time to time I showed her to those who came up and I was watching her from all points of view in order to tell you my impression.'

We can imagine how he watched her, in the flickering light of those torches, like a clever old fox with eyes that missed nothing. It was love at first sight. He goes on to tell Mme de Maintenon that he has never seen such grace or such a pretty figure; she is dressed fit to be painted (no doubt her French mother had seen to that); her eyes are bright and beautiful, her complexion perfect; she has masses of black hair, luscious red lips; white, most irregular teeth (which were to make her short life a martyrdom), pretty hands, rather red as little girls' hands are, and she is thin, which

Cabinet given to Charles II of England by Louis XIV.

is also of her age. Her curtsey very poor, very Italian and there is something altogether Italian about her look; but she pleases. He can see that all are enchanted with her. She is like the first picture they had – not a bit like the others. He will write again after supper when he expects to have noticed some more touches. He hopes he will be able to keep up a certain attitude he has adopted until he gets home, which he is longing to do.

Later in the evening he is still more delighted. They have had a public conversation together, during which she gave nothing away; in other words she was perfect. Monsieur is in a dreadful temper and is now pretending to be ill. (Monsieur was, in fact, furious because his grand-daughter was to take precedence over Madame, who since the death of the Dauphine, had been the first lady in the land. He may also have realized that the King was determined to keep the little girl away from what he regarded as the bad influence of the Court of Saint-Cloud.) The King goes on to send Mme de Maintenon a thousand we don't know whats, because, in accordance with her policy of mystifying posterity, she has here erased two lines. He ends by saying that when the time comes for this princess to play her part she will do so with dignity, poise and charm.

Mme de Maintenon wrote to the Duchess of Savoy, when she had seen Marie-Adélaïde, saying that the King and she herself were in transports of joy at receiving such a treasure. Indeed she now came into her own with a future Queen of France to educate. The little girl was good, but not easy material, astonishingly like that other descendant of Monsieur's who came to marry an heir to the throne, Marie-Antoinette. She was fascinating, spoilt, wilful and proud. Owing to Mme de Maintenon's loving care of her the nobility of her nature blossomed with womanhood – in Marie-Antoinette's case it never appeared at all until brought out by cruel misfortune. Mme de Maintenon and Marie-Adélaïde had a perfect relationship, more intimate than that of most mothers and daughters. *Ma Tante* and *Mignonne* they called each other. The cynics at Versailles to whom human goodness was inclined to be suspect, and who had watched Mme de Maintenon for a lifetime in all her apparent hypocrisy, said that *Mignonne* was servile to *Ma Tante*, that she had seen the way to the King's heart through his old wife and had, with the innate cunning of her race, regulated her behaviour accordingly. Certainly she had been primed before leaving home; she wrote to her grandmother: 'I do as you told me about Mme de Maintenon'. But the respect and confidence of the next sixteen years, such difficult years for any young woman, could hardly have been built on an untruth; and there is no doubt at all that she loved the old lady. She was an affectionate little thing, fond of the King and of her grandfather, Monsieur, not so fond of Madame; even less of her father-in-law, the Dauphin (who never cared for children) and of her aunts the Princesses not at all, and they were furiously jealous of her. While she and Bourgogne were still in the schoolroom they were indifferent to each other. They

One of a pair of cabinets made in France by Cucci, 1683.

Spiritu magno vidit ultima

Previous page: Marriage of the Duc de Bourgogne and Princess Marie-Adélaide of Savoy, 7 December 1697 by Antoine Dieu. Behind the Duc de Bourgogne are the Ducs d'Anjou and Berry. Louis is supported by a stick with his son, the Grand Dauphin, behind him. To the right are Monsieur, with his son the Duc de Chartres and the Duchesses of Orléans and Chartres.

Armand-Jean Bouthillier, Comte de Rancé, Abbé of La Trappe.

Tapestry showing animals drawn from direct observation at the *Ménagerie*; detail from a Gobelins tapestry showing Chambord.

met every day, often dining with Mme de Maintenon, but were never allowed to be alone before the consummation of the marriage which took place when Marie-Adélaïde was fourteen, two years after their wedding. On their wedding night they were put into bed together as part of the ceremony and the Dauphin jokingly told Bourgogne to kiss his wife; but her lady-in-waiting, Mme du Lude, who had been given strict orders by the King, sent the bridegroom packing. The Duc de Berri, pert and forward at eleven years old, said scornfully that nothing would have got *him* out of that bed.

In all his long life the King never loved anybody as much as he loved Marie-Adélaïde. He took her for a walk every day, when the tiny creature looked as if she were coming out of his pocket, and spoilt her totally. At Versailles she had her own private zoo, the *Ménagerie*, in a building by the canal which has now disappeared, so of course she liked Versailles better than all the other residences. She also had her own little theatre where she put on plays with her friends. She asked if she could go to Marly, for the usual two day visit, quite alone with the King and this unheard-of treat was arranged. She lived in Mme de Maintenon's room which the King used as a sort of office. Nothing was forbidden; the word 'no' was never used. She opened his letters, rummaged about among his state papers and is always supposed to have dispatched many a military secret to her father when, having changed sides once again, he was fighting against the French. There is no hint that she did so, however, in her dull little letters to him and her mother; when she mentions the war it is to beg him to stop it; but the letters are mostly concerned with the appalling tooth-aches from which she suffered. By the time she was grown up her manners were more or less under control; as a child they were giddy indeed and it is quite understandable that those who were not entranced by her, Marie-Anne de Conti, for example, and Mme la Duchesse, should have found her unbearably irritating. She could never be

still for an instant, even at meals when she would sing, hop and dance on her chair, make frightful faces and put her fingers in the sauce. In a carriage she jumped about like a little monkey, first on one person's lap and then on another's. She *tu–toy*ed the Dauphin to make him laugh – such a thing had never been known in good society. She could be naughty in rather a horrid way. She was dreadful to Mme du Lude for no reason at all; Mme du Lude was a charming, beautiful person whom everybody liked and who had wonderful manners. The King knew exactly how to treat Marie-Adélaïde when she was impossible; Mme de Maintenon had shown him a better method of forming a young nature than the terrorizing that had made the Dauphin so dull. For instance, when Marie-Adélaïde made loud jokes about the appearance of a very ugly officer at the King's supper, the King abashed her, saying in an even louder voice, 'To me he is one of the best looking men in my kingdom since he is one of the bravest.'

She went to Saint-Cyr three days a week for her lessons; she wore the school uniform and was called Mlle de Lastic. She was never naughty there but good and clever. The day before her wedding, when she was twelve, she came to show them all her wedding dress, so thickly embroidered with silver that she could hardly stand in it. She loved Saint-Cyr and was greatly loved in return, much more, at this time, than she was at Versailles. Mme de Maintenon saw to every detail of her day, even ordering her dinner: a typical menu was crayfish soup in a silver bowl, twisted bread and wholemeal bread, freshly made butter, fresh fried eggs, a sole in a small dish, redcurrant jelly, cakes, a carafe of wine and a jug of water.

The King in his new-found piety now only admitted virtuous men to his Council and as a result public affairs were by no means flourishing. Neither Beauvilliers, Chamillart, nor Torcy would have dreamt of feathering their nests like Colbert, of insulting the King and practically raping the duchesses like Louvois or of quarrelling with and intriguing against each other like the two of them. (Beauvilliers actually refused his salary, a thing which had never been heard of before – it must be said, however, that his nest had already been feathered by Colbert, his father-in-law). But they were not in the same class as their predecessors and a very poor advertisement for integrity in public life. The King was quite contented with them. As he grew older and more authoritarian, he preferred to rule with second-rate advisers whom he thought he could control. When Louvois died, in 1691, he actually seemed rather pleased, saying to James II: 'I've lost a good minister but your affairs and mine will be none the worse for that.'

The army had gone downhill since the days of Condé, Turenne and Louvois. Vauban's favour had declined since he had gratuitously advised the King against the revocation of the Edict of Nantes and had spoken to him about the state of the peasantry. There was a serious shortage of first class general officers; Mme de Maintenon said: 'I don't know if our generals will frighten the enemy – they terrify me.' Louis XIV was not unaware of this situation and realized that now, if ever, was the time to keep the peace. When the Treaty of Loo was invalidated by the death of the Bavarian heir, he entered into another treaty with William III by which the Spanish empire was to be partitioned; the Netherlands, Spain itself, and the American colonies were to go to Austria, while France was only to have Naples, Sicily and Milan. This moderate arrangement shows that the King dreaded another conflict. It came to nought through the folly of the Emperor Leopold who claimed the whole inheritance and would not hear of any partition.

In 1700 the pathetic King of Spain died, in the thirty-sixth year of his life, and of his reign, with all Europe hanging on his will. Charles II was simple but not actually, as has so often been said, idiotic. He knew perfectly well that foreign potentates were consulting together, without any reference to him, to divide the Spanish empire after his death and was, naturally, displeased. Capable of a certain amount of reasoning, he had noticed that whenever news came from the front (a vague place in the Netherlands, dotted with towns whose names he never could learn) it was always of a French victory; from this he deduced that it would be better for Spain to have France as an ally than an enemy. His French wife, Marie-Louise d'Orléans, had given him the only joy he had ever known; and the greatest sorrow of his whole sad life was her death without children. His second wife ruled him like a strict governess; he trembled before her and made faces behind her back. She was a Bavarian, a first cousin of the Grand Dauphin's children but also sister of the Empress and she was doing all she could to further the Imperial cause. She was unpopular in Spain, and the Germans she brought there with her were loathed.

Now the most outstanding personage at Madrid was the French ambassador, the Marquis d'Harcourt who, by his charm and intelligence had overcome apparently insurmountable obstacles there. At the beginning of his mission the Queen had made it impossible for him even to have an audience with Charles. D'Harcourt was not discouraged; he kept a magnificent embassy; little by little, he won over the grandees, the clergy, the *toreros*, the King and even the Queen herself: his task was made easier by the miserliness and tactlessness of his Austrian colleague. D'Harcourt's diplomatic activities were cleverly backed up by neighbourly help to the Spanish king such as French convoys for his ships bringing gold from America and assistance in his running warfare with the Barbary pirates. During the last months of his life Charles II rebelled against his Queen; he only saw her in order to make last, desperate efforts to have a child, and treated secretly with statesmen and ambassadors. He went to Marie-Louise's grave, had her coffin opened and kissed the poor remains. A pro-French Pope did the rest. Still undecided about his will, pious, desperately ill, Charles II wrote and asked the Holy Father what he ought to do and was told to leave everything to his great-nephew Anjou. And so he did, adding a rider that, should Louis XIV not accept on behalf of his grandson, the messenger who brought the will was to go straight on to Vienna and offer the Spanish empire to Archduke Charles. The whole thing was a triumph for French diplomacy; and d'Harcourt was made a duke, to the annoyance of Tallart who had only been rewarded for his success in London by a marshal's *bâton* and the order of the Saint Esprit.

Charles II's will arrived, with the news of his death, at Fontainebleau, 9 November 1700. The King, whose face gave no indication of its contents, put off a day's shooting and ordered Court mourning. He then called a Council in Mme de Maintenon's room to decide whether his grandson should or should not accept the legacy. It seemed almost certain that to accept would provoke a European war. The Dauphin who of course was out hunting, hastened back to attend the Council and surprised everybody by speaking up in favour of his son's rights, using brilliant arguments with an eloquence of which he was not known to be capable. The decision was a foregone conclusion; and indeed it is difficult to see how Louis XIV could have refused, since this would have meant putting his greatest enemy on two French frontiers with only the doubtful Duke of Savoy as a buffer on the third. From the time that Mazarin forced the King to marry Marie-Thérèse, French foreign policy had been based on the hopes that a day would dawn when there would be 'no more Pyrenees.'

Louis went back to Versailles, taking the Duchesse de Bourgogne, the Princesse de Conti and the Duchesse du Lude in his own coach and eating a picnic without stopping. They left at 9.30 a.m. and arrived at 4 p.m. The following morning he sent for the Spanish ambassador whom he received alone with Anjou, and told him that he might salute his King. The ambassador fell on his knee and made a long speech in Spanish which the King understood but the Duke did not (oddly enough he had never been taught the language). Then the double doors of the council chamber were thrown open and the waiting courtiers bidden to enter, a thing which

Mgńr le Duc d'Anjou declaré par le Roy, et reconnu Roy d'Espagne à Versailles le 16.9bre

had never happened before. Louis XIV, having with a long, piercing, majestic look seen exactly who was there, said: 'Gentlemen, here is the King of Spain'. It was a memorable scene.

They went to Mass, Louis taking the new King into the box where he always worshipped alone. He offered the only hassock to the boy who refused it, so they both knelt on bare boards. The King of Spain was given the state bedroom in the Grand Appartement – the only person to sleep there in all the history of Versailles. The Dauphin, delighted at his son's good fortune, went about saying 'few people can speak of the King my father and the King my son!' He seems not to have known a prophecy, made at his birth, son of a King, father of a King, never a King; but the courtiers all knew it and gave each other significant looks.

By a lucky chance this King, Philip V, had more of the Spaniard than the Frenchman. Had the crown fallen on the head of his brother Berri it would most likely have fallen off again, for Berri was a French boy through and through and could never have endured the twilit gloom of the Spanish Court. Philip had the esteem of all who knew him and very quickly captured that of his subjects. He was handsome, with a strong look of Philip II, proud, brave, truthful and generous, rather melancholy, religious, uxorious. His first wife, Marie-Louise of Savoy, was the sister of Marie-Adélaïde. Human beings outside his family meant little to him and after he arrived in Spain the only friend at Versailles he ever enquired for was Mme de Beauvilliers. He tenderly loved his father and two brothers and never got over the death of Bourgogne, perhaps the person he loved most in the world. When he left for Spain the farewell scenes were heartrending: the Dauphin, usually so impassive, was terribly distressed – everybody felt that it was goodbye for ever, although the King said that, when Philip was quite established in Spain and when he had a son, he could pay them a visit on his way to the Spanish Netherlands. It never

200

The Duc d'Anjou recognized as King of Spain.

Dangeau being invested by Louis XIV in the old chapel, 18 December 1695 by Antoine Pezey.

happened. Philip outlived them all by many years, and founded a dynasty which lasted almost exactly a century longer than his brother's. His conscience was to trouble him when he remembered, late in the day, that Marie-Thérèse had renounced the Spanish throne for her descendants. He began to see himself as an usurper, and even abdicated for a while. But during the lifetime of Louis XIV he was ruled by him and assumed what God had sent with sober satisfaction.

After the first shock caused by the will and Louis's acceptance of it the other European countries seemed disposed to leave things as they were. The Emperor wanted to go to war, but could hardly have done so without the maritime powers and they were in favour of peace. Many English politicians rightly thought that once the old King of France was dead there would be little danger of the Spanish ruler taking his orders from Versailles. William III considered that war was inevitable, but he and his subjects were more at odds every day. At this moment Louis XIV was the most fortunate as well as the most powerful monarch on earth.

In his annual report for 1683, Foscarini, the Venetian ambassador, said that the King never expressed either joy or grief but remained imperturbable on all occasions. The death of his wife extracted a few polite sighs; those of his mistress [Mlle de Fontanges], his minister [Colbert] and his child [Vermandois] were endured with noble indifference. 'Whether he would continue in this wonderful tranquillity if fortune went so seriously against him that not only his happiness but also his glory were destroyed can only be known in the event – may it please the Lord God not to put to the proof a Prince who deserves well of the Christian world and especially of our Serenissime state.' God was about to put Louis XIV to the proof and his demeanour never altered through terrible public and private misfortunes any more than it had under the surgeon's knife. He was a man of iron.

XVII

MOURNING

Je vais ou va toute chose
Où va la feuille de rose
Et la feuille de laurier

A. V. ARNAULT

In 1701 Monsieur died suddenly of a stroke which was brought on by a quarrel with the King. For some months he had been furious with Louis (and with good reason) over his treatment of the Duc de Chartres. Monsieur was proud of his son and minded the fact that his undoubted intelligence and military gifts were never put to his country's service. The young man, bored and disillusioned, was fast going to the bad like his cousin Conti. The courtiers thought it was the King's policy to keep young royal princes away from the army and out of the public eye for fear that they should become too powerful. This is perhaps too much of a simplification: it must be remembered that Louis XIV was a man of violent likes and dislikes. Condé was of royal birth, he had actually committed high treason in his youth, but he was one of those whom the King loved: he had trusted him with military commands and much power. Like many old fellows, however, Louis was irritated by his young male relations; no doubt they were at their worst with him from sheer terror. Chartres and Conti were the leaders of the fashionable younger set at Court, which was universally condemned by its elders. La Bruyère wrote that Versailles was a place where old people were gallant, polite and polished, while the young were hard-hearted and ferocious, without any manners at all. Mme de Maintenon: 'I find the females of today insupportable with their ridiculous and immodest clothes, their tobacco, their drink, their greed, their vile manners and their idle hands.' The fact that the two princes outshone du Maine also counted against them. But if by chance the King had taken a fancy to either of them, it is possible that none of these considerations would have weighed with him.

Chartres was having a wild love affair with one of his mother's ladies, yet another 'flower in Madame's nursery,' in full view of his wife and of the whole Court. He had also put an actress and Mme de Chartres in the family way at the same time; Madame describes him going to Paris to visit his two young mothers, who gave

Mme la Duchesse in white mourning, attributed to Pierre Gobert.

birth simultaneously to a son and a daughter. (Unfortunately the legitimate child was the daughter.) The Duchesse de Chartres complained to her father the King and he complained to Monsieur, who answered very boldly. He said the King was hardly the one to blame people for flaunting their mistresses and upsetting their wives – what about the time when he took La Vallière and Montespan to Flanders in the same coach as the Queen? The King was extremely angry at being reminded of those cheerful but sinful days, and the two men began to shout at each other. A servant came into the room, and whispered that a lot of people next door were listening as hard as they could and hearing every word. So Monsieur lowered his voice but continued his attack: he accused the King of having behaved dishonestly to Chartres whom he had lured with many a specious promise, none of which had ever been kept, into a wretched marriage. Naturally a brilliant, energetic young man would be restless with nothing to do but kick his heels at Versailles, what did the King expect? Louis, who had never been spoken to like this, was beside himself with rage. Very well, he said, there was soon going to be a war, he would be obliged to make economies and wouldn't fail to begin by cutting off Monsieur's allowance.

Dinner was then announced and the two men sat down, Monsieur crimson in the face. The King said it was quite obvious that he ought to be bled, and he had a good mind to send him to his room and have it done, if necessary by force. However they both calmed down as they ate the usual enormous meal; when it was over Monsieur went back to Saint-Cloud. Late in the evening Chartres sent the King a *courrier* to say that his father was ill. Normally the King would rush to be with Monsieur if his little finger ached, but he was still in a temper; he took no notice of the message and went to bed. At three in the morning there was another *courrier*; the King hurriedly dressed and left for Saint-Cloud with Mme de Maintenon; they found Monsieur unconscious. He had collapsed at supper, had just managed to tell Madame, when she came running to him, to go back to her room (where she had been in bed with a cold); and he had then fallen into a coma. There seemed to be no hope, so the King went home again. Some hours later, Fagon, who was in charge of the case, appeared and the King knew that his brother was no more. He was greatly upset and naturally felt remorse. He spoke kindly to Chartres, who was now the Duc d'Orléans, and told him that now he must consider him as his father. He showered him with riches.

Many people minded this death, the Duchesse de Bourgogne for one: she and her grandfather had the same sense of humour and amused each other. 'I loved Monsieur very much.' 'We all saw her prolonged grief at the death of Monsieur,' Mme de Maintenon wrote to a friend. The courtiers, both at Saint-Cloud and at Versailles were plunged in gloom. Monsieur arranged parties better than anybody and always kept things in a hum. Athénaïs de Montespan was so sad that she had to

Madame by an unknown artist.

go for long walks in fields; he had been a faithful friend since her retirement from the Court. Mme de Maintenon sent her a kind message, saying that old age, with all its memories, would be insupportable if one did not believe in another life without end.

Madame was in despair. Having detested her husband for years, she had just begun to be rather fond of him and was touched that his last thought should have been for her; but above all she was terrified that she would be obliged to leave the Court and go to a convent. As soon as the breath was out of Monsieur's body she set up shrieks of 'no convent'. Very loyally, the first thing she did was to look through his private papers, all scented with violet; she burnt hundreds of letters to him from boys; only when that business was dispatched did she get into her coach and go to Versailles. There she pocketed her pride and sent for Mme de Maintenon. How could she have had the face to do so? She knew quite well that for years the King, and presumably his wife, had been reading letters in which she had called Mme de Maintenon every name under the sun; old horror, old ape, witch, whore, manure heap and so on, attributing her every action to the vilest motives. Mme de Maintenon came at once; Madame invited her to sit down for the first time in their lives. Then she humbly asked if she would intercede with the King for Madame to keep her flat at Versailles. Mme de Maintenon, who always looked at Madame with a special expression, raising the corners of her mouth and drooping her lower lip, made no reply, but drew a letter from the bosom of her dress and handed it to Madame who was appalled to see that it was in her own writing – she was even more appalled when she opened it. It was to some German relation and said that nobody really knew for certain whether the old brute was the King's wife or his concubine. Almost worse, the letter went on to describe the misery of poor people in France, always a sore subject with the King and one he would not care to have bruited about foreign courts. Madame fell into hysterics. However Mme de Maintenon behaved with the greatest magnanimity and arranged for her to stay on at Versailles. Madame continued to write about her benefactress in exactly the same terms as before, but was probably more careful not to send her letters by the public mail.

In 1699 Racine had died. He had been out of favour for some time; and though he kept his job at the Court and was therefore often at Marly and Versailles the King *never looked at him.* He suspected him of Jansenism, but – what was more damning – Mme de Maintenon had encouraged him to write down his thoughts about the peasants; she showed them to the King who, as usual, was furious. 'Because he writes good verse he thinks he's got the talents of a minister.' Racine reproached Mme de Maintenon who admitted that his disgrace was her fault and said she would make everything all right. 'You never will' he said, sadly, 'because my aunt at Port-Royal, who is even more influential with God than you are with the King, is praying night and day that I shall be chastened.' The aunt won; he was never taken back into favour. He left a wish to be buried at Port-Royal – the courtiers said he would never have been brave enough to have been buried there in his life-time.

Another death, grievous to the King, was that of his body-servant Bontemps at nearly eighty. He had been with him all his life, had been Governor of Versailles for forty years, knew the King's secrets (and those of everybody else) and had been one of the witnesses at his second marriage. Bontemps, too, had a Mme de Maintenon, a woman he lived with who may or may not have been his wife. One of the most powerful men in the land, he never gave himself airs; he spoke his mind to the King like a gruff old nanny and used his influence well. He was succeeded by his son.

Then it was the turn of James II. The King had never shown the nobility of his nature to greater advantage than in his treatment of this sad, charmless cousin during his years of adversity. True, he thought that Kings were different from other people, set aside by their anointing, representatives of God on earth. By honouring King James he was proclaiming his faith in the sacrament of coronation. All the same, he was wonderful to him: he lodged him splendidly, clothed and fed him and all his wretched, plotting, bickering followers; sent him in French ships and with a French army to be beaten in Ireland; gave him and his Queen precedence over everybody at Versailles; allowed him to flaunt the fleur-de-lys on his coat of arms and to touch for King's Evil in his capacity of King of France! Nor did he raise a smile when James clanked into his chapel wearing a sword, drawing it during the Creed, as Defender of the Faith, a post which he said he had inherited from Henry VIII. When Louis XIV had been obliged, for urgent reasons of state, to sign the Peace of Ryswick, which entailed recognizing William of Orange as the English King, he had apologized humbly to James and had more or less said that he had only done so as a matter of form. But his generosity to the 'poor King' on his deathbed went far beyond all this, and led him into making perhaps the most expensive and certainly the strangest mistake of his whole career.

King James had been in church and while the choir was chanting: 'Our inheritance is turned to strangers; the crown is fallen from our head', he fell lifeless to the ground. However he was not dead; he had merely had a stroke from which he recovered enough to go to Bourbon for the waters, accompanied by Fagon, with all expenses paid by Louis. Soon after his return to Saint-Germain-en-Laye he had another stroke, which to the despair of his adoring wife was evidently the beginning of the end. He had two children who would be able to claim the English crown, the Old Pretender, now aged thirteen, and Princess Louise, born in France. Many Englishmen were interested in the boy, and would have been glad to see him acknowledged as heir to William III instead of the uninspiring Anne, with her stupid husband and dead and dying children, but only if he could be educated in England as a Protestant and away from his mother's influence. There was no chance whatever of that.

Louis XIV thought that he must now make up his mind what to do about 'the Prince of Wales'; should he or should he not recognize him as King of England at his father's death? The sensible course, inaction, seems not to have occurred to him: he felt that he must pronounce one way or the other. He called a cabinet meeting at which the ministers were all categorically against recognition. Torcy, his foreign minister, told him that such a step would madden the proud English; and that furthermore, if the child was too obviously the French King's puppet, his cause would be ruined from the start. Louis would have violated the Treaty of Ryswick – and for what? William III was solidly established on his throne; the only people in Europe who questioned the fact were the exiles at Saint-Germain-en-Laye, a pathetic crew, merely concerned with their own prospects. The King had seldom in his reign taken a decision contrary to the unanimous opinion of his Council. Now he paused. He visited his cousin once or twice, always leaving his carriage and walking across the courtyard at Saint-Germain for fear of disturbing the dying man; but he never raised the topic which was uppermost in everybody's mind. Mme de Maintenon meanwhile was working on his feelings day and night. Queen Mary of Modena had become one of her dearest friends; she and King James had never snubbed her like Madame, the Dauphine and nearly all the French royal family. She shared the charming Queen's distress and longed for King James to go in peace. At last Louis heard that his cousin was about to die. He went to Saint-Germain in great state, ordered King James's courtiers to gather round his bed, and then, too late to be much of a comfort to James who was practically unconscious, he announced his decision: 'I come to tell Your Majesty that, whenever it shall please God to take you from us I will be to your son what I have been to you, and will acknowledge him as King of England, Scotland and Ireland'.

Nobody has ever known, because the King as usual never explained, what could have induced him to behave so unwisely. True, the Grand Alliance against him, in view of the Spanish affair, had already been signed; but it is very improbable that the English with their dislike of Continental wars would have implemented it, had they not been infuriated by this unlucky step. The worst fears of Torcy were now to be realized.

The Pope wrote a letter, congratulating Louis on so singular a proof of his piety – that, and the melancholy smiles of Mary of Modena were the only satisfactions he ever had from this decision.

Model of the Ambassador's staircase.

Marble table top showing map of France, 1684.

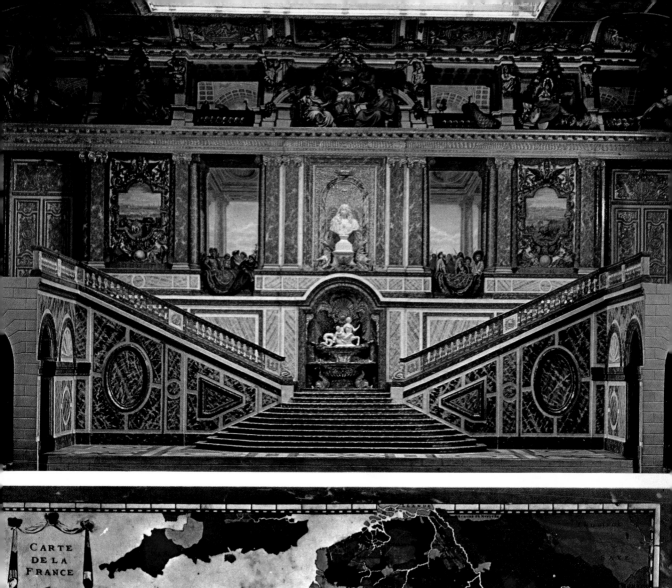

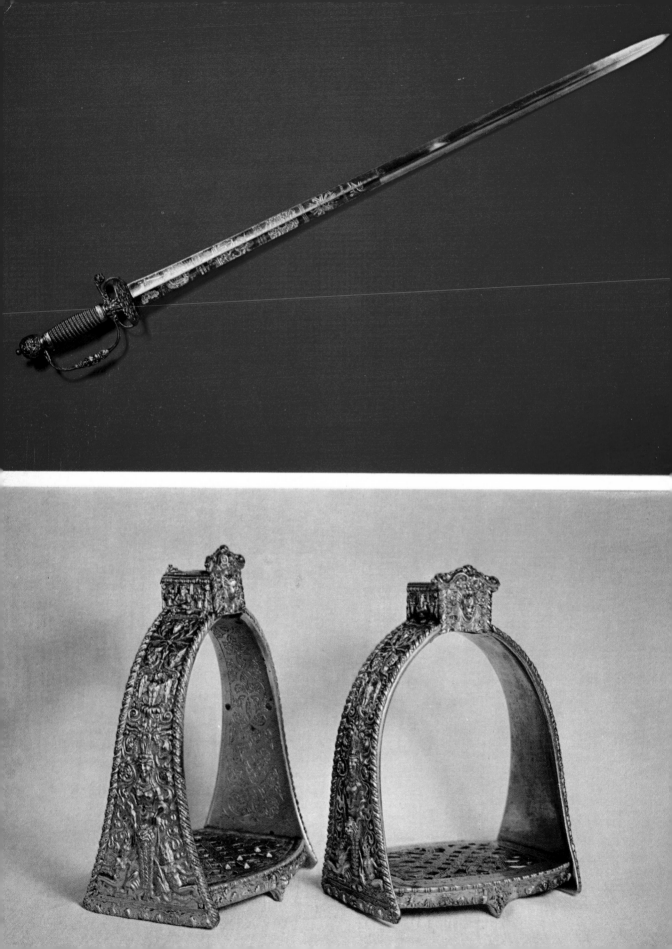

XVIII

MARTIAL NOISES OFF

Du chagrin le plus noir elle écarte les ombres
Et fait des jours sereins de mes jours les plus sombres

RACINE

The War of the Spanish Succession, in which Austria, nearly the whole of Germany, Denmark, Holland and England leagued against France and Spain to dethrone Philip V in favour of the Archduke Charles broke out in 1702. William III, the great animator of the Protestant world, was dead; but his policy was carried on for a while by England under Queen Anne. Like all European wars of those days, it was fought with close relations in the opposing camps – Anne against her half-brother, the Pretender, her other half-brother Berwick and her first cousin once removed Louis XIV; Berwick against his uncle the Duke of Marlborough; the Emperor against his brother-in-law and first cousin Louis XIV; Prince Eugène against his first cousin, the Duc de Vendôme; the Duke of Savoy, once he had changed sides, against both his sons-in-law, Bourgogne and the King of Spain.

For Louis, the news from the front, not too bad at first, was soon punctuated by such desperate defeats as Blenheim, Ramillies, the French retreat from Italy, the fall of Madrid. The large sum of money in his coffers, referred to by Portland, soon melted away. Trade ground to a standstill, the army was expected to perform miracles without pay, without organization, almost without food. Colbert and Louvois might never have existed, their work was so diminished in a few years.

With all this rumbling in the background, life at Versailles went on exactly as usual. A few days after the news of Blenheim there were fêtes at Marly and fireworks at Paris to celebrate the birth of a son to the Duc and Duchesse de Bourgogne. There were continual parties and balls at which the courtiers were encouraged to dress richly and the princesses to sparkle in all their diamonds. The gambling, which Louis XIV had formerly discouraged in war-time, was high because the Duchesse de Bourgogne liked that. The King only put in short appearances, now, at *Appartement*; he was really governing by himself, working nine or ten hours a day. He directed operations at the front, thus making unnecessary difficulties for his generals,

Louis XIV's sword and stirrups.

The Duchesse de Bourgogne
by Jean-Baptiste Santerre, 1709.

who had to wait for a reply when in doubt as to what they were meant to do; he read every one of their dispatches as well as all his ambassadors' reports from foreign capitals; he continually gave audiences.

Most of the work was done in Mme de Maintenon's bedroom. In the evening she would be undressed in front of any minister who happened to be present and put into bed. As the hours went on she sometimes longed for a certain article of bedroom china, and then simply had to wait until the men had gone away. When at last they had said goodnight she used to sigh to her maid, who came to pull the curtains, 'I have only time to tell you that I am done for'. She wrote to the Bishop of Chartres to say that she was extremely tired and to ask whether she might not now refuse to go to bed with the King twice a day: 'These painful occasions' she said, were really too much for her. Godet de Marais replied he would indeed have preferred to see her in the state of virginity of Jesus Christ's wives, but that it was a work of great purity to preserve the King from sins and scandals into which he might fall. Soon, he reminded her, she would be in heaven, able to follow the Lamb.

Both the King and Mme de Maintenon knew that there was somebody at Versailles spying for the English. Mme de Maintenon thought he was probably in an important position at Court. What Sir Winston Churchill calls 'this deadly personage' certainly sent highly coloured accounts of their domestic life to the Duke of Marlborough – his identity remains mysterious.

At Court, now that the King had retired into the wings, the Duchesse de Bourgogne was the star. When she first grew up, she gave every sign of being a deplorable person; she frankly lived for pleasure, was unkind to her husband and to older women, vile to her aunts. She would tease them until they could not help letting out some disagreeable observation upon which she would perform a series of pirouettes: 'I don't care what they think and I shall be their Queen!' She spent half her life in fancy dress as Flora, or a sultana, or an old beggar woman or a dairy maid. When the weather was warm, she bathed in the river and slept in a tent on the bank. Sometimes she was several weeks without seeing the light of day; she would dance all night, go to Paris to sup at Les Halles, then to Mass at St Eustache, back at Versailles in time to kiss the King good morning. Though she had a beautiful body and complexion, and walked like a goddess, her face was really ugly. She cared not a rap. She took no trouble over her appearance, and the other women at Court were amazed to see how quickly she dressed.

The usual staid royal manner was not affected by Marie-Adélaïde; when walking in the park she would take the arm of one lady-in-waiting and dance along preceded by the others, so that, (Madame said, disapprovingly) how could a stranger guess who was in the company? 'It's not like a Court here nowadays'. She describes Marie-Adélaïde 'bounding into my room' to announce the marriage of her brother-in-law, the Duc de Berri, with Madame's grand-daughter; this was such a joy to the old lady that she quite forgave the bounding. Berri was the Duchess's pet, her little page. He spent his life with her and her ladies, winding their wool, running their errands, laughing all the time. Everybody loved him, even Madame, though she could not approve of his *tenue*. Anjou having renounced the French throne when he accepted the Spanish, Berri was next in succession to Bourgogne, but nobody would have thought so by his behaviour. When treated as an important person he was amazed and hardly knew how to respond. He had no notion of etiquette and precedence and fled from ceremonies. He was sent by the King to address the Paris Parlement; when he was on his feet he dried up completely; the President had to come to his rescue; the whole thing was painful. Back at Versailles somebody who had not heard what had happened congratulated him on his speech – the poor fellow burst into tears. His talent was for outdoor sports, he was an excellent rider and an extraordinary shot – he could bring down pheasants with a pistol.

In 1700 Mme du Lude asked permission to enter the King's cabinet during a council of state, and announced that she had seen something at the Duchesse de Bourgogne's toilette which meant that she was now ready to have a child. Bourgogne had fallen furiously in love as soon as they were man and wife, so much so that he embarrassed the bystanders, and Marie-Adélaïde even more. Since he was in every other way remarkably sober, as calm and well behaved as his wife was rampageous, this amorous behaviour surprised everybody. The Duchess often said she was sorry that she made him such an unsuitable wife – he would have done better to have married a Grey Sister. But she never let him see that he loved her more than she loved him. She had various fancies of her own. First there was the Marquis de Nangis, the most fashionable young man at the Court. He, though flattered and touched that she should have singled him out, was in love with one of her ladies, Mme de La Vrillière. In fact he found himself in the same case as the

The Duchesse de Bourgogne with her son the Duc de Bretagne.

Vidame de Chartres in *La Princesse de Clèves* and many of the situations described in that book were re-enacted in real life. After a while the Duchess switched her affections to the Marquis de Maulévrier, a friend of Nangis, and their attachment gave rise to comic scenes worthy of Feydeau. So that he could stay with his love instead of going to the front, Maulévrier pretended to have tuberculosis and to have lost his voice. This also gave him an excuse for whispering into Marie-Adélaïde's ear when they were in company together. Soon, everybody except the King and Bourgogne knew what was going on. Fagon, prompted, most likely, by Mme de Maintenon, took it upon himself to end the affair; he sent for Maulévrier, examined him, shook his old head and pronounced that the only, very slight hope of a cure would be for Maulévrier to go to Spain. Fagon's word was law: to Spain he went. After that the Abbé de Polignac was loved for a while until his superiors sent him to Rome.

The King's adoration for Marie-Adélaïde never altered. She still ran in and out of his room a hundred times a day, as she had done when she was a little girl, and each time had something funny to tell him or found some way of distracting him when he was low. Formerly such a martinet for behaviour, he never scolded her for her fantasies and escapades; when she was not present at his supper table he was sad but not angry. Nanon, Mme de Maintenon's maid, gave the Duchess an enema standing up in front of the fireplace when they were all ready to go to the play. 'What's Nanon doing to you?' said the King and only burst out laughing when he was told. (She held it, says Saint-Simon, all through an Italian comedy.) Louis did once say to Mme de Maintenon 'surely a dinner party, a hunt, a riding party and a banquet are enough for one day without playing cards as well!' He said he would speak to 'those gentlemen her friends'. But he never did speak. His indulgence was remarkable, when it is remembered that his ideal of a woman and a queen was the

A fête at court; a water colour.

exquisitely polished Anne of Austria. He tried to make the Duchess have a day for receiving the ambassadors but seemed not to mind when nothing came of the idea. However on one point he was firm. He insisted that she should communicate five times a year. The courtiers thought this must have been awkward, at her age.

Mme de Maintenon could be quite severe. Once, when the King was out of the room, the Duchess began rummaging about among his papers. Mme de Maintenon told her to stop; she paid no attention. Presently she came across a letter, in which she spied her own name, from Mme d'Espinay, a Princess of Lorraine and great friend of the Dauphin's. 'What's that, Mignonne?' said Mme de Maintenon 'and what's the matter with you?' The Duchess showed her the letter. 'That's what comes of being so curious. One sometimes finds things one doesn't quite like——' then, in a different voice, 'read the whole of it and if you're wise you'll profit by it.' The letter was an hour by hour report of Marie-Adélaïde's doings of the past few days. There was a good deal about Nangis, with many intrigues and imprudences. The Duchess was fit to faint. Then Mme de Maintenon gave her a talking-to which she was not likely to forget. She told her that everybody at Versailles always knew what was going on there and that she, Mme de Maintenon, had reports from all kinds of people on Marie-Adélaïde's behaviour.

Perhaps owing to her flightiness and the fact that she was always over-tired, the Duchesse de Bourgogne only had her first baby in 1704. He died a few months later. The parents behaved beautifully – she, good and resigned, while the Duke, like Abraham, offered up his son as a sacrifice. The King, though sadly disappointed, tried to be pleased for the sake of the child, now in eternal bliss. By degrees, as she grew older, Marie-Adélaïde's nature changed. Public and private·misfortunes sobered her. When her father betrayed his French allies she was perfectly dignified, considering herself as a Frenchwoman, while never forgetting the country she still loved, though she had left it at the age of twelve. From having been indifferent to the point of disliking her husband, she became a devoted wife. She rallied fiercely to him when he had a period of bad luck. True, she was always a tease. Once she told Mme de La Vrillière to get into her bed and then said to Bourgogne that she was sleepy. As he loved going to bed early and she never would, he was delighted – went off to undress in a hurry – came into her room where she was out of sight. 'Where is Madame?' 'Here I am' she said, as though in bed. He threw off his dressing-gown and jumped in. Up came the Duchess. 'What is all this? You're for ever pretending to be such a saint and now I find you in bed with the most beautiful woman in France!' Bourgogne threw himself on Mme de La Vrillière and beat her, so that she had to flee without her slippers.

The Duchess is easy to know, neither her virtues nor her vices surprise us. But her husband is one of those historical enigmas, an heir to a throne who died too soon to succeed. How would he have turned out? From the Black Prince onward such young

　　　　　　　The Duc de Bourgogne by Hyacinthe Rigaud, 1703.

men have generally had a good press. Some of Bourgogne's contemporaries thought that he was going to be a perfect King, a second St Louis. As a small child he was exceptionally violent and naughty; he could not bear to be thwarted; had been known to break a clock when the hour struck for him to do something that bored him; would scream at the rain if it stopped him from going out. He was very unkind about people, shrewd in knowing their weak points. After Fénelon had taken charge of him he changed amazingly, becoming as good as gold. He himself put this down to religion and indeed the turning point seems to have been his first communion. He was brought up by Fénelon and Beauvilliers like a monk, with little knowledge of the world or of how to behave in polite society. He never realized, until Madame told him, that he had a German mother. People noted with amazement that he knew the geography of France better than that of the forests round Versailles. Indeed, he did not care for hunting. He went about the Court with a melancholy and disapproving air, letting the courtiers see that he regarded them as so many lost souls. When he went to Paris it was not for pleasure and amusement but to see a man's brain dissected or to hear a thesis at the Sorbonne. He was for ever at Holy Communion, dressed in his robes of the Saint Esprit to do honour to the Sacrament. He knew Latin and was fond of history – he told the Abbé de Choisy that he had read his life of Charles V (of France) several times. When Choisy was engaged on his next book, *Charles VI*, he asked him, in a disingenuous way, how he would manage to convey the fact that Charles VI was mad? 'Monseigneur, I shall say that he was mad.'

When Bourgogne was sixteen, Anjou fifteen and Berri thirteen, 'Spanheim summed up the characters of the brothers and the Duchesse de Bourgogne thus:

> Bourgogne, a masterpiece. Delicate health. Very gay but not very chatty. Loves to study science, languages, philosophy, mathematics and history ancient and modern. Excellent memory. Never cared for games even as a child. Rather proud and intimidating.
> Anjou, sweeter nature and also a clever boy. People prefer him to Bourgogne.
> Berri, very chatty, lively and full of promise.
> Duchesse de Bourgogne. Sharp and spiteful. Hates Mme du Lude and makes her life a burden. She and Bourgogne completely indifferent to each other. Servile to Mme de Maintenon.

Bourgogne's letters show an amazing piety, they could have been written by a Victorian clergyman; they have no spark of the originality, gift for language and nobility which inform every one of his grandfather's utterances. He greatly disapproved of his father. When the latter nearly died from eating too much fish, Bourgogne hoped that God would take advantage of this illness to make him lead a better life in future. The Duchess fell ill; he wondered what he had done to displease the Almighty; when she got better he made all sorts of good resolutions. He had a faithful, affectionate nature; he never forgot Fénelon though he hardly saw him

The Duchesse de Bourgogne dressed for hunting, by Pierre Gobert.

Overleaf: Louis XIV, with the Grand Dauphin, the Duc de Bourgogne and (supposedly) his second son, and the Duchesse de Ventadour by Nicolas de Largillière.

again after the disgrace (once or twice on his way to the front); he loved his brothers very much and worshipped his wife. Physically he was far from attractive, thin from too much fasting, short, almost hump-backed, often ill. At that time it seemed unlikely that he would make a great King of France. However, Louis XIV placed high hopes on him and admitted him to his Council when hardly out of his teens.

Mme de Montespan, who had been melancholy ever since the death in 1704 of Mme de Fontevrault, died herself in 1707, while taking the waters at Bourbon. She had a fainting fit, was given an emetic and expired a day or two later, calmly, religiously and without fear. The King was told the news at Marly as he was going out hunting; he showed no sign of emotion but, after he had killed his stag, he went for a walk alone. When he returned to the château the Duchesse de Bourgogne asked him whether he felt sad; he replied that he had regarded Mme de Montespan as a dead person from the moment she left Versailles. But Mme de Maintenon hid herself in her privy and wept bitterly.

In 1708, the King thought it time for Bourgogne to take part in the war. He had been to the front with Tallart in 1702 and 1703, but had seen little fighting, merely some camping out and the siege of a small town which had soon fallen. Luckily for him he had stayed at home in 1704 to be with the Duchess when her baby was born, so he had not seen Tallart losing the battle of Blenheim. The Marshal's son had been killed beside him and he himself languished in prison at Nottingham for the next seven years.

Berri was to go with his brother and so was the 'Chevalier de Saint-George', the Old Pretender. These young men had never done any soldiering at all. The three of them were put in charge of the Duc de Vendôme, a great-nephew of Mazarin and a left-handed grandson of Henri IV. Vendôme was very friendly with du Maine, who supported him up to the hilt in order to give an air of importance to the whole species of bastards and who arranged for him to marry the ugliest of M. le Duc's sisters. Saint-Simon said one would have to be very ambitious to marry Mlle d'Enghien, and very brave to marry M. de Vendôme, whose nose was quite eaten away by syphilis. Vendôme was disgusting and, at the age of fifty-four he looked like an old, fat, dirty, diseased woman. He was one of the King's most unaccountable favourites – he treated Louis XIV as nobody else dared to. When they were in the middle of working out the campaign of 1708 Vendôme suddenly left Versailles to go and amuse himself with the financier Crozat and only came back again when it suited him, in spite of urgent messages from the King.

He was enormously rich; his country seat was the Château of Anet; the King bought his town house and built the Place Vendôme on its site.

At the front Vendôme paraded gluttony, sloth, sodomy, and practically all the deadly sins - and amused the soldiers, who adored him. They deserved a little amusement; their lot had never been so hard in any of the King's wars, owing to the

Louis-Joseph de Bourbon, Duc de Vendôme, 1707.

constant breakdown of staff arrangements. Louis XIV thought that Vendôme was his best general; he was a born leader but he had one grave failing. He was too fond of entering the thick of the fight and leaving the operations to take care of themselves. The holy set at Versailles said that God would never bestow victory on one so wicked. Vendôme got to hear of this and observed that he did not imagine that Marlborough went to Church much more than he did. Incredible as it may seem, the King hoped that the presence of Bourgogne would check the licentiousness of this hardened old fellow, who was to be nominally under his orders.

The campaign was a disaster in every way. Bourgogne had no soldierly qualities, he was too sensitive and took no pleasure in the fighting. The cruelty with which Vendôme's soldiers treated the peasants, destroying their crops and raping their daughters, appalled him almost more than the horrors of the battlefield. He soon had only one idea – to stop the whole thing. The officers who were put to look after him also had only one – to bring him back alive. Unfortunately all this was well known at Versailles, so that after Eugène and Marlborough had carried off the great battle of Oudenarde, Vendôme was believed when he said that it had all been the fault of Bourgogne. According to Vendôme's dispatches, night had fallen upon an indecisive field; he intended to stay upon his positions, when he could easily have won the battle the next day; but Bourgogne had insisted upon a retreat. In truth, the French army was beaten and on the run and Vendôme alone was responsible. He had disobeyed strict orders from Versailles and (in the words of Sir Winston Churchill) 'embarked upon the one thing the Great King had always forbidden, an infantry battle in broken and enclosed country.' He had then indulged his love of hand-to-hand fighting, 'crashing about like an enraged animal' instead of remaining at the post of command. Back at his headquarters, after dark, he pretended to think that the soldiers could be rallied to begin again; his officers told him that if he stayed he would be alone upon the field; there was no alternative to a retreat. 'Very well, gentlemen, I see that your minds are made up; so we shall have to retire. As for you, Monseigneur,' he said, staring with bloodshot eyes at Bourgogne, 'you have wanted this for a long time!' Such words, addressed to the eventual heir to the throne, amounted to high treason: the bystanders waited for Bourgogne to order his arrest. But he said nothing, merely looked very sad – and was despised for it. He told Beauvilliers afterwards that he had offered up his deep humiliation as a sacrifice to God. Some of the officers wanted to carry the three princes to a safe place in a coach, escorted by five hundred soldiers, but Vendôme rightly said that this would be too shameful, so finally they rode off the field, while Nangis fought a brilliant rearguard action. Vendôme made straight for Ghent where he fell into bed and slept for thirty hours without bothering to find out what had become of his army. After this *débâcle*, he subsided into a sulky lethargy and left Bourgogne in full control. The young man lost Lille and other towns, entirely by his own fault – after much wavering he generally took an unlucky decision. One of his officers, exasperated, said 'I don't know if you will have the Kingdom in Heaven but as to an earthly one, Prince Eugène sets about it better than you do'.

Meanwhile the King continued his usual existence. Only once was a look of anxiety (*son visage altéré*) noticed on his face. He went out hunting all day, to the despair of the courtiers because the post bags from the front were only opened at his return. Nearly all had loved ones in the army, and it may be imagined how feverishly they longed for letters. In the raging controversy which followed this fatal campaign most people took Vendôme's side. Unfortunately Bourgogne had given the impression of not caring for the outcome: he never looked worried when things went badly, and instead of concentrating on military problems he was often on the tennis court or in church. Even Fénelon said that he had paid too much attention to his confessor, who ought not to have interfered with the conduct of the war. On his return to Versailles and his beloved wife, he was altogether too cheerful and carefree for one whose army had suffered such dire reverses. Mme la Duchesse, now thoroughly embittered by the treatment of her love, the Prince de Conti (still unemployed), wrote an unkind poem about Bourgogne which went the rounds, and was not the only one. The King, much affected by the loss of Lille, talked of going in person to win it back the following summer. One of the fine traits of his character was his generosity to subordinates when things went wrong. He never blamed his generals. He had written and condoled with Tallart for losing the battle of Blenheim and for the death of his son; when Tallart finally returned from England, looking very old, he made him a duke. After Ramillies, all he said to the defeated Villeroy was: 'at our age, M. le Maréchal, one is not lucky'. He now received both Bourgogne and Vendôme most kindly, though a few weeks later, on the insistence of Marie-Adélaïde, Vendôme had a short disgrace, was removed from

Père Tellier.

Flanders and sent to the Spanish front, where he succeeded brilliantly. Bourgogne never went to the wars again. But there was one good result of all this: the Duchesse de Bourgogne, vehemently on her husband's side, was shaken out of her futile existence and began to show the stuff she was made of.

The next year, 1709, was perhaps the most terrible that France has ever known. On 12 January the cold came down. In four days the Seine, all the rivers and the sea on the Atlantic coast were frozen solid. The frost lasted for two months, then there was a complete thaw; as soon as the snow which had hitherto afforded some protection to the land, melted away, the frost began again, as hard as ever. The winter wheat, of course, was killed, so were the fruit, olive and walnut trees and nearly all the vines; the rabbits froze in their burrows; the beasts of the field died like flies. The fate of the poor was terrible and the rich at Versailles were not to be envied – the fires which roared up the chimneys night and day hardly altered the temperature of the enormous rooms; spirits froze on the very chimney-pieces. The Princesse de Soubise died of cold at sixty-one and so did Père de La Chaise.

He had long been failing and had often asked to retire but the King insisted on keeping him, until he was more like a corpse than a man, with no memory or judgment left. He was succeeded by Père Tellier, a Jesuit, who came to be loathed so much so that he was perhaps chiefly responsible for the expulsion of his Order from France. A sort of Rasputin, with ardent, black eyes in a false, terrible face, ignorant and wildly ambitious, he was a peasant and boasted of it to the King, who was unimpressed since in his eyes the peasantry and the bourgeoisie rated exactly the same – the only non-royal people slightly superior, in his eyes, to the rank and file of his subjects, were dukes. Fagon, who witnessed the first interview between the King and his new confessor, said 'What a bird of prey – I wouldn't care to meet him on a dark night. The public which has forgiven the King all his mistresses will never

Detail from the choir stalls at Notre Dame.

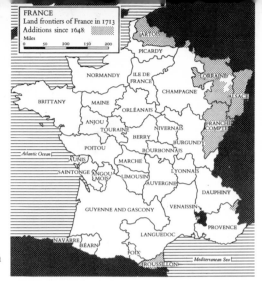

Samuel Bernard.

The frontiers of France in 1713.

forgive him this confessor'. Dear old Père de La Chaise was regretted by everybody; this sinister figure was ever at the King's elbow. He made his influence felt pretty soon be sending the twenty-two holy women, who were all that were left at Port-Royal, to other convents. A few months later, in 1710, the convent buildings of Port-Royal were destroyed and the graveyard was desecrated. Louis XIV hesitated a good long time before taking such violent action. Tellier told him that the convent was a nest of republicanism and this dreaded word may have decided him. He had much better have left the dying sect alone. The pointless persecution – especially the violated tombs of holy and famous people – only gave it an impetus. Jansenists attributed the King's family tragedies of the next two years to this deed; but the King probably thought that the victory of Denain was his just reward for it.★

On 21 February the Prince de Conti died, at forty-five, to the intense grief of nearly all Frenchmen except the King, M. le Duc and the Duc du Maine. His death was particularly poignant because the King, despairing of his generals, had at last decided to put Conti in command of an army. The news came too late, and indeed only served to make his last days even sadder by giving him an intense desire for life. Conti had some obscure digestive trouble; he lived for a time on milk but finally could no longer swallow anything. His old friend the Dauphin having infuriated the Parisians by driving past the Hôtel de Conti to go to the Opéra while his cousin was receiving the last rites, was told of his death as he was setting out for the hunt. He made no observation and galloped off; but who knows what memories of childhood and youth may have passed through his fair head as he followed his hounds up and down the icy glades that day? (Like his grandson, Louis XV, he hunted whatever

★ However, the excellent appointment of Bishop Fleury to be tutor of Louis XV, is to the credit of Père Tellier.

the weather, taking no account of the horses' legs). Mme la Duchesse concealed her grief as best she could and decided to be a perfect wife to M. le Duc, possibly because she knew she could never love again or possibly from ambition, since M. le Duc was bound to become an important personage at the death of the King. But the tiny fellow himself died a year later, making horrible faces. He had become terrifyingly mad, and was found to have a tumour on the brain. A son and a daughter of Mme la Duchesse eventually married a daughter and a son of the Prince de Conti; they are among the ancestors of the present French pretender.

As the winter dragged on there was a shortage of bread in Paris; after several bad riots a mob of women set out for Versailles. Louis XIV had them stopped at Sèvres and escorted back to Paris by the army. The Venetian ambassador wrote home to say that the King had better make peace, because the French nation had no stomach for defeat and privation and soon he would not be safe in his own house. (All the same, the King's personality was such that a revolution in his lifetime would have been unthinkable.) The conversation at Versailles was of nothing but wheat, oats and barley; and Mme de Maintenon was suspected by her enemies of speculating in these commodities – without a scrap of evidence. No doubt some people really did so though on the whole there was a wave of solidarity in the land and the little that could be done, was done for the poor. Saint-Cyr, for example, was put on to reduced rations, and the surplus distributed.

Horrible stories went the rounds, for instance, of starving children found by a magistrate huddling under the body of their father, who had hanged himself. People stayed indoors sooner than see the faces in the street, black with hunger. Public and private finances were in a desperate way; the currency lost a third of its value in a few months; the famous financier Samuel Bernard was declared bankrupt, in spite of backing from the exchequer. The King asked people to give up their silver, either to send it as a loan to his goldsmith, M. de Launay, or to sell it to the mint. Launay was to keep a list and when times improved the King would give back the weight of the metal and the permission (which in those days was always required) to make it up. In short it would be an advantage to the lender, since eventually he would have silver of the very latest style. Only about a hundred sent to Launay; more sold outright, especially dirty old family silver which was out of fashion. Many bought pottery and used it ostentatiously while hiding their silver. The King himself melted his gold plate and ate off silver gilt. He made a few other economies: indeed he was obliged to – he did not know where to turn for cash. He seemed completely unmoved, and declared that the balls and parties must go on as usual. But the Duchesse de Bourgogne, plunged in sadness, put a stop to them.

Mansart's beautiful chapel at Versailles was practically finished and the King went every day to see Coypel painting the ceiling. Mme de Maintenon, who never thought that Versailles would survive Louis XIV, and who cared not a rap for works of art, did her best to stop any more expenditure on the house and especially on this chapel, but fortunately she was not heeded. It is rather a pity that the famous sermons of the reign were preached either in one of the two temporary chapels at Versailles or at Saint-Germain-en-Laye, so that the visitor to the existing chapel cannot conjure up Bossuet, pointing at Louise de La Vallière, fit to sink through the floor, and booming out: *Vide hanc mulierem!*, or preaching the great funeral orations on Henrietta of England and Condé. Or Massillon: 'It's not the sovereign but the law, Sire, which must reign over the people; you are only the Prime Minister.' Or Mascaron, bravest of all: 'A conqueror is no better than a thief.' And it was not here that the King frowned furiously at giggling courtiers, to double up himself with laughter when the joke was repeated to him after the service; nor here that some wag gave out that His Majesty would not be coming to evensong, so that when he did he was amazed to find exactly three people in the congregation. This chapel only served for the five, sad last years of his life. Mr Dunlop, in his book on Versailles, says quite rightly that the tour of the château ought to end, instead of beginning, with the chapel. Its plain white stone purposely affords a contrast with the gilded bronze and coloured marbles of the state rooms; it is of Gothic inspiration, calm and religious. One hopes that the King found comfort there in the trials that lay ahead.

After the appalling winter of 1709, Louis XIV realized that he must sue for peace. Having made various preliminary moves, he was still negotiating when the season for resuming hostilities opened with the indecisive battle of Malplaquet and the loss of Mons. The Grand Alliance, thinking that France was beaten to her knees, proposed terms of unexampled severity which the King felt obliged to accept. But then they went too far. It was not enough that Louis XIV should give up Alsace, destroy the fortifications of his frontier cities, including Dunkirk, give Lille, Tournai, Ypres, Menin, Furnes, Condé and Mauberge to the Dutch, and recognize the Archduke Charles as King of Spain. They also insisted that the French Army should be used to chase Philip V off his throne. When this was explained to the King he said 'Since I must go on fighting I would rather it were against my enemies than my grandchildren'. Then he appealed to his people. The Allied demands were sent to the governors of all his provinces and published in the churches. The result was an extraordinary upsurge of patriotism; men flocked to the colours. The Spaniards, too, were still fighting like demons for Philip – heroes of resistance, said the French; a rascally foot militia, said General Stanhope. Feeling that both he and his grandson had the moral support of their subjects, Louis XIV decided to continue the war. His courage was to be amply rewarded.

The Salon d'Or in the Comte de Toulouse's Paris house (now the Banque de France).

XIX

THREE IN ELEVEN MONTHS

Me sera–t–il permis d'ouvrir un tombeau
devant la cour?

BOSSUET

For half a century Frenchmen had assumed that, at the death of Louis XIV, they would be governed by the Grand Dauphin. In 1711 the King, though in excellent health, was over seventy while his son, though no longer young, had hardly ever known a day's illness. The Dauphin's heir was a young man with two brothers and two little boys of his own. Louis used to say that the succession to the French throne had not been so well assured for hundreds of years. The schemers and plotters who always surround pinnacles of power were divided into two factions, looking either to the Dauphin or to Bourgogne. It was not possible to be well with both of them: the two men disliked each other to such a point that the Dauphin's entourage had taken Vendôme's side after Oudenarde. Those who paid their court to the father had an eye on the immediate future, whereas the son stood for the present, through his wife's influence over Louis XIV, and the more distant future when he would reign. In a way this seemed the better investment, especially as the Dauphin led a curiously enclosed life, mostly at Meudon, into which it was not easy to penetrate. His companions were his wife Mlle de Choin, fatter and squashier than ever, and his two sisters, the once beautiful Princesse de Conti and the ever adorable Mme la Duchesse. Even among his intimates the Dauphin spoke so little that it seemed as if he counted his words, only allowing himself a limited number – impossible to tell if he were pleased or displeased or how much or how little he knew of public events. He certainly knew what went on in the countryside, and though so submissive and timid with the King he was among those few who dared to broach the unpopular topic of the peasant and his dreadful lot. He got a resounding snub for his pains. His servants were devoted to him and so were his two younger sons. Mlle de Choin must have loved him since she got no advantage whatever from her position except that of sitting in an armchair, when the Duchesse de Bourgogne only had a footstool at Meudon, and referring to her as *la Duchesse* instead of *Mme la Duchesse de Bourgogne*.

The Chapel.

Mlle de Choin was not interested in politics, dressed like a poor person and did not own a carriage; she used to go from Paris to rejoin the Dauphin at Meudon, when he had been absent, in a hackney cab. She slept in the state bedroom next to his but when the King visited Meudon she was relegated to an *entresol*. She and Mme de Maintenon (the two sultanas as Saint-Simon called them) were on pretty good terms. But Mme de Maintenon despised the Meudon set and was very much afraid that Mme la Duchesse would take the Duchesse de Bourgogne's rightful place when the Dauphin succeeded to the throne.

The speculations, cabals and intrigues round father and son, which occupied the Court for years and gave Saint-Simon material for some of his most telling pages, represented a total waste of time. In 1711 the Grand Dauphin fell ill with smallpox, at Meudon. He held his own and presently seemed to be out of the wood. Saint-Simon describes a conversation he had with the Duchesse d'Orléans when the news from Meudon was much better. Both he and she were against the Dauphin; he admired Bourgogne and she was jealous of her sister Mme la Duchesse. In the same funny, languishing family voice, in which her mother once told Mme Voisin that she only had time for one black mass, the Duchesse d'Orléans said it really was bad luck that the Dauphin, at his age (fifty-three) and fat as he was, seemed to be getting over such a dangerous illness – those wretched doctors were so careful not to forget the smallest little remedy that he could hardly help recovering. One might have hoped for a nice apoplexy but there – unfortunately he had been following a strict diet for the last year or so. In short, it looked as if they had better make up their minds to a long life and reign for their enemy. While they were going on like this at Versailles, the Dauphin's heart, strained by constant blood-letting and purges, gave way and he died so suddenly that he only just had time to receive absolution from a *curé* who had happened to look in.

The King, who had been at Meudon from the beginning of the illness, was having his supper. He was stunned by the unexpected news and ran to his son's room, but the Princesse de Conti and Mme la Duchesse, who had done the nursing, forcibly prevented him from going in. When he knew for certain that all was over, he sent word to Versailles that he would go to Marly and would like to have a word with the Duchesse de Bourgogne if she would meet him in the town on his way through. The news of the death went round Versailles like lightning; and, with a curious, instinctive, crowd movement and the terrible noise of a stampede, the courtiers ran from all over the château to the Bourgognes' apartment. The Duchess, whose face gave nothing away, picked up a shawl and went down the Queen's staircase to her coach. She sat in it between the two stables and had not long to wait before the King arrived; she got down and was going to him when Mme de Maintenon put her head out of the window, crying 'What are you doing, Madame? Don't come near us, we are infectious.' So Marie-Adélaïde went back to the château. She found

Meudon: engraving by Le Pautre
after Mariette.

her husband, with the Berris, as she had left them, seated most uncomfortably in
the middle of a huge, curious crowd. Berri, who was truly sad, was crying and
sobbing. Bourgogne, white as a sheet, put on no false sentiments, but was visibly
shaken to find himself suddenly so near the throne. Husband and wife whispered
together for a long time. The Duc d'Orléans cried like anything, and when Saint-
Simon asked him why, since he and the Dauphin had long been estranged, he said,
almost apologetically, that the Dauphin was a good man whom he had known all
his life – perhaps his grief would not last long but he was his first cousin, blood was
thicker than water and he felt the sorrow in his bowels. Madame, dressed up as for a
party (she had not got a dressing-gown), and looking very odd since everybody
else was in *déshabillé*, was howling at the top of her voice. The Duc de Beauvilliers,
cold and impassive, stood by the Dauphin's two sons keeping the crowd at a certain
distance. This extraordinary scene went on from midnight until 7 a.m. when
Beauvilliers said it was time to go to bed and they all retired, but only for an hour
or two.

The next day the Bourgognes went to join the King at Marly where precautions
against infection had been taken – those who came from Meudon had changed
their clothes and herbs were burnt all over the house. The saddest person there was
the Princesse de Conti; she fell so ill with sorrow that she had to be confessed. The
King went to her bedroom, where he had not been for a long time as it was up a
steep staircase; he noticed that various improvements would make it more
comfortable and these were soon put in hand. For many years the Dauphin had not
been specially nice to Marie-Anne: she had had to swallow the pill of his marrying
a woman she had dismissed from her own household, and Mme la Duchesse had
managed to make her feel out of it. But she was a faithful soul, possibly rather
thick-skinned, like her mother, to whom she had always been so good and who had

227

died some months before the Dauphin. Marie-Anne had done her best to make the King go and say goodbye to his old love but Mme de Maintenon would not allow it. She went herself, instead.

Mme la Duchesse was in despair, but her tears were more for her lover than for her brother. The tragedy of Conti's death was harder to bear than ever, now that, having lost the Dauphin and on bad terms with the Bourgognes, she found herself a lone widow with many young children and no protector. Had Conti lived, and done well at the war as he surely would have, she would have shared in his glory and had a solid support to lean on. She had always been his permanent attachment; he loved her deeply in spite of many other affairs both natural and unnatural; and he was her only love. As things had turned out she was almost inclined to regret M. le Duc, terrifying though he was at the end of his life. However, Mme la Duchesse was not made for sorrow and soon put it from her. She took up with a monkey-faced Marquis de Lassay and lived with him, quite openly after the death of her father, for another thirty years. Mlle de Choin lived until 1730. The Dauphin had once shown her a will he had made leaving her a huge fortune, but she had torn it up saying that if he was there she needed nothing, if she lost him a tiny income would suffice. The King saw to it that she was comfortably off. Her widowhood was spent modestly, she was given over to good works and saw her friends but eschewed society.

The Duc de Bourgogne was now the Dauphin. His father's death changed him amazingly; he lost his shyness and his disapproving look and became affable and easy. He attended all the Councils, received ministers and generals and prepared himself for the huge destiny which lay ahead. He had none of the faults which older people thought typical of his generation; he was grave and virtuous; not a pleasure-seeker; polite to everybody, and unlike his grandfather he understood the gradations of rank in the French aristocracy. He became popular with the notables, a popularity which soon spread to all sections of the community. Oudenarde and Lille were forgotten; Bourgogne, his fascinating wife and pretty little boys were placed on a pedestal and almost worshipped. This current of feeling reacted on the King himself who, for the first time in his life, began to delegate a substantial part of his work. The ministers were encouraged to meet in the Dauphin's apartment; he was informed of everything that happened. He went to Paris, where the King had not set foot for four years, and was enthusiastically received there.

The new Dauphine had become quite staid and dignified; she began to hold a court in her own apartment instead of dashing here and there for her amusements. Mme de Maintenon wrote: 'After having been preached at for bringing her up badly and blamed by everybody for her flightiness, after having seen her hated at the Court because she would not talk to people, after having known that she was accused of horrible dissimulation on account of her attachment to the King and the goodness with which she honoured me, I now find that everybody sings her praises'.

Although the King showed a new side to Bourgogne, age had done nothing to soften him towards other people. When he was preparing to go to Fontainebleau in 1711 two members of his family were in no condition to follow him there. The Duchesse de Berri was expecting her first baby, ill all the time. The doctors said she must be kept quiet and that it would be madness for her to go to Fontainebleau. Neither the little girl herself nor her father the Duc d'Orléans dared speak to the King about it. Berri tremblingly put in a word and had his head bitten off. Madame and Mme de Maintenon had the humanity to speak up, although neither of them liked the Duchess. The King merely became angry – said she must go and that was that. She was sent by boat in order to avoid the vibration of a coach. Unluckily the boat ran into the foundations of a bridge and snapped in two – the Duchess was badly shaken; immediately gave birth to a dead daughter, and never thereafter had a child which lived more than a few months. (Most of her babies were still-born.) The King remarked that as the baby was only a female no great harm was done. Almost worse, he forced the Comte de Toulouse, in frightful agony from stone, to go to Fontainebleau, also against medical insistence. Both these young people were so ill that the King hardly saw them during the whole visit.

The transformation of character which we have seen in the Duc de Bourgogne and his wife often happens with ardent and very personal young creatures, when they have found their place in the world. He was happy in his work and she with her babies: it now seemed that when the old King disappeared his realm would be in excellent hands. The events of February 1712 are almost too heartrending to relate.

In 1711 the Court had been away from Versailles for several months on account of smallpox there; hardly had the King returned than people began to go down with measles. During a long comfortable chat with two of her ladies, the Dauphine had been saying that many people had died at Versailles since she first came there fourteen years ago. How strange to be old and find oneself with hardly any contemporaries with whom one could talk about the past. Already she was twenty-six and she felt that her youth had gone! Soon after this she caught measles. She had always been delicate, had had three children and six miscarriages, and had never led a reasonable life. The first day or two of her illness she got up, feeling wretched, then she was put to bed; nine doctors came, gave her emetics and bled her. Madame was beside herself when she saw what was going on, and at last she burst out, imploring them to let the Dauphine alone. Mme de Maintenon sharply rebuked her for this impiety in medicine and told her to mind her own business. Presently Marie-Adélaïde was advised to confess. Although she felt very miserable she was surprised to learn that her condition was thought to be so desperate. Her Jesuit confessor came

Mausolée pour la Cérémonie ... funèbre de tres haut et tres puissa ...
...nce, Loüis de Bourbon, Duc de ... Bourgogne, Dauphin de Fran...
...edé le 18. Fevrier 1712. et de tres ... haut et tres puissant Princ...

Duchesse de Ventadour; engraving.

but she hesitated. He was a good, understanding sort of man; he saw at once that she did not want to confess to him – asked her if this was so, and when she said 'yes' asked whom he should send for. She said she would rather not have a Jesuit and named a priest from the Versailles parish church; he could not be found so another was brought, to whom she made a very long confession. The stupefaction at Court when all this became known may be imagined. There has never been an explanation: some thought it was because the Jesuits were too strict, others because they were not strict enough – in any case Marie-Adélaïde was known not to like them. Her sister, the Queen of Spain, did exactly the same thing when she died two years later.

'You are going to God, Madame' said Mme de Maintenon. 'Yes, aunt' she said, obediently swallowing two more glasses of emetic.

'Goodbye, beautiful Duchess' she said to Mme de Guiche. 'Today Dauphine and tomorrow nothing.' It was too true.

The grief of the King and his old wife was terrible; she had been the joy of their existence. In their panic and misery they seem not to have noticed that the heart-broken husband was also very ill. The King fled to Marly and the Dauphin was persuaded to follow him there; his gentlemen dreaded that he might hear sinister noises coming from his wife's room. When the King saw him he was struck by his look and most lovingly urged him to go to bed. He did so and never rose again. 'I die with joy' he said – suffered horribly and said he knew now what his poor darling had had to endure.

Their two children caught the illness. Somebody addressed the elder boy, who was five, as 'M. le Dauphin'. 'Don't' said the child, 'it's too sad!' The doctors then dispatched him into the next world: three Dauphins of France had died in eleven months. As for the younger boy, his governess, the Duchesse de Ventadour, was determined not to let the doctors near him. While they concentrated on his brother,

The mourning catafalque for the Duc and Duchesse de Bourgogne.

François de Neufville, Duc de Villeroy;
engraving.

she took him to her own room, pretended that he was quite well, put him back to breast feeding, although he was two, kept him warm and saved his life.

Although five hundred people in Paris and several at Versailles died of measles with the same symptoms as those of the princes, there was much hysterical talk of poisoning. Madame, who never let a death go by without crying poison found herself hoist with her own petard, because the culprit this time was supposed to be the Duc d'Orléans, and his motive, to put the Duchesse de Berri on the throne. He was thought to be carrying on an incestuous love affair with her: certainly he loved her more than anybody, and the Duchesse d'Orléans and the Duc de Berri were furiously jealous of the relationship. One might believe that the Duchesse de Berri was a poisoner – she was a pathetic, mad little person – but her father was incapable of such a crime. The worst thing old Fagon ever did was to try and arouse the King's suspicions against Orléans – probably in order to excuse his own incompetence. Father, mother and son, all sent to Saint-Denis in the same hearse, was quite a good score even for those days. But the King, greatly as he had always disliked his nephew and son-in-law, knew him well enough to be certain of his innocence and as, many years ago, he had defended Monsieur from the same accusation, now he defended Orléans. The bodies were opened with the usual horrifying ceremonial, and the surgeon Mareschal, who was present, asserted that there was not a trace of poison.

Nobody expected the new little Dauphin to live; for years he was a particularly delicate child, although he grew up to be very strong. The next heir, Philip V, was told that he must choose between Spain and France and chose Spain, though with many a mental reservation. France was his love and he never ceased to pine for his native land. So the future Regent and probably the future King seemed to be Berri whom nobody had bothered to educate. He and Louis XIV had nothing whatever

Louis-Auguste de Bourbon, Duc du Maine; engraving.

Claude-Louis-Hector, Duc de Villars, Maréchal de France, after Rigaud.

in common, and the King could hardly bear the sight of his Duchess. However the two young people pulled themselves together and made a real effort. Berri began to attend Councils; he was not very clever but made up for it by his extreme sweetness – everybody loved him. His wife held a Court and did all she could, quite honestly, to take the place of Marie-Adélaïde. In 1713 she was pregnant. At seven months the water broke and three days later, after a shattering confinement, she had a boy, born alive. Mme de Maintenon said that everybody who saw Berri at this time seemed to have been born at seven months, and to have known hundreds of healthy people born several days after their mother's water had broken. But the baby died.

Louis XIV was now not only sad but also bored. Mme de Maintenon, to try and amuse him, brought two old, long neglected friends back into his little circle: Madame twice descended from William the Silent, was, like William himself, a wonderful chatterbox and sometimes succeeded in making the King smile, and the Maréchal de Villeroy, who had lost many a battle but was a jolly soul and had been brought up with the King; (the courtiers used to say that Villeroy was irresistible to women but not to the enemy). The three of them gossiped about days long ago and tried to forget the dreadful present. The King gave up his efforts to keep the courtiers amused and busy; the evening parties had stopped; the iron discipline of every hour relaxed. Both Madame and Mme de Maintenon said, in all their letters, this is no longer a Court. Mme de Maintenon: 'We have no more Court here. Madame is not well and very low; Mme la Duchesse de Berri still has a temperature; Mme la Duchesse d'Orléans is down with every sort of affliction; Mme la Duchesse is always whining for favours; Mme la Princesse de Conti is lazy, hardly ever leaves her room, seems unwell and doesn't bother to be elegant any more; other members of the royal family are never at Versailles; in short I have nothing good to tell you except the King's wonderful health and courage.' Versailles was only inhabited by the old; it had become unfashionable and the smart set escaped to Paris, which hummed with pleasure and vice. The Princesse de Conti, the Comte de Toulouse and the Duc d'Antin all bought themselves houses there; this would have been out of the question formerly and was considered an interesting sign of the times.

The only person who really managed to amuse Louis XIV was the Duc du Maine who now resumed his position of prime favourite from which he had been ousted by Marie-Adélaïde, ever since her arrival in France. He was in and out of his father's room as much as he used to be. The old King, pushed by Mme de Maintenon, made another of those resounding mistakes to which he was so unaccountably prone, and forced the Paris Parlement to declare his bastards eligible for the throne of France if the legitimate branch of his own descendants should die out. This was monstrously unfair to the Duc d'Orléans. No harm was done in the event, since Bourgogne's baby grew up and reigned as Louis XV, but the result might well have been that division of Frenchmen which it had always been the King's policy to prevent.

Louis XIV still had three years in which to put his house in order, and ought to have applied himself to reforming the constitution of France. In half a century he must have noticed how badly it worked, but he was tired, would do anything for a quiet life and instead it was the 'Constitution *Unigenitus*' which now occupied his attention. More and more under the influence of Mme de Maintenon, he used his remaining strength to force the papal Bull *Unigenitus* on the French bishops. The Bull was supposed to bury Jansenism for ever. No other government took it seriously. The Serenissima Republic of Venice locked it up in a cupboard and never mentioned it; in Savoy, Spain and Poland its acceptance or refusal was left to individual bishops. Only the King of France made a national issue of it. The Archbishop of Paris, Noailles, formerly such a great friend of Mme de Maintenon and now her enemy, led the opposition to the Bull with the result that Louis XIV exiled him from Versailles. Jansenism had begun to flourish again, especially in Paris and the King's action was the source of endless difficulties for his successor.

Meanwhile the fortunes of war had been slightly turning in favour of the French ever since the King's courageous decision in 1709 not to capitulate. He had managed to raise some cash, (notably in bullion from the New World, which he borrowed from the Spanish bankers), with which to feed and clothe his soldiers. English public opinion was beginning to agree with Lord Peterborough who said 'We are all great fools to get ourselves killed for two such boobies [the Archduke Charles and Philip V]'. There was a change of government which took England out of the war and she signed preliminaries of peace with France in 1711. The Italian states and the Papacy banded together to resist the Emperor and his tool the Duke of Savoy; the Emperor himself died of smallpox and was succeeded by the Archduke Charles; and Vendôme established Philip V in Spain with several resounding victories.

The French army in the North was now commanded by Maréchal de Villars, one of those picturesque, boastful soldiers who are sometimes, to the annoyance of their colleagues, as good as their own opinion of themselves. He was a man of great courage; his knee was shattered by a bullet at Malplaquet; in agony he continued to direct the battle until he fainted away. He refused to allow the surgeons to cut off his leg and by a miracle he was soon well again, except for a stiff knee. At Versailles he was considered a slightly comic figure, partly because he insisted on taking his young wife, of whom he was inordinately fond, to the front with him. It was a sensible precaution: she was nothing if not flighty. At the death of M. le Duc, Mme la Duchesse, distracted, sent urgently for Toulouse; he was found in bed with Mme de Villars, to the general merriment. Later she was to be an early love of Voltaire's; he stayed with her and her husband at their château, Vaux-le-Vicomte, renamed Vaux-Villars, and collected much information from the Marshal for the *Siècle de Louis XIV*. The courtiers saw this Marshal as a *cocu*, not to be taken seriously, but the King believed in him.

At the end of July 1712 the Court was at Fontainebleau. For some days there had been no dispatches from Villars; then rumours began to come in that he had won a decisive battle against the Austrians and the Dutch, led by Prince Eugène and Lord Albemarle, and that Albemarle was taken prisoner. It was many years since such news had come from the front: now nobody paid much attention, it seemed far too good to be true. However it was soon confirmed. Villars had not only beaten the apparently invincible Eugène at Denain but he followed up this action by taking Douai, after which Eugène and his allies lost more territory in three months than they had won in the past three years. Napoleon was always to say, speaking of those times, 'Denain saved France'. The King, who had held firm during ten of the most difficult years in French history, now had his reward. God had remembered him at last; and he gave thanks to God.

The various treaties of Utrecht were all signed by 1713 and concluded the war. England was awarded Newfoundland, Nova Scotia and Gibraltar. France kept her pre-war frontiers intact. France and Spain declared that their two crowns were always to be kept separate. Louis recognized the Protestant succession in England and was obliged to refuse to harbour the Old Pretender in France. He also agreed to destroy the fortifications of Dunkirk. The Duke of Savoy regained Savoy and Nice which the French had taken. The Netherlands were returned to the Empire. There were also various trade agreements between France and England. The cause of this long war, Philip V, remained on the throne of Spain, and it was occupied by his descendants until 1931.

XX

THE END

*Le dernier acte est sanglant quelque belle que soit la comédie
en tout le reste*

BLAISE PASCAL

There was to be one more bereavement before the end. In 1714, while the little,
delicate Dauphin lived, though with difficulty and always ailing, his hearty young
uncle Berri died. He was hurt out hunting, by the pommel of his saddle – his horse
slipping and rearing. He had just been having a particularly bad time with the
doctors: he had had an abcess on a tooth and they had inflicted various torments on
him, and now he was not brave enough to say what had happened. He drank quantities of hot chocolate and the next day went out hunting as usual. A peasant, who had
seen the accident, said to one of the King's men, 'How is the Duc de Berri?' 'I
suppose he is quite well, since he has gone out hunting.' 'If he is quite well princes
must be made of different stuff from the rest of us – I saw him take a blow yesterday
which would have split a peasant in two.' But when he got home he began to bring
up black blood. Of course he was given the usual emetic and soon was clearly dying.
He said not to bring the Holy Sacrament until the King had gone to bed as he did
not want to upset him – then he realized how urgent it was. The King went and
fetched the priest himself. Next morning the Duke, who thought he was better,
died.

A few weeks later the Duchesse de Berri had another dead baby. Louis XIV now
only had one legitimate descendant eligible for the throne. If the little Dauphin
died, the choice would be between Orléans and the bastards unless, which was most
probable, Philip V were to go back on his word and present himself. When Mme de
Ventadour saved the life of Louis XV, she almost certainly prevented civil war in
France.

Later that year the Duc de Beauvilliers died, broken by the deaths, in a single week
from smallpox, of his two sons, by that of his brother-in-law Chevreuse and above
all of the precious and adored Bourgogne. The Duchess survived another twenty-
four years.

Louis XV by Hyacinthe Rigaud, 1715.

In May 1715, the members of London clubs, kept informed by the English ambassador, Lord Stair, were betting that Louis XIV would not live much longer. In July he went to Marly; when he returned the courtiers were shocked to see how ill he looked. He had become not only thin but very small and had lost his appetite. Only Fagon and Mme de Maintenon seemed to notice nothing: when Mareschal told them that he was worried they sent him packing. The King's consitution was undermined by years of indiscriminate purging, bleeding, enemas, doses of opium and quinine and other remedies of the day by which the doctors sought to make this healthy man live for ever. For a good while now Fagon had ordered him to sleep enveloped in feather beds so that he should sweat, which he did so freely that he had to be washed down twice in the night. It made the King very uncomfortable but he was too pious in medicine to refuse to do it. On 9 August he went out hunting from Marly in the little *calèche* which he drove so brilliantly; came back to Versailles that evening; and never saw Marly, or went out hunting again.

His death was long and dreadful and conducted, like his life, with perfect self-control. On 11 August he began to have pain in his leg. Fagon diagnosed sciatica. The leg got more and more painful. The King had to be carried about in a chair, but he led a fairly normal existence until about 24 August when Mareschal noticed black spots on the leg and realized that there was gangrene. The King was made to keep his leg in a bath of Burgundy. Four doctors came from Paris and consulted lengthily with Fagon: they ordered ass's milk. Then Mareschal, saying that gangrene was a matter for surgeons rather than physicians, called in half a dozen of his own colleagues. They decided that it was now too late for amputation and that Mareschal must make a few incisions in the leg. The King, who knew quite well that he was dying, asked Mareschal if he really thought it right to hurt him so much, since it was useless. Mareschal was careful after that to spare him any extra suffering. His eyes were full of tears, and the King asked how many more days he gave him. It was a Monday. Mareschal said, 'Sire, we may hope until Wednesday'. Though in fact he lived until the following Sunday he made all his dispositions to be ready to go on the Wednesday.

It cannot be said that Mme de Maintenon made the King's last days on earth very easy. The Duc d'Orléans was the Dauphin's nearest legitimate relation in France, and as such would automatically become regent at the child's succession. Mme de Maintenon had never liked the Duke and was now scandalized by the gossip she heard about him. The more he was accused of an incestuous love affair with the Duchesse de Berri, in pamphlets and songs, the more idiotically he behaved with his daughter, probably out of bravado. Mme de Maintenon dreaded his influence on the future King; she could not bear to think of him ruling France. So when Louis XIV was too tired and ill to stand up to them she and du Maine forced him to add a codicil to his will, putting du Maine in charge of the new King's education.

Philippe, Duc d'Orléans as Regent. French school, eighteenth century.

This was a clever move to render Orléans virtually powerless, since the King's person was the magic which made all wheels turn in France. Louis XIV knew that it was very wrong of him to sign; but he also knew that political testaments are not worth the paper on which they are written. Two people, Président de Mesmes and Lauzun, told Saint-Simon that the King was heard to say 'I have bought some rest. They gave me no peace until I signed – it will become what it becomes; but at least they won't torment me any more!' An even greater worry to him was his estrangement, also the fault of his wife, from the Archbishop of Paris. If he died without being reconciled to this prelate many tongues would wag; he asked to see him. Père Tellier and Mme de Maintenon kept the two men apart, however, and the Last Sacraments were given by the young Cardinal de Rohan, son of the Princesse de Soubise and, it was generally thought, of Louis XIV himself.

The King was in agony, day and night. He wanted to make his adieus and then be left in peace. He heard his daughters wailing in the antechamber. It was the fashion at Versailles to grieve out loud: a woman who had lost husband or son at the war was expected to appear in the public rooms and make as much doleful noise as possible. Madame, the Princesse de Conti, Mme la Duchesse and the Duchesse d'Orléans were all admitted to the King's bedroom together; but the shrieks of his daughters tired the dying man, who had long ceased to have much feeling for them, and he said good-bye as quickly as he decently could; after advising them to make up their differences he let them go. But he spoke affectionately to Madame, saying he had loved her more than she ever knew.

Then he sent for his great-grandson, a charming little boy of five, with big, round black eyes. He came with his governess, Mme de Ventadour. She lifted him on to the bed and the two men who between them reigned in France for a hundred and thirty-one years, looked gravely at each other for the last time. 'Mignon', said Louis XIV, 'you are going to be a great King. Do not copy me in my love of building or in my love of warfare; on the contrary, try to live peacefully with your neighbours. Remember your duty and your obligations to God; see that your subjects honour Him. Take good advice and follow it, try and improve the lot of your people, as I, unfortunately, have never been able to do. Do not forget what you owe to Mme de Ventadour. Madame, I would like to kiss him.' As he kissed him he said 'My dear child I give you my blessing with all my heart.' From now on it was noticed that he spoke of the little boy as the King and of himself as already gone:

'In the days when I was King'.

Louis XIV said to those courtiers who had the *entrée*: 'Gentlemen, I ask your forgiveness for the bad example I have set you. I must thank you for the way in which you have served me and the faithful attachment you have always shown me. I am sorry that I have not been able to do as much for you as I would have wished to: the difficult times we have had are the reason for this. I ask you to be as faithful and

Louis XIV receiving the Elector of Saxony at Fontainebleau, 27 September 1714 by Louis de Sylvestre.

Versailles in 1722 by Jean-Baptiste Martin.

as diligent in serving my great-grandson as you have been with me. The child may well have troubles ahead of him. My nephew will govern the realm. Follow his orders. I hope he will do it well, I also hope that you will all remain united and do what you can, if any should stray, to bring them back to the fold. I feel that I may break down and that you also are moved – I beg your pardon. Good-bye, gentlemen – I believe you will sometimes think of me.'

My nephew will govern the realm. These words show how much importance the King attached to the famous codicil, forced out of him by Mme de Maintenon.

Next to be summoned were the two bastards, du Maine and Toulouse. They were some time alone with their father and then it was the turn of the Duc d'Orléans. The King had not seen him alone, had hardly exchanged a word with him, since they had had a painful interview after the deaths of the Bourgognes, when Orléans had hysterically begged to be tried in a court of law so that he could prove that he was not guilty of poisoning them. Now his uncle spoke kindly to him, and seemed to take it for granted that he would be sole Regent. 'You are about to see one King in his tomb and another in his cradle. Always cherish the memory of the first and the interests of the second.' He told him the identity of the Man in the Iron Mask – which was only known by two other people after them, Louis XV and Louis XVI, who took the secret to the scaffold with him. The King said that, after he had expired, Orléans must carry the new King to Vincennes where the air was good. He had ordered the castle to be got ready, and had even allocated the rooms, since the Court had not been there for fifty years. He asked Orléans to see that Mme de Maintenon was all right. 'She has been a great help to me, especially as regards my salvation.'

Now he was left to the priests, the doctors and his wife. She seems to have been strangely cold, but probably she was worn out. She had scarcely left his room, since the illness had taken a serious turn. Some say that he saw her crying and remarked 'Why do you weep – did you imagine that I was immortal?' but others that these words were addressed to two lacqueys. He did say 'I think I'm going to cry (*m'attendrir*), is there anybody else in the room? Not that it matters, nobody would be surprised if I cried with you.' And also 'I had always heard it is difficult to die but I find it so easy.' He said he was sorry he had never been able to make her happy. He spoke of her future and she said 'I am nothing. Don't waste your time over nothing.' He said that his great comfort was to think that, given her age, they would soon be united. She did not reply. Hours before he was dead, before he had even relapsed into unconsciousness, she had gone down the Queen's staircase for the last time and was soon comfortably in her own bed at Saint-Cyr.

The King's room was like a church, filled all the time with religious music and the murmuring of prayers, in which he joined with a loud firm voice during his moments of lucidity, asking God to help him. On 1 September 1715, after three weeks of intense suffering, Louis XIV's life went out as gently as a candle.

The gardens at Versailles in autumn.

SOURCES

SOURCHES, Marquis de, *Mémoires Secrets et Inédits de la Cour de France*, Paris 1882-93

SPANHEIM, Ezékiel, *Relation de la Cour de France*, Paris, 1882

CHOISY, Abbé de, *Mémoires pour servir à l'histoire de Louis XIV*, Utrecht, 1727

QUINTINIE, M. de La, *Instructions pour les Jardins Fruitiers et Potagers*, Amsterdam, 1692

PRESCOTT-WORMLEY, Katherine (editor), *Correspondence of Madame, Princesse Palatine, of Marie-Adélaïde, Duchesse de Bourgogne and of Mme de Maintenon*, London, 1899

STEVENSON, G. Scott (editor), *The Letters of Madame*, 2 vols. Arrowsmith, 1924

PALATINE, Princesse, *Lettres Inédites*. Translated A. A. Rolland. Paris, 1863

GRIMBLOT (editor), *Letters of William III and Louis XIV 1697-1700*, London, 1848

DANGEAU, Marquis de, *Journal, avec les additions du Duc de Saint-Simon*, Paris, 1854

CAYLUS, Mme de, *Souvenirs*, Paris, 1806

RABUTIN, Roger de, Comte de Bussy, *Correspondance*, Paris, 1859

BOURDALOUE, le Père, *Exhortations & Instructions Chrétiennes*, Paris, 1721

BOSSUET, *Oeuvres Oratoires*, ed: Abbé Lebarq, Paris, 1890-6

FÉNELON, *Letters*, London, 1964

MAINTENON, Mme de, *Correspondance Générale*, Paris, 1865

MAINTENON, Mme de, *Lettres Inédites à La Princesse des Ursins*, Paris, 1826

SÉVIGNÉ, Mme de, *Lettres*, various editions

SAINT-SIMON, Duc de, *Mémoires*, Pléiade, Paris, 1950

VISCONTI, Primi, *Mémoires de le Cour de Louis XIV*, Paris,

LA BRUYÉRE, *Caractères*, various editions

BOURGOGNE ET BEAUVILLIERS, Ducs de, *Lettres Inédites 1700-1708*, ed: Vogüé

BOURGOGNE, Duc de, *Lettres Inédites*, Paris, 1900

VRIGNAULT, Henri, *Généalogie de la Maison de Bourbon*, Paris, 1957

Journal of the Extraordinary Embassy of H.E. the Earl of Portland in France. The Hague, 1851

TORCY, Marquis de, *Mémoires*, Paris, 1828

Calendar of State Papers, 1698

Duke of Portland Historical Manuscript Commission Report 15, 1897.

PICAVET, Camille Georges, *La Diplomatie française au temps de Louis XIV*, Paris, 1930

DUCLOS, Charles, *Mémoires secrètes sur les règnes de Louis XIV et Louis XV*, Paris, 1791

LUYNES, Duc de, *Mémoires sur la cour de Louis XV*, 1861

LAFAYETTE, Mme de, *Histoire de Madame Henriette d'Angleterre*, Paris, 1853

WITTKOWER, R., *Bernini's Bust of Louis XIV*, London, 1951

NOLHAC, Pierre de, *Versailles, Residence de Louis XIV*, Paris, 1925

VERLET, Pierre, *Versailles*, Paris, 1961

MARIE, Alfred, *Marly*, Paris, 1947

VOLTAIRE, *Le Siècle de Louis XIV*, 1751

LANGLOIS, M., *Louis XIV et la Cour*, Paris, 1926

OMAN, Carola, *Mary of Modena*, London, 1962

MAURIAC, François, *La Vie de Racine*, Paris, 1928

MACAULAY, Lord, *History of England*, 1849-1861

LOUGH, John, *Introduction to Seventeenth-Century France*, London, 1954

CHATEAUBRIAND, François René de, *Vie de Rancé*, Paris, 1955

LAVALEE, Théophile, *Histoire de la Maison Royale de St Cyr*, Paris, 1853

MONGREDIEN, Georges, *Mme de Montespan et l'affaire des poisons*, Paris, 1953

MONGREDIEN, Georges, *Vie de Colbert*, Paris, 1963

MONGREDIEN, Georges, *La vie quotidienne sous Louis XIV*, Paris, 1948

D'HAUSSONVILLE, G. P. Othenin de Cléron, *La Duchesse de Bourgogne*, Paris, 1898

ST GERMAIN, Jacques, *La Reynie*, Paris, 1962

LAVISSE, Ernest, *Histoire de France*, vols. VII and VIII, Paris, 1911

BRÉMOND, Abbé, *Apologie pour Fénelon*, Paris, 1910

BOISLISLE, Jean de, *Portraits et Caractères dans Bulletin S. H. de France*, Paris, 1896

BRETANO, Funck, *L'Affaire des Poisons*, Paris

MARESCHAL, Georges, *Mareschal de Bièvres*, Paris, 1906

LA FORCE, Duc de, *Les Caumont de La Force*, Paris, 1960

CHURCHILL, Rt. Hon. Sir Winston, *Marlborough, his Life and Times*, London, 1947

KNOX, Mgr., *Enthusiasm*, Clarendon Press, 1950

LENOTRE, G., *Versailles au Temps des Rois*, Paris, 1950

LENOTRE, G., *En France Jadis*, Paris, 1938

Louis XIV, *Oeuvres de*, 6 vols. Paris, 1806

INDEX

Figures in **bold type**, indicate pages opposite or between which plates in colour are to be found; figures in *italic type*, indicate pages on which illustrations in black and white are to be found.

Bernini, Giovanni Lorenzo (1598-1680), Italian sculptor and architect; designs for the Louvre not approved, 23; bust of Louis XIV, 23-24, detail from, *23*, **24**; equestrian statue of Louis XIV, **25**, 25

Berri, Charles of France, Duc de (1685-1714), 3rd son of the Grand Dauphin, 66, 125; portrait with his parents between **152** and **153**; Fénelon appointed his tutor, 168; suggested by Louis XIV·as heir to Spanish crown, 186; at marriage of Bourgogne, *194-195*; 196, 200; his marriage, 211; character by Spanheim, 216; 219, 225; grief at Grand Dauphin's death, 227; 229, 232f.; death, 237

Berri, Marie Louise Elisabeth d'Orléans (Mlle de Valois) (1695-1719), m. Charles Duc de Berri 1710, 211; and the Grand Dauphin's death, 227; gives birth to a dead daughter, 229; 232; the King's dislike of, 233; birth and death of a son, 233; 237f.

Berry, Province of, 169
Berwick, James Fitzjames, Duke of (1670-1734), 183, 209
Béthune, Duchesse de, 18
Bibliothèque Nationale, The, 92
billiards; Louis XIV's preferred game, 65; Louis XIV playing, 65; 142
Black Masses for Mme de Montespan, 73, 76, 90ff., 226
Black Prince, Edward, The (1330-76), 214
Blainville, Marquis de (son of Colbert), 37
Blenheim, Battle of, 1704, 209, 217, 219
Blois, Mlle de; see Orléans, Françoise Marie, Duchesse de
Blood-letting, 149f.; instruments used, *150*
Boileau (called Boileau-Despréaux), Nicolas (1636-1711), satiric poet, 159, 161f.
Bolingbroke, Viscountess Marie-Claire Deschamps de Marcilly, (1665-1750), Marquise de Villette; married Henry St John, Viscount Bolingbroke (1678-1751), 163
Boneuil, Monsieur de, 185
Bonnard, Robert; sketch of the Siege of Tournai,1667, by, *37*
Bonne; one of Louis XIV's shooting dogs, *21*
Bontemps, Alexandre (1626-1701), Louis XIV's head valet, 43, 119; death 207
Bontemps family, Other members of, 43, 207
Bordes, Père, 145
Bosse, Abraham (1602-76), French engraver; engraving of a childbirth scene by, *111*
Bosse, Mme; involved in poisons scandal, 85ff.; death by burning, 88; 91
Bossuet, Jacques Bénigne (1627-1704), Bishop of Meaux from 1681, 40, 56, 69; tutor to the Dauphin, 69; 70f.; portrait by Rigaud, *72*; 73; quotations from 95, 225; 95, 114, 128, 142; praises Revocation of the Edict of Nantes, 143; death, 152; 163f., 171, 173; and Mme de La Maisonfort, 174, 176; 191, 224
Boufflers, Louis François, Marquis, later Duc, and Maréchal de (1644-1711), 178, 182
Bouillon, Emmanuel Théodore de la Tour d'Auvergne, Duc d'Albret, Cardinal de (1643-1715); exiled from court, 129; 136
Bouillon, Marie Anne Mancini, Duchesse de (1646-1714), 87ff.
Bouillon, Maurice Godefroy de La Tour d'Auvergne, Duc de, 88f.; exiled from court, 129
Boulle (or Buhl), André Charles (1642-1732), cabinetmaker, 105f.; furniture, 176
Bourbon (spa), 71, 74, 152, 163, 207, 217
Bourbon, Louis de (son of La Vallière) (1663-6), 25
Bourbon, Louis III de Condé, Duc de (1668-1710), Monsieur le Duc, gambling, 65; 96; portraits, *124*, *132*; marries Louise-Françoise, eldest daughter of Mme de Montespan and the King, 130; appearance and character, 133; his sisters, 133; 155, 192, 222; madness and death, 223; 228, 235
Bourbon, Louise Françoise (Mlle de Nantes), Duchesse de (1673-1743), eldest daughter of Mme de Montespan and

the King, Madame la Duchesse; gambling, 65;· *124*, *134*; marries Louis III de Condé, Duc de Bourbon, at 12, 130; description, 133; nursed through smallpox by the Grand Condé, 133, 155; love for Prince François Louis de Conti, 133, 223, 228; Louis XIV's love for, 196; in white mourning, *202*; 219, 225; nurses the Dauphin in smallpox, 226; 227, 235, 240
Bourbon-Condé family, 87
Bourbons, The, 18; as *parvenus*, 51
Bourdaloue, Louis (1632-1704), preaches Lenten sermons at court, 1675, 71; 114, 168
Bourdon, Sébastien (1616-71); portrait of the Marquis de Louvois by, *63*
Bourgogne, Louis de France, Duc de (1682-1712), eldest son of the Grand Dauphin, 66; birth, 111, 116; portrait with his parents between **152** and **153**; Fénelon appointed tutor to him and his brothers, 168; 174, 176; marriage, 180, 192; 191, 193; picture of marriage by Antoine Dieu, *194-195*; consummation of marriage, 196; his brother Anjou's love for him, 200; birth of a son, 209, 214; in love with his wife, 211; 213; portrait by Rigaud, *215*; character, 216; with his father, grandfather and others, by Largillière, between **216** & **217**; at the war, 218f.; 221, 225f.; his father's death, 227; becomes Dauphin, 228; 229; mourning catafalque, *230*; catches measles and dies, 231, 237, 241
Bourgogne, Marie-Adélaïde of Savoy, Duchesse de (1685-1712), 25, 185; character and appearance, 192f., 196; marriage picture by Antoine Dieu, *194-195*; lessons at Saint-Cyr, 197; 199; grief at Monsieur's death, 204; birth of a son, 209, 214; becomes the star at court, 210; portrait by Santerre, *210*; way of behaving, 211; and the Marquis de Maulévrier, 213; with the Duc de Bretagne, 213; change in her character, 214; portrait by Pierre Gobert, 216; Spanheim's estimate of her character, 216; insists on disgrace of Vendôme, 219; 221; stops balls at Versailles, 223; 225-229 *passim*; catches measles, 229; mourning catafalque *230*; confession and death, 231; 233f., 241
Boyne, Battle of the, 1690, 145
Brancas, Louise Françoise de Clermont-Gallerande, Duchesse de, widow of Louis Antoine, Duc de Villars-Brancas, 96
Brandenburg, 143
Brazil, 177
Bretagne, Louis, Duc de (1707-12), elder brother of Louis XV; with his mother, the Duchesse de Bourgogne, *213*; 225, 228; catches measles and dies, 231
Brémond, Abbé Henri (1865-1933), 171, 173
Breteuil (magistrate), 86
Breteuil, Louis Nicolas Le Tonnelier, Baron de (1648-1728), 164
Bretonvilliers, Hôtel de, *187*
Brinon, Marie de (d. 1701); and the Saint-Cyr school, 157-163 *passim*; writes words of 'God Save the King', 160; removed by a *lettre de cachet*, 163, 176
Brinvilliers, Antoine Gobelin, Marquis de, 84
Brinvilliers, Marie Madeleine d'Aubray, Marquise de (1630-76), poisoner; on the way to execution, *82*; 83ff.
Brinvilliers, The Hôtel, *84*
Brouais, Comte de; defender of Lille, 1667, 98f.
Brown, John (d. 1883), Scottish servant of Queen Victoria, 41
Brussels; flight of the Comtesse de Soissons and the Marquise d'Alluye to, 88
Buckingham Palace, London; Author's presentation at, 58
Builders of Versailles, The, 33-43
Bussy, Roger de Rabutin, Comte de (1618-93), 88
Cabinet Doré, Versailles, 58
Caesar, François Louis, Prince le La Roche-sur-Yon (later Prince de Conti, q.v.), compared to, 126
Calais [Pas-de-Calais], 188
Cambrai [Nord]; Fénélon made Archbishop of, 173; 174
Candida, Saint; relics sent by the Pope to Mme de Maintenon,

244

119; taken to the school of Saint-Cyr, 160

Caravaggio, Michelangelo Amerighi da (*c.* 1570-1609): *St John the Baptist* by, 64

Carmelite, Louise de La Vallière becomes a, 63

Carnavalet, The Hôtel (town house of Mme de Sévigné), 78

Carracci, Annibale (1560-1609); *Aeneas carrying his Father; St Sebastian* by, 64

Carracci Gallery, Palazzo Farnese, Rome, 38

Cassini, Giovanni Domenico (1625-1712), astronomer, 36

Castel del Rios, Marquis de, Spanish ambassador, 199

Cavendish, Lord, 180

Cavoye, Louis d'Oger, Marquis de (*c.* 1639-1716), 162

Caylus, Marthe Marguerite Le Valois de Villette de Murçay, Marquise de (1673-1729), cousin of Mme de Maintenon,119 censorship of the post, 128

Cessac, Comte de; involved in poisons scandal, 87ff.

Chaillot, Convent of, 48, 51

Chaillot, Palais de, 48

Chambord [Loir-et-Cher], 17

Chambre Ardente, The, set up 1679, 86-89; closed 1682, 91; judgements, 91

Chamillard, Michel (1652-1721), contrôleur général des Finances, 1699, ministre d'Etat, 1700; playing billiards, 65; 142, 197

Champaigne, Philippe de (1602-74); portrait of Cardinal Mazarin by, 26

Champs Elysées, Paris, 40

Chantilly [Oise], 40, 129

Chapel, The, at Versailles, 225

Chapelin (abortionist), 91

Charles II (1630-85), King of England, Scotland and Ireland from 1660, 29; death, 129; 144; silver table given to him, **161**; 183, 185; cabinet given to him, **192**

Charles II (1661-1700), King of Spain from 1665, 165, 177, 186; death, 198; leaves everything to Anjou, 199. For his wives see (1) Marie-Louise d'Orléans; (2) Maria Ana of Neuburg

Charles V (of France); life by the Abbé de Choisy, 216

Charles V (1500-58), Holy Roman Emperor from 1520, 24f.

Charles VI (of France); life by the Abbé de Choisy, 216

Charles VI (1685-1740), Holy Roman Emperor from 1711, 177, 199, 209, 224, 234; succeeds the Emperor Joseph I, 234

Charles, The Archduke of Austria; see Charles VI, Emperor

Charost, Armand II de Béthune, Duc de (1663-1747), 99

Chartres [Eure-et-Loir], Bishop of; see Godet des Marais, Paul

Chartres, Duc de; see Orléans, Philippe II, Duc d'

Chartres, Duchesse de; see Orléans, Françoise Marie de Bourbon, Duchesse d'

Chartres, Vidame de; character in *La Princesse de Clèves*, 213

Chateaubriand, François René, Vicomte de (1768-1848); quotations from, 33, 191

Châtelet, Gabrielle Emilie Le Tonnelier de Breteuil, Marquise du (1706-49), 164

Chevreuse, Charles Honoré d'Albert, Duc de (1646-1712), 141, 171, 174; death, 237

Chevreuse, Jeanne Marie Colbert, Duchesse de, 62, 141, 171, 174

childbirth scene; engraving by Abraham Bosse, *111*

Choin, Marie Thérèse Joly de (*c.* 1670-*c.* 1732); portrait, *124*; marries the Dauphin, 130, 225ff.

Choisy, The Abbé de, 216

Christ at the column; one of Louis XIV's jewels **152**

Churchill, Arabella (1648-1730), 183

Churchill, Sir Winston (Leonard Spencer) (1874-1965), 210, 218

Citizen King, The; see Louis-Philippe

Clagny, Château de (near Versailles), 18; Mme de Montespan at, *44*; house built for Mme de Montespan, 50; drawing of, *50*; 71, 73, 75, 80, 90, 92; appropriated by the Duc du

Maine, 191

Clement XI, Giovanni, Francesco Albani (1649-1721), Pope from 1700, 208

Clément (surgeon); delivers the Dauphine, 110-112

Clérambault, Mme de, 151

Clermont-Chaste, François Alphonse, Comte de (1661-1740), 87; three-cornered affair with Marie-Anne de Conti and Mlle de Choin, 130

Clermont-Chaste, Comtesse de, 130

clothes worn at Versailles, 97

Colbert, Jean Baptiste (1619-83), 21, 23, *28*; portrait, 33; his influence on Mazarin, Louis XIV, France, 33-36; his emblem, *34*; descent and relations, 36f.; death, 38; 48, 50, 62; his prestige affected by the poisons scandal, 91; 95, 114, 135, 141, 197f., 201, 209

Colbert, Richard (d. 1300), 36

Colbert de Croissy; see Croissy, Charles Colbert, Marquis de

Commerce, Council of, instituted by Colbert, 34

Compans, Monsieur de (Président of the Chambre Ardente), 86

Condé [Nord], 224

Condé, Louis II de Bourbon de (1621-86), the Grand Condé, 29; retirement, 32; one of his cooks, 43; 62; crossing the Rhine, 1672, 99; 105, 126; marries his granddaughter to François Louis de Bourbon, Prince de Conti, 129; his grandson, Louis III de Condé, marries Louise Françoise, eldest daughter of Mme de Montespan and the King, 130; she captivates him, 133; likeness by Antoine Coysevox, *154*; death, 155; 198, 203, 224

Condé, Louis III de (1668-1710); see Bourbon, Louis III de Condé, Duc de (Monsieur le Duc)

Confessors of Louis XIV; see François de La Chaise; Michel Le Tellier

Constantinople, 128

Conti, Anne Marie Martinozzi, Princesse de (niece of Mazarin), 126

Conti, Armand, Prince de (1629-66), father of Louis Armand and François Louis de Conti, *54*, 126

Conti, François Louis de Bourbon, Prince de (1664-1709), portrait, *124*; character, 126; friend of the Dauphin, displeasing to Louis XIV, 128; goes to fight the Turks, 128f.; succeeds brother, marries granddaughter of the Grand Condé, exiled from Versailles, 129; restored to favour, 133; in love with the Duchesse de Bourbon, 133; fails to secure throne of Poland, 134; 136, 155, 203, 219; death, 222, 228; *223*

Conti, Louis Armand de Bourbon, Prince de (1661-85), 29, 126; goes to fight the Turks, 128f.; death, 129; portraits, *124*, *127*

Conti, Marie, Anne de Bourbon, Princesse de (1666-1739), daughter of Louise de La Vallière and the King, 25; refused as wife by William III of Orange, m. to Louis Armand, Prince de Conti, 29; 48, 58; gambling, 65; *124*; on the Dauphine, 125f.; rebuked by the King, 128; contracts smallpox, widowed at 19, 129; 130; portrait, *131*; 133; turns to religion, 136; 191, 196, 225f.; nurses the Dauphin in smallpox, 226; *227*; Maintenon on, 233; buys a house in Paris, 234, 240

Conti, Marie Thérèse de Bourbon-Condé, Princesse de (1666-1732), granddaughter of the Grand Condé; portrait, *124*; 129, 199

Cour Royale, Versailles, 103

Cousinet, J. M.; silver font by, *186*

Coypel, Antoine (1661-1722), French artist, 223

Coysevox, Antoine (1640-1720), sculptor, 25; works by; relief for the Salon de Guerre, *97*; the Grand Condé, *154*; Louis XIV praying, *172*

Crenan, Mlle de, sent to the Bastille, 1685, 129

Croissy, Charles Colbert, Marquis de (*c.* 1626-96), 110, 182

Cromwell, Oliver (1599-1658), Lord Protector of the

245